CHAMPION
OF THE LARK

CHAMPION OF THE LARK

Harold Churchill and the Presidency of Studebaker-Packard, 1956–1961

Robert R. Ebert

McFarland & Company, Inc., Publishers
Jefferson, North Carolina, and London

ISBN 978-0-7864-7420-2
softcover : acid free paper ∞

LIBRARY OF CONGRESS CATALOGUING DATA ARE AVAILABLE

BRITISH LIBRARY CATALOGUING DATA ARE AVAILABLE

© 2013 Robert R. Ebert. All rights reserved

No part of this book may be reproduced or transmitted in any form or by any means, electronic or mechanical, including photocopying or recording, or by any information storage and retrieval system, without permission in writing from the publisher.

Harold Churchill stands next to the Lark by Studebaker (photograph courtesy of the author's collection)

Manufactured in the United States of America

*McFarland & Company, Inc., Publishers
Box 611, Jefferson, North Carolina 28640
www.mcfarlandpub.com*

To my wife, Marcia Ebert.
Her love, support, encouragement, and patience
throughout my teaching and research career,
and especially in this current book endeavor,
are appreciated beyond what words can express.

Acknowledgments

It is always difficult to attempt to acknowledge all those who have assisted in a particular body of research. A general statement of appreciation is in order for the many librarians, student assistants, and Studebaker-Packard historians and enthusiasts who have contributed to this research. However, special mention of gratitude must be made to several people and organizations including Andrew Beckman, Archivist of the Studebaker National Museum, and his staff. A number of picture images were made available courtesy of Studebaker historian Richard Quinn and are credited individually to him in the captions. The staff of the University of Indiana at Bloomington Oral History Project gave generous provision of time and resources that helped make this project possible. Niccole Pamphilis, who, as my student research assistant, co-authored an earlier article with me on Studebaker-Packard, contributed significantly to our understanding of Harold Churchill's thinking as he took over the leadership of S-P. The assistance of Chris Ritter, Librarian of the Antique Automobile Club of America (AACA) Library and Research Center, for the courtesy of providing numerous Studebaker-Packard Corporation factory photographs, is acknowledged in the captions. Sandra Wojtalewicz and Amanda Gawne assisted in the preparation of the manuscript.

Table of Contents

Acknowledgments vi
Preface 1
Introduction 3

1 • From Boy Tinkerer to Automotive Engineer 9
2 • Erskines, Rocknes, Champions, Weasels and Merger 14
3 • Accepting and Facing the Challenge 28
4 • The Lark Miracle 55
5 • Evolution of the Lark 73
6 • Churchill — Beyond the Presidency 91
7 • Churchill Era Studebaker-Packard Products: An Assessment 99
8 • Harold E. Churchill in Retrospect and Perspective 131

Appendix A: Studebaker Sedan Styling Evolution, 1953–1966 157
Appendix B: Studebaker Sport Coupe Styling Evolution, 1953–1964 162
Appendix C: Studebaker-Packard Vehicle Specifications, 1953–1966 166
Chapter Notes 175
Bibliography 181
Index 187

Preface

Harold E. Churchill was a career engineer at the Studebaker-Packard Corporation when he became its president in July 1956. The question examined here is whether Harold E. Churchill was an effective and successful president of the Studebaker-Packard Corporation. Although all histories of Studebaker-Packard mention Churchill's singular achievement, which was bringing out the compact Studebaker Lark in 1959, there has been insufficient analysis of Churchill's thinking, motivation, and struggles as he endeavored to save the Studebaker-Packard Corporation from almost certain bankruptcy.

Presented here is neither a detailed corporate history of the Studebaker-Packard Corporation nor an in-depth review of the 114 years of vehicle products built by the firm. As president of Studebaker-Packard, Churchill was the chief executive officer of a major industrial enterprise that was the fifth largest automobile manufacturer in the United States. Therefore, this book sets its focus on the corporate leadership of Harold E. Churchill as he dealt with the challenges confronting Studebaker-Packard in the crucial 1956–1961 period.

To analyze the contributions of Harold Churchill to the operations of Studebaker-Packard during the 1956 to 1961 period, use is made of corporate records, including Board of Directors minutes, internal documents, oral histories, and media reports. The use of these resources enabled an analysis of the motivations, pressures, and even personal thoughts of Churchill as he assumed leadership of Studebaker-Packard. The cars built by Studebaker-Packard during Churchill's tenure as president are discussed in the context of analyzing whether his presidency was successful.

Also, lacking in the automotive history literature is a comprehensive comparison of Churchill's presidency and leadership style to that of James J. Nance, his immediate predecessor, and Sherwood H. Egbert and Byers A. Burlingame, his successors in the 1960s. The approach taken here is to demonstrate that Nance, Churchill, Egbert, and Burlingame had distinctively different philosophies and visions for the automotive division of Studebaker-Packard. Among the questions raised, then, is how these differing philosophies and visions were manifested in the policies undertaken during each man's time as president of the company and the extent to which those policies were or were not successful.

Resources used in the preparation of this book include, in part, a substantial amount of material from my personal library. In some ways, both this book and the accumulation of those resources can be blamed on the January 1957 issue of *Motor Trend* magazine. My purchase of that magazine as a teenager was motivated simply by the fact that it profiled all of the 1957 automobiles, including the 1957 Packard. My mother always claimed that the first word I ever spoke was "car." A love for automobiles, therefore, was part of my DNA from day one. However, in my early youth my automotive interests were fickle: Chevrolet one day, Lincoln the next, De Soto the next, and Rolls-Royce the week after that. However, that picture of the 1957 Packard in the January 1957 issue of *Motor Trend* was an instant cure for my fickleness. I was totally captivated by the 1957 Packard (or "Packardbaker," as some would call it). That picture changed my life as well as the focus of my automotive interests.

From my interest in the 1957 Packard grew my fascination with the entire Studebaker-Packard line of cars and trucks. By 1958 I had bought stock in Studebaker-Packard, visited the factory, and even convinced my father to buy stock in the struggling automaker. During this time, of course, a great accumulation of corporate annual reports, Studebaker-Packard literature, and various other official corporate documents was acquired, and with it an awareness that Harold E. Churchill was involved in trying to save the company. By my senior year in high school I had written a major term paper and a book-length manuscript on the history of Packard. It was, in many respects, a life-defining experience because my growing interest in corporate affairs and finance caused me to change my career objectives from medicine to being an economist. My master's thesis was an economic analysis of the decline of the Packard Motor Car Company.

The obsession with Studebaker-Packard never left me. There were distractions, of course, including writing a doctoral dissertation on a totally unrelated subject, engaging in a career in college teaching, and research into a number of different areas, but always the lure of Studebaker-Packard seemed to beckon to me. There were occasional articles on Studebaker-Packard written for both professional journals and hobbyist magazines, including a three-part series on Studebaker's last ten years (1956 to 1966) for *The Bulb Horn*, magazine of the Veteran Motor Car Club of America, in 1991–1992. But seemingly more urgent tasks, including three books on various aspects of automotive history, kept me from fulfilling the desire to write something extensive on Studebaker-Packard.

Although through the years I had owned a dozen Studebaker and Packard products, perhaps it was the fulfillment of a 52-year desire in 2010 with the acquisition of a 1958 Packard, a car that can legitimately be called a "Churchill-era car," that finally provided the motivation to find out more about the man who led Studebaker-Packard during some of its most tumultuous years. What follows is his story—the story of Harold E. Churchill.

Robert R. Ebert

Introduction

When he became president of the Studebaker-Packard Corporation in the summer of 1956, Harold E. Churchill inherited a company that was near bankruptcy and in need of reorganization, refocusing, and inspired leadership. Yet for all the difficulties S-P found itself in, Churchill could draw on a rich history of two companies that had long and respected pasts that, between them, totaled over 150 years of experience in the automobile industry. Studebaker traced its roots back to 1852. The heritage of Packard went back to 1899.

Although Studebaker and Packard had long and distinguished histories in the automobile industry, their beginnings were dramatically different. On February 16, 1852, Henry and Clement Studebaker with $68 in capital opened a blacksmith shop in South Bend, Indiana, called H & C Studebaker. Before long they were building wagons and carriages but needed capital to expand their business. One of their brothers, John Mohler Studebaker, had gone to California in the gold rush to seek his fortune, but soon found that there was more money to be made in building wheelbarrows than in actual mining. In 1858, with $8000 in gold, John M. Studebaker left California and joined his brothers in the business at South Bend. In time, five Studebaker brothers, Henry, Clement, John, Peter, and Jacob, became involved in the firm. Added capital provided by John, orders from the U.S. Army, especially during the Civil War, and entrepreneurial vision soon made the Studebaker Brothers Manufacturing Company the largest builder of horse-drawn wagons in the world.[1]

In contrast to the somewhat humble beginnings of Studebaker, the Packard Motor Car Company began as a result of the desire for an automobile by a Warren, Ohio, industrialist. James Ward Packard and his brother, William Doud Packard, were successful businessmen who ran the Packard Electric Company, a manufacturer of electric lamps, in Warren, Ohio. James Ward Packard became interested in automobiles when, dissatisfied with one he purchased in 1898 from the Winton Motor Carriage Company of Cleveland, Ohio, decided to build one himself. Thus, on November 6, 1899, the first Packard automobile was test driven successfully on the streets of Warren. The car performed well enough that several more were built, and with investment from others, under the name of the New York & Ohio Company, what became the Ohio Automobile Company and then the Packard Motor Car Company was launched.[2] With investment from Detroit industrialist Henry B. Joy and others, by 1903, Packard operations had moved to Detroit. James Ward Packard began to take a lesser role in the affairs of the company by this time and resigned as president in 1909.[3]

At about the time that the Packard Motor Car Company was taking shape, Studebaker Brothers Manufacturing Company was celebrating its 50th anniversary in 1902. By this time, John M. Studebaker was the only one of the five brothers who was still living. His son-in-law, Frederick Fish, became influential in the company, and eventually president, and convinced his father-in-law that the wagon maker should enter the horseless carriage era. In 1902, Studebaker began to build electric automobiles.[4]

Before long, in the 1904–1905 period, Studebaker realized it needed a presence in the gasoline motorcar field and affiliated with the Garford Company of Elyria, Ohio, which was building gasoline automobiles. By 1908, Studebaker had taken a controlling interest in the Garford firm and changed its name to Studebaker-Garford. However, the Studebaker-Garford association, which was building relatively higher-priced luxury cars, did not last long because Fish became interested in engaging in the manufacture of lower-priced cars on a mass-production basis. In 1909, Fish maneuvered for Studebaker to take controlling interest of the Everett-Metzger-Flanders (E-M-F) Company of Detroit, which built cars in the $1100 range — less than half the price of a Studebaker-Garford. So, in 1911, Studebaker divested itself of Garford, which became independent again, and Studebaker began to focus its automotive interests on the E-M-F operation.[5]

While Studebaker was striving to find its position in the automobile market, Packard was becoming one of the leaders in the luxury car field. Under the leadership of Henry B. Joy and Alvan Macauley, who had become Packard's general manager when Joy became president in 1910, and later became president when Joy relinquished the position in 1916, Packard built some of the legendary luxury cars of the era, including the Packard Twin-Six (12 cylinders) and the Packard straight 8 models. However, with the onset of the Depression in the 1930s, Macauley realized Packard would have difficulty surviving building only high-priced luxury cars. From production of 49,698 cars in 1928, Packard output had declined to only 6265 units in 1934. Macauley then made the momentous decision to have Packard enter the medium-priced field with the production of the Packard 120 eight-cylinder models for 1935, and then the Packard Six 115 models in 1937. The result was Packard set a production record of 109,518 units in 1937 and stayed in the medium-priced market for the rest of its existence while continuing to build a line of luxury cars as well.[6]

Although Studebaker had entered the lower-priced gasoline automobile field with the acquisition of E-M-F, it did not stay in that price class for long. Reliability problems were encountered with the E-M-F models and a related car, the Flanders, and those nameplates were dropped by 1912. The Studebaker brand emerged as a major nameplate of its own in 1913 and soon established itself as a major competitor in the $625-to-$1500 price class of gasoline-powered automobiles with some models priced as high as $2000. Studebaker continued in the medium-priced to upper-priced range of the automobile market through most of the 1920s, during which time it built cars such as the Studebaker President 8, which held its own in competition with some of the luxury brands of the time. In the late 1920s, Studebaker also assumed control of the Pierce-Arrow Company of Buffalo, New York, a builder of luxury automobiles, but later divested itself of Pierce-Arrow during the Depression. Studebaker output during the 1920s consistently was in the 110,000- to 140,000-unit range.[7]

Studebaker's president in the 1920s was Albert R. Erskine, who had joined the company as treasurer in 1911 and became its president in 1915. Erskine believed that Studebaker should be in a lower-priced range than the basically middle and higher-priced cars it was building at the time. The result was the failed introduction of the Erskine, which is discussed in more detail in Chapter 2 of this book. With overall sales at only about a third of the levels of the 1920s, Studebaker made another attempt at entering the low-priced market during the Depression in the 1930s with the introduction of the Rockne — also discussed in some detail in Chapter 2.

It was during this period of Studebaker's experiments with lower-priced cars that Harold Churchill joined Studebaker as an engineer and was influenced by the company's efforts in the low-priced field. Although the Erskine and Rockne were not significant successes, the company's vision of itself and its future became increasingly focused on the lower-priced end of the market.

Studebaker went through bankruptcy reorganization in 1933 with the result that Harold Vance, Studebaker Vice-President of Manufacturing, and Paul Hoffman, a leading Studebaker dealer, assumed operational control of the company as president and board chair. In a move paralleling that of Macauley's decision to bring out the medium-priced Packard 120 in 1935, Vance and Hoffman decided to change the focus of the company by bringing Studebaker into the low-priced field in direct competition with Ford, Chevrolet, and Plymouth. The result was the very successful Studebaker Champion, introduced for 1939. Development of the Champion and its influence on the thinking of Harold Churchill are elaborated upon in Chapter 2.

With the success of the Champion, for the remainder of its automobile-building years, which lasted until 1966, Studebaker became associated with cars built to compete in the low-priced market. Although Studebaker continued to offer models in the lower end of the medium-priced range as well as models designed to appeal to buyers interested in sporty-type cars following World War II, the company's bread-and-butter models were the Champion and derivatives of the basic Champion.

Both Studebaker and Packard prospered in the early years following World War II when the auto industry in general was enjoying a sellers' market. Due to wartime shortages and lack of civilian automotive production from 1942 almost to the end of 1945, after the war the automakers could sell virtually anything they produced. Studebaker's peak year was 1950, when its worldwide sales totaled 334,554 units. Packard's peak year after the war was 1949, with sales of 104,593 units. By 1954, however, the sellers' market had turned into a buyers' market, and both Studebaker and Packard began to suffer sharp declines in output. Although both firms remained marginally profitable through 1953, in 1954, sales of Studebakers declined to only 100,604 units and sales of Packards declined to 27,583, with the result that the two companies each lost between $26 million and $27 million.[8]

Meanwhile, management problems began to manifest themselves at both Studebaker and Packard. In 1939, Macauley stepped aside as president of Packard to become its board chair. Macauley was replaced by Packard marketing executive Max Gilman, who quit Packard in 1942, with the result that Packard manufacturing expert George

Christopher became president. Christopher lasted until his forced resignation in 1949, having failed to deliver on promises to stockholders to build 200,000 Packards a year. Replacing Christopher was Hugh Ferry, Packard's executive vice-president, who made no secret of the fact that he saw his primary task as finding a dynamic executive to replace him as president.[9]

In 1952, Ferry found his replacement in the person of James J. Nance, a dynamic General Electric executive, who was looking for new challenges. He certainly found those challenges at Packard. As Packard's problems began to multiply in the early 1950s, the realities of the automotive industry were catching up with all of the independent automakers. By 1954, Kaiser and Willys had merged, Nash and Hudson had merged to form American Motors Corporation, and Studebaker and Packard merged to form Studebaker-Packard Corporation. The mergers of Nash and Hudson, and then Studebaker and Packard, were part of a larger scheme discussed by Nance and George Mason of Nash. The idea was to eventually merge all four of those makes to form the fourth large full-line automobile company in the U.S. to compete with Ford, General Motors, and Chrysler. Unfortunately, the sudden death of George Mason and the emergence of George Romney as head of AMC put an end to that plan, and Nance found himself facing the future alone as head of Studebaker-Packard.[10]

The merger of Studebaker and Packard has been characterized as a "shotgun wedding." That description may not be too far from the truth. The merger was arranged in haste as the market for the cars of the two companies was declining sharply. The merger was a friendly one and not underwritten by outside investment houses, so no in-depth investigation was made into the financial and industrial health of the two companies.[11]

In later chapters of this book, a more thorough discussion is undertaken of the situation confronting Studebaker and Packard as they merged in 1954, and of the subsequent two model years, 1955 and 1956. In brief, major problems included loss of government contracts by Packard as the Korean War came to an end. At Studebaker, the leadership of Harold Vance and Paul Hoffman had begun to weaken as the postwar sellers' market gave way to the buyers' market. While Vance and Hoffman made many excellent moves at Studebaker in bringing the firm out of bankruptcy during the Depression, including introducing the Champion and then developing the postwar Studebaker with dramatic new styling, their handling of labor relations was viewed by many as too accommodating to the United Auto Workers.

In his analysis of the decline of Studebaker, Donald Critchlow concluded that Vance and Hoffman had allowed the union to define labor standards, job rights, and grievance issues without countervailing pressure from management.[12] As a result, by the time of the merger, Studebaker's labor costs were considered out of line with the rest of the industry and confronted Nance with the need to try to bring them under control. The result was a period of several years of labor unrest at Studebaker.

Compounding the problems of Vance and Hoffman in the early 1950s was the crisis with the introduction of the 1953 Studebakers. The successes that Vance and Hoffman had enjoyed with the Champion and then the 1947 Studebakers were not repeated in 1953. Featuring very stylish coupes with sporty styling by the Raymond Loewy organization, the 1953 Studebakers created a great deal of public interest. Unfortunately, the planning for the manufacture of the cars left something to be desired, resulting in parts not fitting as the cars came down the assembly line. The consequent delays in production resulted in thousands and perhaps tens of thousands of units of lost sales. The problems were serious enough that Vance felt compelled to apologize and explain the problems to the stockholders in the company's annual report for 1953.

With the merger of Studebaker and Packard, and Nance's emergence as the president and chief executive officer, the company embraced a full-line philosophy, even though the original plan of merger with American Motors could not be implemented. Studebakers were to be the lower-priced and lower-medium-priced cars, Clippers (built by Packard) were to be the upper-medium-priced line, and Packards were to be the luxury high-priced cars. Complementing this was the line of Studebaker trucks. It was an ambitious plan that very quickly took Studebaker-Packard nearly into bankruptcy.

One of the most ambitious parts of the full-line philosophy of Nance for Studebaker-Packard was the plan for the 1955 Packards. The 1955 Packards featured a significantly facelifted body shell, an all-new V8 engine, a totally new Torsion-Aire suspension system, a new Twin-Ultramatic transmission, and assembly operations in an entirely new plant. The results echoed the problems at Studebaker in 1953. Production delays occurred, product quality was not up to Packard standards, and the result was a loss of public confidence in the company. Factory sales of Packard and Clipper cars virtually collapsed from over 62 thousand units in 1955 to only 19 thousand units in 1956. Studebaker was not doing much better. Although Studebaker sales rose from the depressed levels of 1954 to nearly 139 thousand units in 1955, they fell to under 108 thousand units in 1956.[13]

Nance had developed a grand plan of building a whole new line of Packard, Clipper, and Studebaker cars off a common body shell beginning in 1957. The estimated cost of the plan was in the neighborhood of $50 million — cash which Studebaker-Packard simply did not have — and in the end, the plan was scrapped as the company's fortunes reached a new low.[14] Instead of Nance's grand plan, the minutes of the Board of Directors meetings during this time show the focus of the Board was on saving the corporation from bankruptcy. Banks were not inclined to lend the firm any more money than they already had. There were attempts to merge with other firms, but none of those came to fruition. What emerged from the crisis was the decision to close the Packard plants in Detroit, consolidate all Studebaker and Packard production in South Bend, Indiana, at the Studebaker plants, and engage in a management advisory agreement with Curtiss-Wright Corporation. Curtiss-Wright also provided an infusion of cash to Studebaker-Packard by purchasing some of its idle production facilities in the Detroit area and South Bend that could be used for defense production by C-W.

It was in the midst of this crisis that James Nance resigned and Harold Churchill became president of Studebaker-Packard Corporation in July 1956. He was to face a myriad of challenges in his five years as president. For example, what he could not know in the summer of 1956 was that, as he worked to restore the confidence of the public in both the products of S-P and the financial integrity of the corporation, the United States would face a major recession in economic activity in 1958. In that year gross national product declined by about 1.1 percent and the unemployment rate rose from 4.3 percent in 1957 to 6.8 percent in 1958 and never fell below 5.5 percent for the remainder of Churchill's tenure as president of Studebaker-Packard through 1960.[15]

It is important to note that through this period of time the market for passenger cars in the United States fluctuated in a narrow range around 6 million units per year. From 5.5 million cars sold in 1954, sales jumped to 7.2 million cars in 1955, which was an excellent year for the industry. Subsequent years were not nearly so robust, with sales dropping to 5.9 million units in 1956, and then to 4.6 million in the recession year of 1958. Sales did recover somewhat to 6 million units in 1960 and 6.5 million in 1961, but did not reach the levels of 1955 until 1963, which was after Churchill had left the presidency of Studebaker-Packard. With the market for automobiles essentially flat, all of the car makers were in a battle for market share. To succeed, Churchill was going to have to increase the market share of Studebaker-Packard, which meant taking sales and market share away from other companies. The combined market share of Studebaker and Packard had reached a postwar peak of 6.5 percent in 1948 and 1949, had declined to 2.44 percent at the time of the merger in 1954, and to 1.08 percent during the recession year of 1958.[16]

Throughout his engineering career at Studebaker, which began in 1926, Churchill had been interested in the potential for economy cars in the automotive market. He had worked on and been impressed with the development and success of the 1939 Studebaker Champion. That experience led Churchill to institute policies that led, first, to the development of the Studebaker Scotsman in 1957, and then to the introduction of the compact Studebaker Lark. This model enabled the automaker to survive a close brush with bankruptcy in the crisis of 1958, which saw the termination of the Curtiss-Wright agreement and a restructuring of the company's finances. The Lark did its job, though. The S-P market share rose to 2.4 percent in 1959. As the fortunes of Studebaker-Packard deteriorated again in the early 1960s, and the company's market share declined to the 1.6 percent range, Churchill ended up relinquishing the corporate presidency but stayed on the Board of Directors in an active consulting role through 1967.

In emphasizing the economy cars, Churchill's policies and vision for Studebaker-Packard Corporation differed dramatically from that of his predecessor, James J. Nance, as well as that of his immediate successor, Sherwood H. Egbert, and Egbert's successor, Byers A. Burlingame. The approach these four men took to running the automaker differed significantly from each other, which created a rather tumultuous decade for Studebaker-Packard in the ten-year period of 1956 to 1966. Of the four presidents who occupied the office in that last ten years of Studebaker automobile production, Churchill was an automotive executive for the longest period. It is an interesting, but also challenging, period in automotive history to examine.

1

From Boy Tinkerer to Automotive Engineer

It was a Sunday morning much like any other Sunday morning in 1914 in Penn, Michigan, except that two eleven-year-old boys, one of them Harold E. Churchill, decided they did not want to go to church. Professing to have stomachaches, Harold and his friend were allowed to stay home while their parents went off to Sunday services. In reality, the boys had much more grandiose plans than to recover from "stomachaches." Clandestinely the two boys had put together what Churchill later described as an "automotive piece of machinery" consisting of the running gear from an International Harvester mower, pieces of a four-wheel buggy, a stationary gasoline engine, and a driving belt they found along the railroad tracks that was off the dynamo of a Pullman car. That Sunday morning was the date for the inaugural test drive of their machine. Shortly after their parents were on their way to church, the boys started up the machine and drove it down a large hill. There was one problem, though: the belt slipped and they could not get the machine back up the hill. They figured they were in for big trouble when their parents came home. Instead, Harold's father, with a big grin on his face, said: "Well, boys, let's go home and eat. I'll come back and help you get this thing back home, 'cause we got to pump water."[1] Thus was born the automotive career of the man destined to become president of the Studebaker-Packard Corporation in 1956, and developer of the "Lark by Studebaker."

Harold E. Churchill was born July 4, 1903, on a 288-acre farm in Penn, Michigan, the second of six children (two girls and four boys). His father and grandfather were farmers, but Harold developed an interest in mechanical things very early in life. He described his father as being interested in mechanical objects only as a means to an end in running his farm, but who encouraged Harold's interest in them.[2]

In another mechanical experiment during his boyhood, Churchill and his friend built a telephone line from the Churchill house to the other boy's house about a half mile away. The two youngsters even had to forge the climbers to get up the poles, then salvaged wire that hung on the poles and strung the line. In Churchill's words: "And it worked. I don't know why, but it did."[3]

In the oral history interview conducted by the University of Indiana, Churchill stated that his mechanical aptitude also was nurtured by the local blacksmith who let him come into his shop and use his tools. The blacksmith ordinarily did not let youngsters use anything in his shop, but Harold always put the tools back where they were supposed to be. So a combination of an encouraging father, an accommodating blacksmith, and his own ingenuity fostered Churchill's interest in things mechanical; to quote him: "So this thing went on from that time on. I never lost that desire and inquisitiveness."[4]

Detailed information on the early years and personal life of Harold E. Churchill does not exist in any significant quantity. However, the aforementioned oral history of Churchill does give insights into his views on his early experiences in education and engineering. In the interview he related that after high school he spent two years at Western Michigan University, where he took courses in math and physics with an objective of becoming a mechanical engineer. After receiving what he described as a "life certificate" to teach math and industrial arts, he taught for two years and then decided to work in industry.

In 1925, Churchill took a summer job in the engineering department of Dodge Brothers Manufacturing Company in Detroit on drawing-board layout work. His intent was to go back to school at the end of the summer, but he was asked to teach at the high school in Jackson, Michigan, where he spent another year teaching math and mechanical drawing. After attending a summer session at the University of Michigan in Ann Arbor, he was offered a job at Studebaker in Detroit for 30 days at $100. That job offer happened almost by coincidence. After attending that summer session in Ann Arbor, Churchill and a friend were invited to a house party north of Pontiac, Michigan. The chaperone of the party, who was a group leader in the engineering department at Studebaker, talked to Churchill and offered him the job. At the end of the 30 days, Studebaker wanted Churchill to stay, but he wanted to go back to school. The Studebaker offer of $200 per month if he would stay was too tempting, and he spent the next 42 years there.[5]

Besides his becoming an engineer at Studebaker, the late 1920s were significant for Harold Churchill in a personal way. On August 17, 1929, he married Josephine Thompson. Harold and Josephine enjoyed 51 years of marriage and raised four children, including three daughters, Deborah, Catherine, and Cindy, and one son, Alan. By the time he became president of Studebaker-Packard, Churchill and his wife lived on a farm on Shively Road outside South Bend. He enjoyed raising beef cattle, pursuing do-it-yourself projects, and hunting, while his wife, Josephine, was known around South Bend as an avid golfer.[6]

Official corporate portrait of Harold E. Churchill as president of Studebaker-Packard Corporation.

The perspectives Churchill presented, in the oral history interview, on the opportunities he had at Studebaker are both interesting and revealing. His first several months at Studebaker were spent in Detroit, where the engineering operations were located at that time; and then, in November 1926, he moved with engineering to South Bend. The group he worked with at Studebaker was a small group, which he said gave him advantages that his lack of a mechanical engineering degree would have prevented him from having at a larger firm. Specifically, he said that in those early years he worked on product testing and chassis elements including suspension, steering, wheels, and tires.

Churchill's early years at Studebaker coincided with the later years of the reign of Albert R. Erskine as president of the firm. Erskine joined Studebaker as treasurer in 1911, and, upon the advice of Wall Street financier Henry Goldman, was made president of the company. Erskine had a significant impact in building Studebaker into a major automobile manufacturer by the 1920s. Adaptation of new technologies and the use of scientific management techniques under Erskine's leadership made Studebaker an important force in the automobile industry.[7]

During Churchill's formative years at Studebaker, he benefitted from the engineering strength of the company. Among the things that Erskine did at Studebaker was to bring in a dynamic engineering team. In 1911, Erskine set up an engineering laboratory under chief engineer James G. Heaslet and his assistant, Fred M. Zeder. Zeder was an engineering graduate from the University of Michigan who became chief engineer when Heaslet was appointed vice-president for engineering. Zeder later brought on Owen R. Skelton, who had been with Pope-Toledo and Packard, and Carl Breer, who had worked at Allis-Chalmers. These three men gave Studebaker a reputation for innovative engineering. Although Zeder, Skelton, and Breer left Studebaker in 1920 to set up their own consulting firm and later went to Chrysler, they left an indelible mark at Studebaker as innovative engineers.[8] Churchill referred to them as an impressive group of people.[9]

Succeeding Zeder, Skelton, and Breer was Guy P. Henry, who did not leave much of a mark at the company. When he left in 1926, he was replaced by Delmar G. (Barney) Roos, a Cornell graduate who was an articulate and colorful head of the company's engineering department. Among Roos's accomplishments was the creation of the legendary Studebaker President 8.[10] Therefore, Churchill arrived on the scene at Studebaker the same year as Roos and came into an engineering department that had developed a heritage for excellence and innovation.

Churchill's earliest tasks in the Studebaker engineering department were testing chassis elements including steering, suspension parts, and tires. In reflecting on the somewhat primitive state of automotive testing in the 1920s, compared to the latter half of the twentieth century, Churchill said: "We didn't have the advantage of sophisticated electronic equipment in those days that later came about, but we did have a chassis dynamometer, and we did a lot of laboratory work that duplicated road conditions to get accelerated testing and controlled conditions of testing so that you could duplicate tests."[11]

The stock market crash of 1929 and the Great Depression took their toll on Studebaker and Erskine. After a failed merger attempt with the White Motor Company of Cleveland, a major truck manufacturer, Studebaker was faced with severe financial problems and declared bankruptcy in March 1933. Compounding the problems of bankruptcy was the banking crisis that occurred during March 1933. Erskine expected to remain as president of Studebaker, but the judge overseeing the receivership, Thomas W. Slick, appointed Paul Hoffman, a successful California Studebaker dealer who had become vice-president of sales at Studebaker; and Harold Vance, Studebaker's vice president of manufacturing; and A.G. Bean, president of White Motors, as trustees. Deeply in debt personally, owing back taxes, and depressed over the turn of events at Studebaker, Erskine took his own life on July 1, 1933.[12] Although Churchill characterized himself as a "little laboratory technician" at the time, far removed from Erskine, he viewed Erskine as the person who inspired the building of smaller, more compact automobiles, a topic to which we return in the next chapter.[13]

So in 1933, Churchill, now working at Studebaker in South Bend, having moved there in November 1926, found himself an employee for a company in bankruptcy. He recalled that on the day bankruptcy was declared everyone except the vice-president of engineering was terminated. That situation prevailed for about ten days, after which the receivers realized that product planning had to go forward, and eight people, including Churchill, were rehired. In reflecting on the company's recovery from bankruptcy and receivership, Churchill noted that at the time Studebaker was the only auto company that had fully recovered from receivership. He attributed the successful emergence from receivership to the employees' having faith in the company. According to Churchill, the employees had roots in the South Bend community and there were not many opportunities for employment other than at Studebaker, all of which led to great community *esprit de corps*. So, only seven years into his career at Studebaker, Churchill had a lesson in dealing with financial crises. At the time of the financial crisis and reorganization of Studebaker in 1933, Churchill was a group leader in product development in charge of all chassis components except the power plant but including the transmissions and drive train.[14]

By 1936, Barney Roos had left Studebaker to join Rootes Motors in England. Roos was replaced by W.S. James as chief engineer under vice-president of engineering Roy Cole. Cole, along with Ralph Vail, had come to Studebaker in 1930 after having been at Willys-Overland at just about the time Erskine was beginning to think about producing the Rockne (more on that in the next chapter).[15] One of James's first tasks as he became chief engineer in 1936 was to begin work on yet another light car for Studebaker that was to become the Champion.[16]

Over the subsequent years Churchill was promoted steadily and rose to the rank of chief research engineer in 1944, director of research in 1948, and vice-president of engineering in 1952. He received the title of vice-president of engineering after his predecessor in that position, Stanwood W. Sparrow (who had replaced Cole in the late 1940s), was killed in an automobile accident.[17]

Asked what his philosophy was and what changes he made when he became V.P. of engineering, in the interview Churchill responded that his concerns were performance and energy efficiency, which he believed had been Studebaker's strengths all along. He stated: "I knew very well that we didn't have the money to compete stylewise [*sic*] with a skin change every two years. We had to do something different. So we sold economy of operation, and we had a pretty good performance record in that respect."

In 1955, under then Studebaker-Packard President James J. Nance, Churchill became vice-president in charge of Studebaker operations at South Bend, Indiana.[18] Then, in 1956, he became president of Studebaker-Packard Corporation. But before many of these promotions occurred, Churchill was exposed to and deeply influenced by the concept of the smaller, compact car.

2

Erskines, Rocknes, Champions, Weasels and Merger

Very early in his career at Studebaker, Churchill became acquainted with smaller, more compact cars. In the 1980 oral history interview he related how Albert Erskine, president of Studebaker in the 1920s, challenged the product design department to create a smaller car. Studebaker, up to then a builder of upper- and medium-priced cars, introduced its smaller car as the Erskine for the 1927 model year.

The Erskine featured a 146-cubic-inch engine yielding 40 horsepower. Studebaker advertising claimed the Erskine was capable of achieving 60 miles per hour with safety and 25 to 30 miles per gallon of gasoline. It was built on a relatively small 107-inch wheelbase.[1]

Initially, the Erskine sold well, but problems with its six-cylinder engine (built by Continental Motors and not by Studebaker, which did build its own President 8 and Commander 6 engines) caused sales of the Erskine to fall from a peak of over 37,000 units in 1928 to 11,500 in 1929. The Erskine subsequently evolved into simply the Studebaker 6 by mid-year 1930.[2]

Under the direction of Barney Roos, in 1930 Studebaker developed freewheeling.[3] Churchill was part of the team that worked on Studebaker's freewheeling feature, which was an innovation that eventually led to the development of automatic overdrive and the automatic transmission.[4]

In his early years at Studebaker, after the Erskine efforts, Harold Churchill experienced two more attempts of the company to enter the smaller, economy car market. In 1932, Studebaker introduced the Rockne, named for Notre Dame football coach Knute Rockne. The Rockne, originally built in Detroit at Studebaker's old E-M-F plant and later in South Bend, had two six-cylinder Studebaker-built engine options of 190 and 205 cubic inch displacement. There were two wheelbases available, 110 and 114 inches. The Rockne had a starting price of $585. The price was $100 more than Ford and Chevy and comparable to Plymouth.[5] Studebaker sold over 22,000 Rocknes in 1932 — about half of the firm's Depression-reduced output. As mentioned in Chapter 1, Studebaker was facing serious financial problems during the Depression. A victim of the Depression, the fact that it offered buyers little that couldn't be obtained in a Ford or Chevrolet at a lower price, and the reorganization at Studebaker, the Rockne was discontinued in July 1933.[6]

The 1928 Erskine Six Sedan shows the car's attractive styling for small cars of its era. Even though promoted in advertising as "The Little Aristocrat," its styling was not enough to make it a sales success.

Perhaps the Studebaker product that influenced Churchill the most was the Champion, introduced for the 1939 model year. In the 1980 interview, Churchill stated that planning for the Champion began immediately after the company emerged from bankruptcy in the mid–1930s. Studebaker's vice-president for engineering, Roy Cole, and engineer Ralph Vail were responsible for the mechanical development of the Champion. Raymond Loewy's industrial design firm was instrumental in designing the Champion body.[7]

The Champion was designed for the low-priced field. Unlike the Erskine and Rockne, which also had been aimed at the low-priced field, with the Champion, Studebaker undertook serious market analysis before building the car. Studebaker did not study the Big Three low-priced cars as much as it studied the people who bought the cars. The marketing and product-planning staff at Studebaker studied how much these people earned, what they could afford, and how many people were in the income class at which the Champion would be aimed. What Studebaker's study of the market found was that people were having difficulty affording the operation of cars in the low-priced class. The reason for that problem was that standardized low-priced quality automobiles that could be operated at low cost were unavailable because of interchangeability. The

The 1932 Rockne "65" coupe was available in either a two-passenger model or four-passenger version with rumble seat models.

interchangeability situation was the result of the Big Three's practice of building engines and parts big enough to be used in two or more cars in different price classes. An example of this would be interchangeability of parts between Chevrolet and Pontiac at General Motors. Also, the study found that there were eleven million car-owning families that earned thirty dollars or less a week and that this number was increasing at the rate of a million families per year. For these families, the automobile accounted for about ten percent of their budget. Studebaker engineers were given a clean sheet to create an entirely new automobile that would appeal to this market without having to worry about interchangeability with other Studebaker models.[8]

According to Churchill, Cole and Vail worked closely with Hoffman and Vance to develop the Champion as a light and efficient vehicle. Churchill also noted that major changes in production technology were employed to produce the Champion. A new machine line was put in for the engine. The engine was designed around single-purpose machine tool equipment rather than around old multi-purpose tools. The tooling for the Champion was a major step in automation at Studebaker, with the engine and the tooling being designed together. According to Churchill: "These machine tools were not usable for anything else. And to make them universally adaptable to any other engine besides the Champion engine was almost an impossibility."[9]

Designing and tooling the Champion was a relatively expensive undertaking for Studebaker. In April 1938, Vance told the Board of Directors that the tooling costs would be $3 million and that it was, in essence, a great risk. The company would have serious problems if sales did not materialize. Yet Vance believed that market circumstances and the prospects for the future warranted taking this risk.[10]

The Champion six-cylinder, 164.3-cubic-inch displacement flathead engine ended up serving Studebaker well in the Champion and, with modifications, for almost the rest of its participation in the automobile industry. Churchill pointed out that the Champion engine was purposely designed to provide flexibility to increase its performance over time. The increase in the cubic inch displacement of the Champion engine

The 1939 Studebaker Champion was introduced to compete with the "Low-Priced Three" and was an outstanding success. It made a lasting impression on Harold Churchill.

in 1941 became the basis for many Studebaker six-cylinder cars through the 1964 model year. By 1961, engineering modifications had converted it to an overhead valve, 169-cubic-inch engine.

Churchill, in his interview, viewed the development of the Champion as a team effort at Studebaker. The Champion represented a change in philosophy in that the company was now staking its future on the low-priced field as opposed to having only the larger and medium- to high-priced Commanders and Presidents that had anchored the Studebaker product line since the demise of the Rockne.

The Champion sold well. Studebaker sales of 114,196 cars and trucks in calendar year 1939 more than doubled 1938 output of 52,605 units. The Champion was the principal reason for the increased output, with sales of 72,791 units the first year. In the *Studebaker Corporation Annual Report for 1939*, management spoke in glowing terms of the success of the Champion. The company observed that, although the Champion was introduced in April 1939, which was very late in the model year, the Champion soon accounted for 3.8 percent of U.S. registrations of cars in the low-priced field. Initially priced at $660, the Champion was competing directly with the so-called Low-Priced Three of Ford, Chevrolet, and Plymouth. By early 1940, the Champion accounted for 60 percent of the company's passenger car business. The 1939 *Studebaker Corporation Annual Report* notes the important effect of the increased production levels on Studebaker's profits, which rose from $1.8 million in 1938 to $2.9 million in 1939. Output increased to 119,509 units in 1940, but profits declined to $2.1 million due, according to the *Studebaker Corporation Annual Report for 1940*, mostly to competitive pricing pressures and increased costs associated with gearing up for defense production. The *Studebaker Annual Report for 1941* boasted that output increased to 133,855 cars and trucks, in part as a result of the continued success of the Champion, but also as a result of increased truck production for military purposes.

Harold Vance summed up the success of the Champion as follows:

> We couldn't ignore the tremendous need for low-cost transportation.... We had a loyal body of Studebaker owners. What we set out to do, and did, was to expand that number of owners as fast as possible, keeping both the old and new owners loyal with a quality car the average family could afford to buy. We believed the low-price car was the answer to the transportation needs of the country and that we ought to build it.[11]

Churchill noted that the success of the Champion was such that General Motors and Ford bought Champions to try to figure out how Studebaker was able to develop the Champion, with its reduced weight and increased operating efficiency. He said GM and Ford wondered how Studebaker did it, "but we did."[12]

Given the tremendous success of the Champion, and Churchill's stated commitment to performance and efficiency and economy of operation, it is clear that the Champion played a key role in shaping his attitude about what kind of automobiles should be offered to the American people. The experience with the Champion, then, became a key influence on Churchill when he became president of Studebaker-Packard and had to determine in what segments of the market the company would participate.

By the beginning of 1942, a substantial portion of the manufacturing facilities of Studebaker was devoted to production of a variety of war materials. The company's report for 1941 pointed out that three of the firm's plants, in South Bend, Chicago, and Fort Wayne, Indiana, were devoted to the manufacture of Cyclone aircraft engines for the B-17 Flying Fortress bomber. The South Bend automotive facilities were being devoted to the manufacture of six-wheel-drive heavy-duty military trucks, many of which ended up being utilized by the Soviet armed forces in the Eastern European campaigns.

One of the major engineering accomplishments of Studebaker and Churchill during World War II was the development and production of the M-29 cargo carrier known as the Weasel. By World War II, Churchill had advanced to the position of director of engineering research. One of the products developed under his leadership in that position was the Weasel.[13] The Weasel was a type of amphibious Jeep that had tracks like a tank and was powered by the Champion engine. It was a small but very versatile vehicle that could carry soldiers and cargo just about anywhere. The Weasels were used in the Aleutian Islands, the Italian campaign, the Normandy Invasion, and the Philippine campaign.[14]

In the oral history interview of Churchill, he indicated very clearly that he and the whole Studebaker organization were particularly proud of the work done on the Weasel. He related that the Weasel development was done under the sponsorship of the Office of Scientific Research and Development as a high-priority and classified project. The Weasel was designed, prototypes built, tested, tooled, and put in production in a period of seven months. Studebaker Corporation itself was quite proud of the Weasel, which it called in its *Annual Report for 1944*, "a new offensive weapon for the allied armies ... which could travel where no other land carrier could. Over the severest kinds of terrain ... the Weasel inscribes new records in the history of military transportation." According to Churchill, about 13,000 Weasels were built. Along with the Weasel, the *Studebaker Corporation Annual Report for 1945* reported 197,678 six-wheel-drive military trucks and 63,789 Cyclone aircraft engines were built by Studebaker as part of the war effort.

With the production of Cyclone aircraft engines, military trucks, and Weasel amphibious assault vehicles, Studebaker made a significant contribution to the World War II effort.

Following World War II, Studebaker initially produced a car for the 1946 model year that was essentially the same as the 1942 Studebaker Champion. But that was an interim product, and ultimately Studebaker produced what it said in its advertising made Studebaker "First by Far with a Postwar Car!" The 1947 Studebaker was sleek by mid–1940s standards and a clear departure from the design of prewar vehicles. Churchill attributed the rapidity with which Studebaker was able to get back in production and bring out a newly designed car after the war to the fact that the corporation's production facilities in South Bend had been employed primarily in building automotive-related vehicles during the war. He said in the interview that the assembly lines were changed to fit the bigger components of the trucks but required only minor modifications to readapt to producing the automobiles, which were a smaller product. He also pointed out that the Weasel utilized the Champion engine, enabling that component to be in continuous production during the war, which made conversion back to auto production easier. In addition, Churchill observed that planning for postwar production had gone on during the war, according to him, with government blessing.

From 1926 through World War II — indeed, constituting about half of Harold Churchill's career with the firm — he was involved in engineering during critical times

Following World War II, Studebaker got back into production quickly with the 1946 Skyway Champion, which was basically the same car as the 1942 Champion (AACA Library and Research Center).

Top: Following World War II, from 1946 to 1948 Studebaker continued its line of M Series trucks, originally introduced before the war. In the immediate postwar period, Studebaker was very successful with its line of trucks (AACA Library and Research Center). *Bottom:* A short model run for the 1946 Studebakers gave way to the car that stunned the automobile world and set the pattern for much of postwar automotive design. Pictured here is the 1947 Studebaker Commander Starlight Coupe. "First by Far with a Postwar Car" was Studebaker's advertising slogan for its dramatically new 1947 models. The basic styling of the 1947 Studebakers continued through the 1952 model year with major facelifts in 1950 and 1952 (AACA Library and Research Center).

in the development of the philosophy of the company. The need to be flexible in operations was apparent in the development of the defense production for the war effort. The attraction of low-priced, lightweight, more compact cars in the marketplace was evident in the 1939–1942 success of the Champion. These experiences of Studebaker, and especially the success of the Champion, left a major impression on the automotive thinking of Harold Churchill. That thinking became the core of his philosophy when he became president of the Studebaker-Packard Corporation.

As noted in the introduction, the primary focus of this volume is Studebaker-Packard Corporation under the presidency of Harold E. Churchill, and the events and thinking that shaped both his management style and his product philosophy. That presidency begins with events in 1956. However, it is difficult to analyze the situation in which Churchill found himself when assuming the presidency in July 1956, without having a brief discussion of conditions at Studebaker and Packard in the decade following World War II.

What follows is only a cursory summary of the Studebaker and Packard situation prior to the merger of Studebaker and Packard in 1954 (or, more accurately, the purchase of Studebaker by Packard). The topic of the merger has been carefully and analytically discussed in detail in books by Kimes (1978), Beatty, Furlong and Pennington (1984), Ward (1995), Critchlow (1996), and Bonsall (2000).

Table 1 summarizes the serious production and financial crisis that began to engulf both Studebaker and Packard as 1954 approached. Production of vehicles by both firms had undergone a sharp decline since the glory days of the postwar sellers' market in the late 1940s and early 1950s. Although earnings had held up reasonably well for a few years in the early 1950s, they had been supported at both firms by defense contracts related to the Korean Conflict. With the winding down of that conflict, defense business was declining, and the effects of declines in automobile sales were beginning to be felt. Mergers were very much in the wind at the time. Kaiser and Willys had merged and American Motors Corporation (AMC) had been formed by combining Nash and Hudson.

There had been a plan conceived by Packard President James Nance and Nash President George Mason to combine Studebaker, Packard, Nash, and Hudson into one large corporation, hopefully the fourth major automobile company in the United States. The first steps were to be the separate mergers of Studebaker and Packard on one hand and then Nash and Hudson on the other. However, the sudden death of Mason in October 1954 brought an end to that plan as George Romney, who succeeded Mason, would have nothing to do with the idea of combining AMC with Studebaker-Packard.[15]

Adding to the problems at Studebaker-Packard was the fact that the marriage of the two companies was done in haste. *Fortune* magazine reported that each of the companies was losing $2.5 million a month. Studebaker's production costs turned out to be much higher than had been estimated by the company's accountants. Packard production volume had slipped sharply in 1954. Then, after the merger, the company undertook an ambitious expansion program even though losses were mounting. James Nance, who had come to Packard as its president in 1952 from General Electric's Hotpoint Division, decided that S-P should become the fourth full-line producer of autos in the U.S.[16]

Sales of the company's products continued to languish in 1955 and 1956, although

Top: The 1953 Studebaker Starliner coupes were beautiful automobiles designed principally by Bob Bourke of the Raymond Loewy organization. Unfortunately, manufacturing difficulties prevented them from achieving their full sales potential. The Starliner basic hardtop coupe served as the basis for Studebaker sports coupes from 1953 through 1955, the Golden Hawks and some Silver Hawk models, and again for the 1962 through 1964 Gran Turismo Hawks (AACA Library and Research Center). *Bottom:* The Champion Starlight coupe for 1953 had the sports coupe design of the Starliners but had a fixed B-pillar. They served as the basis for pillared sports coupes through the 1961 model year, when the last pillared Hawks were built (AACA Library and Research Center).

Packard had a brief surge in sales in 1955, with a major facelift of the body, a new V8 engine, and a new suspension system called Torsion-Aire. Operating losses for Studebaker-Packard were $31 million in 1955 and $43 million in 1956.[17]

During this period, of course, Churchill was moving up the ranks at Studebaker to vice-president of engineering during the Korean Conflict, and then to general manager of the Studebaker Division following the merger of Studebaker and Packard. Asked in the oral history interview what his major contribution was during this period, he responded that he had been concerned with performance and energy efficiency, which had been Studebaker's strong point all along. He said he knew that Studebaker did not have the money to compete on the basis of styling. But he believed Studebaker could compete with something different — specifically, on economy of operation. Also, he believed that Studebaker was competitive in terms of its product's mechanical specifications. Studebaker had a good V8 engine, introduced in 1950, as well as a good automatic transmission. In 1980, when pressed by his interviewer, R.T. King, on what his (Churchill's) specific contributions were during this period, Churchill responded that he had always been cost-conscious, quality-conscious, and performance-conscious, and that "I still practice that scrupulously."

Churchill's view that Studebaker could not compete on the basis of styling indicates that he had a good grasp of the economics of the automobile industry as they existed in the 1950s. In order to put the remainder of the discussion of the situation that confronted Churchill at Studebaker-Packard into the proper context, the economies of scale in production of automobiles need to be examined.

An integrated automobile producer manufactures most of its components and assembles finished cars. A nonintegrated producer purchases parts from outside suppliers and only assembles vehicles. In the process of building these vehicles, both integrated and nonintegrated producers incur fixed and variable costs. Fixed costs are those that the firm incurs regardless of the level of production and include amortization (depreciation) of the production facilities and tooling, property taxes, capital equipment expenditures, administrative costs and salaried labor, etc. Variable costs increase as the level of output increases and include the costs of production labor, parts and components, and other production supplies. The integrated producer must build sufficient automobiles in a year to cover both the variable and fixed costs of a complex plant with high overhead. An assembler has a minimum of fixed costs and is concerned with direct unit costs only when parts are purchased from outside vendors.

Economist Joe S. Bain estimated in the 1950s, with production techniques existing then, that an integrated firm with a single assembly plant producing 100,000 to 150,000 cars per year might not achieve maximum efficiency, but could be profitable.[18] Another economist analyzing the auto industry at about the same time, Charles E. Edwards, noted that the Big Three set volume targets of 200,000 units per year for new models during the 1950s. For example, Ford targeted 200,000 units per year for the Edsel, introduced in 1958. The General Motors Chevrolet Corvair, the Ford Falcon, and the Chrysler Corporation Plymouth Valiant compact cars were introduced in 1960, when it appeared the annual sales rate would be at least 200,000 units for each make.[19] The 200,000-unit target suggests the industry believed in the 1950s that low per-unit manufacturing costs could be achieved for reasonably integrated manufacturers at that level

Styling introduced in the 1953 sport coupes was continued into 1955, but with facelifted styling. Top of the line for Studebaker in 1955 was the Speedster, built in limited quantities, but viewed as an experiment to test the market for the future introduction of the Hawk models. They featured the 259-cubic-inch V8 engine, a leather interior, and a new-styled sports car engine-turned metal instrument panel with complete instrumentation. This picture features a Speedster parked inside the Studebaker assembly plant in South Bend (AACA Library and Research Center).

of production. Evidence from data in *Ward's Automotive Reports* in the mid–1960s indicates that average output per U.S. automotive assembly plant was between 190,000 and 200,000 units per year, which serves as confirmation of the estimates by Edwards.

Studebaker was an integrated manufacturer in its South Bend, Indiana, plant through 1963. The firm built most of its own major components including bodies and engines. Although some body components were outsourced to suppliers, Studebaker had its own stamping plant and body assembly plant. Outside suppliers furnished some items including electrical components and various drive train components other than engines.

Data shown in Table 1 confirm the estimates of both Bain and Edwards in terms of levels of production that enabled Studebaker to operate profitably. When output reached the 120,000 level, profits occurred, and as output rose above the 200,000 level, profits became robust. Although it gets ahead of the story, comment is relevant at this point on the situation Studebaker faced in 1963, when all output was transferred to

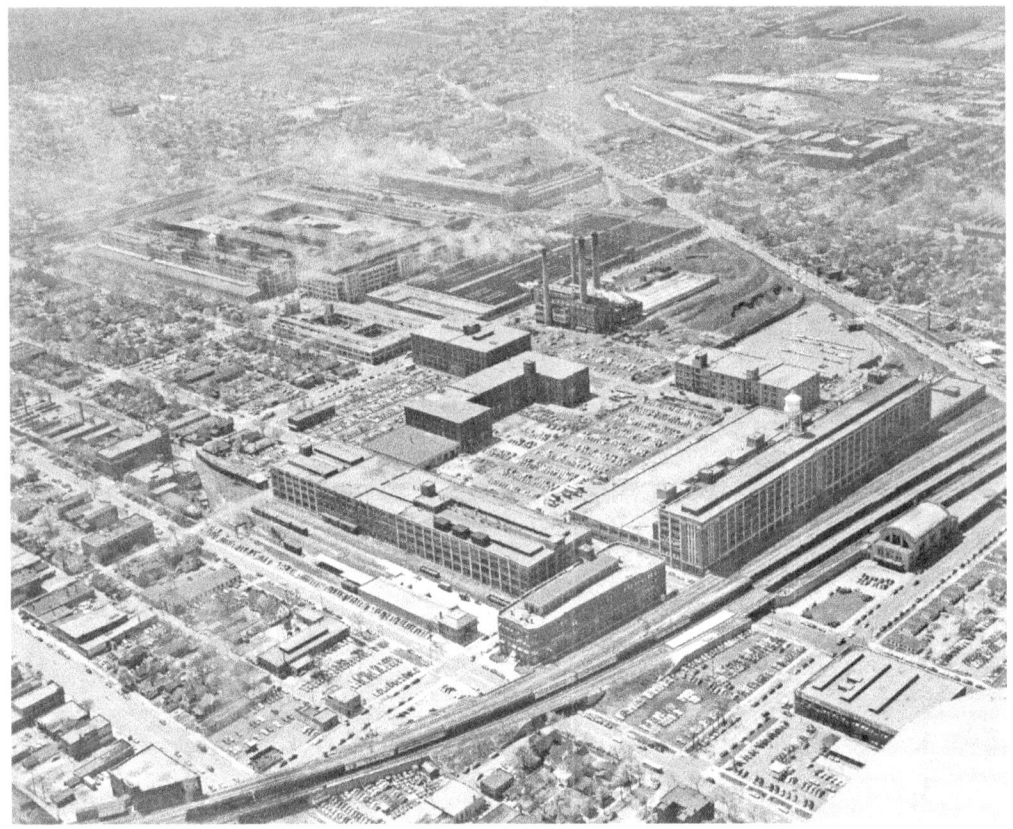

Upon taking over as president of Studebaker-Packard, Harold Churchill was faced with the need to oversee consolidation of all domestic production of Studebaker and Packard cars and trucks into the Studebaker plants in South Bend, Indiana, pictured here.

Hamilton, Ontario, with the closing of the South Bend plants. At the Canadian plant, Studebaker became a nonintegrated producer, purchasing engines from General Motors, for example, and body stampings from outside suppliers. Evidence indicates that Studebaker could be profitable in that plant with output of 20,000 units per year, although capacity on a two-shift basis was about 36,000 units annually. (Table 2 and discussion thereof in Chapter 3 elaborate on these points.)

Churchill, then, appears to have understood the trap in which Studebaker was caught during the late 1950s and the early 1960s. The automobile industry was engaged in frequent major style changes during that period. To maintain a volume sufficient to operate profitably would have required investment in styling and tooling that would have stretched Studebaker's resources beyond the firm's capabilities. Whereas the Big Three could amortize those tooling investments over hundreds of thousands of units, Studebaker's output was at a much lower level. However, the other part of the trap was that failure to make those style changes cost the firm volume. The future for Studebaker, as Churchill affirmed in his interview, was not even to attempt to compete on the basis of frequent styling changes, but rather on the basis of building cars that were mechanically superior and economical to operate.

Table 1: Studebaker and Packard Financial and Production Data 1945–1954a

Year	Factory Sales Studebaker	Factory Sales Packard	Profits/(Loss) Millions of Dollars Studebaker	Profits/(Loss) Millions of Dollars Packard
1945	1,309	2,720	$3.3	$1.1
1946	120,763	41,706	$0.9	$3.9
1947	191,451	52,273	$9.1	$1.1
1948	233,457	98,898	$19.1	$15.1
1949	304,994	104,593	$27.6	$7.7
1950	334,554	72,138	$22.5	$5.1
1951	285,888	76,065	$12.6	$5.6
1952	231,837	62,820	$14.8	$5.6
1953	218,080	81,341	$2.4	$5.4
1954	100,604	27,583	($27.0)[b]	($26.2)

[a]Sources: Annual Reports, Studebaker Corporation, Packard Motor Car Company; Proxy Statement, Packard Motor Car Company, July 9, 1954; selected issues of *Ward's Automotive Reports* and *Automotive News*.

[b]Estimates for Studebaker alone from published four month earnings prior to merger. The Packard loss of $26.2 million for 1954 was reported in the Studebaker-Packard *Annual Report for 1954*, as including Packard for all 12 months of 1954 and Studebaker for the last three months — an accounting procedure consistent with Packard's technically not having merged with Studebaker but having bought the company.

In his early career between 1926 and the outbreak of World War II, Churchill was involved at Studebaker as it evolved from a builder of Presidents, Dictators, and Commanders in the medium to luxury classes, to a builder of economy cars from the Erskine to the Rockne, and finally to the very successful Champion. The lessons of those years had a profound effect on Churchill. Near the end of his life in 1980, looking back on his career, he was able to reflect that he had been driven by a desire to be cost, performance, and quality conscious. It was to be that philosophy that guided his decisions as he took the next big step in his career.

3
Accepting and Facing the Challenge

"Well, Church, I'll tell you what we're going to do. We want you to become president of Studebaker-Packard. Will you accept it?"

With those words, J. Russell Forgan, member of the Studebaker-Packard Board of Directors, which was meeting in New York on Thursday, July 26, 1956, broke the news to Harold E. Churchill (whose nickname was "Church") by telephone that the Board wanted Churchill to take over running of the company. Churchill responded as follows: "Well Russ, I can't tell you 'no.' I'll do the best I can. But I'll only accept it under one condition; that there be no strings attached to it at all; that I'm coming to try to do the best I can as I think I've always done for Studebaker."[1]

It needs to be noted that there is a difference between the S-P Board minutes and Churchill's recollections of the dates on which this sequence of events occurred. In the Indiana University oral history interview of Churchill, he stated the call from Forgan came on August 5, 1956. However, the Board minutes state Forgan called him and the decisions were made on July 26, 1956. Churchill may have been confused with the fact that the minutes show he presided over his first S-P Board meeting on August 6, 1956, in New York.

The *New York Times* reported on Churchill's appointment as head of S-P with the following headline on August 8, 1956: "Studebaker Chief Faces Big Job; President's Task to Lead Company Back to Prosperity." Studebaker-Packard Corporation was in extremely serious financial trouble by August 1956. One unnamed South Bend city official even said that Churchill, viewed as one of their own in South Bend, was pitied when he was made president of the firm.[2] Table 2 summarizes the rapid decline of the company's fortunes following the merger of Studebaker and Packard in late 1954. Output and sales were in a precipitous decline with very serious financial losses being incurred. The discussion presented here will summarize the events that led up to the crisis of 1956, and then will analyze the events subsequent to that crisis as Harold Churchill assumed administrative control of the firm.

In his telephone response to Forgan, Churchill stated he would accept the presidency of Studebaker-Packard only if there were no strings attached. Given his position with the company at the time, he certainly was acquainted with the agreements being reached with Curtiss-Wright Corporation at that July 26, 1956, Board meeting and which would have an important influence on the affairs of Studebaker-Packard for the next two years. Although the Curtiss-Wright-Studebaker-Packard Management Advisory Agreement gave C-W considerable influence in the affairs of Studebaker-Packard, the fact that Churchill accepted the presidency suggests that the C-W influence was at a level with which he (Churchill) could live.

Table 2 Studebaker-Packard Corporation Financial and Production Data During the Presidency of Harold E. Churchill[a]

Year[a]	Factory Sales Studebaker Thousands of Units[b]	Factory Sales Packard Thousands of Units[c]	Studebaker Canadian Production Thousands of Units[d]	Sales Millions of Dollars	Profits/(Loss) from operations Millions of Dollars
1955	138.5	62.6	8.7	$482.2	($30.9)
1956	107.6	19.1	8.7	$303.4	($43.3)[e]
1957	88.6	5.4	5.5	$215.9	($11.1)
1958	77.6	1.7	4.5	$183.7	($13.4)
1959	182.3	—	8.3	$387.4	$28.5
1960	134.0	—	5.7	$323.2	$0.7
1961	102.9	—	6.2	$298.5	($3.1)
1962	115.6	—	8.1	$365.5	$0.5
1963	89.6	—	8.1	$403.3	($16.9)[f]
1964	—	—	17.4	$261.8[g]	$8.1[g]
1965	—	—	18.6	$192.7[g]	$10.7[g]
1966	—	—	2.0	$172.9[g]	$16.5[g]

[a]Harold E. Churchill became president of Studebaker-Packard Corporation in 1956 and relinquished the position of president effective February 1, 1961. Other years are shown for comparative purposes.

[b]Studebaker cars and trucks worldwide, including Canada, 1955–1963; cars only 1964–1966 in Canadian plant.

[c]Packard and Clipper cars.

[d]Canadian output also included in Studebaker factory sales column for 1955–1963.

[e]An additional charge of $60 million was made in 1956 for the closing of the Detroit Packard plants.

[f]An additional charge of $52.4 million was made in 1963 for the closing of the South Bend Studebaker plants.

[g]Dollar value of automotive sales is estimated at $120.6 million in 1964; $46.2 million in 1965; and $1.8 million in 1966. Income from automotive operations is estimated at $0.6 million in 1964; a loss was incurred by automotive operations of about $0.3 million in both 1965 and 1966.

Sources: Studebaker-Packard Corporation *Annual Reports*, 1955–1961; Studebaker Corporation *Annual Reports*, 1962–1966; Studebaker Corporation *Notice of 1967 Annual Meeting of Stockholders May 10, 1967*; Minutes of Board of Directors Meetings of Studebaker-Packard Corporation; *Ward's Automotive Reports*.

Top: The Hawk line of sport coupes, introduced in 1956, featured a significant change in front-end styling and was promoted as a family sports car. The 1956 Studebaker Golden Hawk, with its 352-cubic-inch, 275-horsepower Packard V-8 engine, was the top model in Studebaker's line of Hawk models. *Bottom:* The President Classic was the top of the Studebaker standard passenger car line for 1956. It had the Studebaker 289-cubic-inch, 210-horsepower engine. Although its front and rear-end styling was given a less streamlined look than the 1953–1955 models, its basic body was that of the Studebaker Land Cruiser of 1953.

To understand the agreement with Curtiss-Wright and the position in which Churchill found himself in August 1956 as president of Studebaker-Packard, it is helpful to examine what the Board of Directors had done during the early part of 1956 to attempt to manage the rapidly deteriorating sales and financial position of the corporation. A July 31, 1956, report by the consulting firm Robert Heller and Associates, titled *Record of the Efforts Directed at Preserving the Corporation*, summarizes the steps taken by the Board.

According to the Heller Report, when a request to insurance companies for additional capital was denied in January 1956, the Board undertook a program to explore ways to continue operations and protect the interests of stockholders. Approaches to Ford Motor Company to obtain Ford body shells for 1957 Studebaker cars and Lincoln body shells for 1957 Packard cars, originally designed to be based on the Packard Predictor show car, were rejected. Approaches to American Motors, Chrysler, and International Harvester for merger also were rejected. After a series of negotiations, the only viable plan that was developed was the Management Advisory Agreement with Curtiss-Wright Corporation.

In fact, the situation at S-P in early 1956 can only be described as dire. The minutes of the January 20, 1956, Board meeting record that Nance stated the company faced two basic problems. The first was that added financing was needed. As a result, the Board organized a finance committee to act in an advisory capacity to the Board and the President.[3]

The second problem Nance conveyed to the Board was that sales of the company's cars were not keeping up with production and the dealers had a substantial increase in the inventory of cars. In fact, the stock of cars in dealers' hands was twice that of January 1955, and was at an all-time high. The result was what Nance described as "disorderly retail selling at little or no profit, [and] exhaustion of dealers' finances." Furthermore, Nance reported that banks were reluctant to furnish Studebaker-Packard dealers floor plan and capital loan credit due to concerns about the financial condition of the company. The deteriorating financial condition of S-P was also viewed by Nance as having an adverse affect on sales and leading to a defection of dealers to competitive makes.

At the February 27, 1956, Board meeting, the minutes state that Nance reported sales of Packard and Clipper cars had deteriorated to the point that Packard plant production had been shut down and would open again on March 5, only to produce cars on a limited basis to meet orders that could not be supplied out of warehouse inventories. In terms of the company's finances, Nance stated that if the tooling program for the planned redesigned 1957 cars with a common body shell for all three makes (Packard, Clipper, and Studebaker) was undertaken, the company would run out of cash sometime between July and September.

At that February 27, 1956, Board meeting, Nance introduced Mr. D.C. Borden, a former vice-president of the First National City Bank of New York who had been suggested by S-P's creditor banks as a financial advisor to the company. Borden advised the S-P Board that he believed it to be impossible to get additional loans from insurance companies and that the corporation should not go into the originally planned $35 million to $40 million tooling program for the 1957 cars. At that same meeting, the Board

Top: The 1956 Packards were the last to be built in the Detroit Packard plants. Shown here is a 1956 Packard "400" Hardtop. *Bottom:* The 1956 Clippers, built by Packard, had the same basic body shell utilized by Packard from 1951 through 1956. After consolidation of Studebaker and Packard production in South Bend, this body shell and the Packard running gear were abandoned. However, the taillight assembly, first introduced on the Clippers for 1956, was used on both the 1957 and 1958 Packards built on the Studebaker body shell.

also discussed briefly the possibilities of disposing of the Packard portion of the corporation's business because of the severe deterioration in that division's sales.

Minutes of the meeting reveal the idea of merger with Curtiss-Wright was first mentioned to the Board at its March 23, 1956, meeting by Board member J. Russell Forgan, who chaired the Board's finance committee. Forgan stated that Curtiss-Wright had asked for more information regarding S-P's affairs. At the April 16, 1956, Board meeting, it was announced that discussions were continuing with Curtiss-Wright. At the May 2, 1956, Board meeting it was announced that Nance, Forgan, and Roy Hurley, president of Curtiss-Wright, had met several times with officials in Washington to see if additional defense orders could be secured if S-P and Curtiss-Wright joined together in some sort of joint program. Nance outlined a program that had been presented to officials in Washington involving the possible consolidation and financing of the corporation's operations. That program would have seen the consolidation of all of the S-P defense business in Detroit and all automobile production in South Bend. Also part of the plan would be for S-P to receive as much as $200 million in defense business for 1957 and the sale of automobile facilities in Detroit to other automobile companies. However, Forgan reported that it became clear from those meetings that S-P could expect no help whatever from the automobile industry. Meanwhile, Hurley of Curtiss-Wright was meeting with some of his directors and officials in Washington because it appeared C-W continued to have interest in some sort of an arrangement with Studebaker-Packard.

At a May 8, 1956, meeting of the S-P Board, Forgan outlined plans for an arrangement with Curtiss-Wright whereby banks would extend an added $15 million of credit to S-P, and extend the maturity on the existing $45 million of credit. The plan, however, would have been contingent on S-P's obtaining substantial added defense business and entering into a management advisory agreement with C-W. Also included in the plan would have been an arrangement whereby Daimler-Benz of Germany would agree to buy 1,000,000 shares of S-P stock and Curtiss-Wright would receive warrants to buy 6.5 million shares of S-P stock over a period of two to three years. The agreement contemplated that Daimler-Benz automobiles would be distributed through the Studebaker-Packard dealers in the United States beginning as early as August 1, 1956. Forgan noted that meetings with banks and insurance companies indicated they were prepared to go along with the plan. The consensus of the Studebaker-Packard Board members was that the plan was the only viable alternative available to the company other than reorganization or liquidation. These arrangements with Curtiss-Wright, the banks, and the insurance companies were reaffirmed at the May 29, 1956, S-P Board meeting.

What happened next is interesting historically, given that the early part of the 21st century saw the United States government engage in bailouts and, for a period of time, take ownership of stock in Chrysler Corporation and General Motors. On June 2, 1956, the Studebaker-Packard Board was advised that Curtiss-Wright did not believe there was enough auto and defense business for S-P to make a joint program between the two firms successful. The bottom line was that C-W was pulling out of the deal. However, during that meeting, Forgan conferred several times with unnamed government officials and Hurley of Curtiss-Wright, who said in essence that some sort of joint program might be put into effect if there was some assurance new defense orders could be completed, i.e., that some sort of financially sound defense business subsidiary be established.

A key element of the plan was that it proposed that S-P borrow $15 million from the Federal Reserve Bank of New York. That $15 million would then be loaned by S-P to the defense subsidiary. All defense business would be transferred to the subsidiary, and Curtiss-Wright would provide executive management to the subsidiary and would appoint some members to the S-P Board of Directors. At the June 7, 1956, Board meeting, Forgan reported that an application for a Federal Reserve loan of $15 million was in process and that the Federal Reserve had agreed to give prompt consideration to the matter.

How, then, could the Federal Reserve loan money to a private corporation in this manner? The answer is that in 1934, the Industrial Advances Act added Section 13(b) to the Federal Reserve Act, allowing Federal Reserve District banks to make advances of working capital to established businesses if those enterprises were unable to secure such capital from usual sources. (Section 13[b] was repealed in 1958 as part of the Small Business Investment Act.[4])

Thus it was, about six weeks before Churchill was to become president of Studebaker-Packard, the company applied for what would have been, in essence, a Federal Reserve bailout. However, on June 27, 1956, Forgan reported to the S-P Board that the Fed had agreed to make the loan, "but had established conditions precedent to such loan which were regarded both by the Corporation and by Curtiss-Wright as being too onerous for acceptance." Those conditions would have included complete security for the loan by pledge of real property assets and by restriction against any dividends being distributed by the new defense subsidiary back to S-P itself.

In the meantime, negotiations continued with Curtiss-Wright in hopes that some sort of joint program could be put into effect. As a side note to these discussions, Nance told the Board on June 4, 1956, that both he and the directors knew that there would be no place for him in any joint program with Curtiss-Wright. He said he would cooperate in any way possible to initiate the program and would stay on for 30 days in an advisory capacity with the new management. So it was clear that Nance's days at S-P were quickly being numbered as the negotiations proceeded with C-W. At that June 4 Board meeting a resolution was passed stating: "RESOLVED, That the negotiations with Curtiss-Wright and other parties concerned be continued as expeditiously as possible."

In the end, even without a loan from the Federal Reserve, S-P and C-W were able to pull together a joint agreement that was to be inherited by Churchill as he took over. By the June 27, 1956, S-P Board meeting, Forgan reported that in discussions, Roy Hurley of Curtiss-Wright had proposed a joint program that was essentially the one that in the end was approved and implemented.

At the July 25, 1956, S-P Board meeting there was further considerable discussion of the joint program with Curtiss-Wright. One of the questions raised by the Board was Hurley's intentions with respect to continuance in the automobile industry. Forgan replied that Hurley had stated that he would recommend the continuance of manufacture and sale of automobiles but on a concentrated basis operating from South Bend alone. The Board then unanimously approved the joint program with Curtiss-Wright in principle, subject to further detailed review. That review took place the following day, July 26, 1956, as the Board met once again to consider the Curtiss-Wright proposal. At that meeting, the Board concluded that there were no other alternatives to the Curtiss-Wright program other than bankruptcy for the corporation, which would have been a far less promising situation for the stockholders of Studebaker-Packard. A resolution approving the joint program with Curtiss-Wright was then passed.

Significant for Harold Churchill, at that July 26, 1956, Board meeting of Studebaker-Packard Corporation, Paul Hoffman resigned as board chair and James Nance resigned as president of the corporation. Upon acceptance of the resignations of Hoffman and Nance, the Board minutes read: "On motion duly made and seconded, and unanimously carried, Mr. Harold E. Churchill was elected President and a director."

A summary of the 1956 agreement with C-W was given to Studebaker-Packard dealers in an August 8, 1956, letter, and more details can be found on the agreement in the July 26, 1956, Minutes of the Board of Directors of S-P and in the September 4, 1958, letter and proxy statement to S-P stockholders, which described both the agreement and its subsequent termination. A general summary of the Management Advisory Agreement between Studebaker-Packard Corporation and Curtiss-Wright follows:

1. Packard production was terminated at the Detroit plants on June 25, 1956, and all automotive production was consolidated in South Bend.
2. Utica-Bend Corporation, a subsidiary of Curtiss-Wright, leased S-P's plant at Utica, Michigan (Packard engine and transmission), and the Chippewa Avenue plant in South Bend for twelve years for an advanced rental payment of $25 million to S-P. The S-P subsidiary in Santa Barbara, California, the Aerophysics Corporation, was sold to C-W. These three properties were obtained by C-W for the purpose of fulfilling various defense contracts. Total value of these transactions was $35 million in cash, which S-P obtained and was instrumental in S-P's being able to continue operations.
3. Curtiss-Wright obtained an option on five million shares of Studebaker-Packard stock at $5 per share which, had it been exercised, would have meant an added $25 million in working capital to S-P.
4. Studebaker-Packard and Curtiss-Wright entered into a three-year management advisory agreement, whereby C-W agreed to advise S-P on the operation of the business.

As he became president of S-P, Churchill found himself in the position of running an automaker in serious trouble and having to deal with Curtiss-Wright, whose chair and president, Roy T. Hurley, had a reputation for doing things efficiently by increasing productivity.[5] Also, as President of S-P, for the first time in his life, Churchill found himself having to answer to a different group of corporate stakeholders than the employees or administration. In his own words:

> Well, I had a shocking experience. I think I was and still am ... a loyal Studebaker individual; my devotion and responsibility was centered on my fellow Studebaker employees. The first thing you do when you become president of an organization, your loyalties immediately change. Your responsibility is to the owners of the business. I knew this was going to happen, but it takes a little adjusting to do.[6]

According to people who knew Churchill well, he made the transition from being an engineer who was in charge of the Studebaker Division to corporate executive smoothly and gracefully. *Business Week* magazine, in its June 20, 1959, issue, quoted him as saying that he missed regular contact with his engineer friends once he became president of the company.

That engineering background and way of thinking, though, influenced a great deal of what he did at Studebaker, where he created a compact, flexible management team that ultimately produced the Lark compact car. Churchill had accepted the presidency of Studebaker-Packard with the understanding that there be no strings attached. In a sense, the Management Advisory Agreement with Curtiss-Wright carried with it the potential for interference in the affairs of S-P. However, in the minutes of the August

6, 1956, S-P Board meeting, which was the first Board meeting for which Churchill was the presiding officer, it is recorded that the Studebaker-Packard directors recognized that, while Curtiss-Wright had agreed to furnish advisory management services to S-P, the activities of Curtiss-Wright were still subject to the direction of the Board of Studebaker-Packard, which was charged with the responsibility of managing the affairs of the corporation in the best interests of the shareholders.

Stockholders became a major issue for Churchill in his first two months as S-P chief executive. To build confidence in the company on the part of the media and community, he held a September 5, 1956, news conference for automotive and financial editors in New York City, and a national press demonstration day at South Bend on September 12, 1956. The transcript of his remarks at both events show that he spelled out a three-step plan to make the S-P automotive operation profitable:

1. A cost reduction plan;
2. A market development plan to give dealers new marketing strength;
3. A product development plan to provide dealers with highly competitive lines of products for 1957 and 1958.

In his remarks at both press conferences, Churchill highlighted what he saw as the strengths and weaknesses confronting Studebaker-Packard. His observations reflect both a sense of optimism as he assumed the presidency of the company and a realistic assessment of the challenges being confronted. Some of his remarks at the September 5, 1956, press conference are quoted below:

> At the time of the completion of agreements with Curtiss-Wright Corporation on August 6, we had certain factors working for us, some that were against us.
> On the one hand, we had competitive labor costs with a union contract still having two years to run; we had a very loyal employee group; a highly competitive line of automobiles and trucks; a large and loyal dealer organization with good sales potential; a series of plants that were up to averages for the industry; plenty of floor space in these plants; and a latent reserve of experienced management personnel.
> On the other hand, we frankly had too much floor space in the light of our auto manufacturing requirements; we had a separated, three-city, high overhead production situation; a lack of working capital; and a lack of diversification.[7]

In outlining his three-step program, listed above, for bringing the corporation back to profitable operations, Churchill also stated: "We have a new program in which the main ingredients are 'realism and common sense' and we are putting it into effect with all possible speed."[8] The reference to realism and common sense suggests that Churchill fully realized that the earlier plans under the Nance administration at the time of the Studebaker-Packard merger were unrealistic and probably beyond the capabilities of the company with its then existing line of cars and financial resources. Rather than aiming for S-P to be a fourth full-line producer, throughout the remainder of his service to the company, Churchill pushed for a model lineup that served specific, narrow segments of the automobile market.

Although he was having some success in meeting with the press and telling them the Studebaker-Packard story, Churchill's diplomatic skills were to be challenged as he tried to convince stockholders to approve the agreement with Curtiss-Wright. The proxy statement for a special meeting of stockholders on October 31, 1956, to vote on the C-W agreement, went out on September 26, 1956. Along with the proxy statement, Churchill wrote a letter to stockholders urging a favorable vote on the C-W agreement because it would permit continuation of the business.[9] That agreement was challenged by a group of minority stockholders led by Sol A. Dann, who accused S-P of misleading statements in the proxy solicitation. In the end, Federal Judge Andrew F. Lederle refused an injunction against use of proxy votes at the meeting because the plaintiffs failed to show they would suffer irreparable damage if the court did not grant the request.[10]

Following tabulation of the proxies, Churchill issued a press release on November 2, 1956, that 90 percent of the votes cast approved the C-W deal. In that press release he confirmed that auto production had been discontinued permanently at both the Detroit Packard and Los Angeles Studebaker plants. All United States auto production of Studebaker-Packard Corporation had been consolidated at South Bend, and all truck production had been consolidated at one plant in South Bend. (Previously, some truck manufacturing had been at the South Bend Chippewa Avenue plant leased to Curtiss-Wright as part of the refinancing plan.)

Dealing with stockholders and the press was not the only matter of concern to Churchill. He had an auto company to run, which required some very immediate decisions. Primary among those decisions was the future of the Packard automobile. The original plan, developed under James Nance, was for Studebaker-Packard to be the fourth full-line producer of automobiles in the United States, with the styling of those cars based on the 1956 Packard Predictor show car. Tooling costs for this plan were estimated to be $48.3 million for the 1957 and 1958 model years. Inability of Studebaker-Packard to get the needed financing put an end to that plan in early 1956, and led to the consolidation of all Studebaker and Packard production in South Bend.

While Churchill had been chief engineer at Studebaker, his involvement with actual product planning from a styling, development, and marketing standpoint had been limited. As an engineer, his role was more to adapt the engineering of the Stude-

Studebaker-Packard Corporation initially planned to build an all-new line of 1957 Packards based on the styling themes of the Packard Predictor show car. The financial crisis of 1956 made these plans impossible to fulfill.

baker vehicles to the desires of the styling and marketing folks. Thus, as he became president of S-P, his experience in bringing new cars to market was limited to his experience as an engineer. He was appointed to the position of head of the Studebaker Division of Studebaker-Packard in August 1955, which meant he had no direct influence on product planning for the 1955 or 1956 model year Studebaker-Packard products. Also, by July 1956, when he was appointed president of S-P, Churchill would have had minimal influence over product policy for the 1957 Studebakers, which were ready to go into production and be introduced to the public in the fall of 1956. Although, as general manager of the Studebaker Division, he may have had some input in product decisions, the minutes of the Board of Directors clearly show that the product decisions, such as the full-line philosophy, had been in the hands of Nance and the Board.

The question of what to do with the Packard automobile, though, put Churchill in the position of having to make a very quick and important decision regarding the Packard part of the 1957 Studebaker-Packard Corporation model lineup. In his decision to produce a 1957 Packard, it can be argued that we see in Churchill the ability to be decisive and act rationally under considerable pressure. Details of the Packard decision are discussed in a two-part article in 2006 and 2007 in *Automotive History Review* by Ebert and Pamphilis, who concluded that Churchill's decision to build the 1957 Packard on the Studebaker body shell and chassis was both economically rational and successful for the 1957 model year.

Churchill announced the decision to build a 1957 Packard to the Board on August 20, 1956. He told the Board that the 1957 Packard would be built on the Studebaker President Classic chassis with the Studebaker Golden Hawk supercharged 289-cubic-inch V-8 engine and that the front and rear end styling would embody many features of the Packard and Clipper styling. He estimated that the car would sell for about $150 less than the 1956 Packard Executive model (which was a late 1956 model year Packard entry into the market, positioned between the top-of-the-line Patricians and medium-priced Clippers), and about $450 more than the Studebaker President Classic. Tooling costs for the 1957 Packard were $1 million, which Churchill estimated would be amortized over 4000 to 6000 units. With production of 4809 units, S-P made an estimated operating profit of about $1.8 million on the 1957 Packards.[11]

Of course, Churchill was not starting with a completely clean slate in making the decision to build the 1957 Packards based on the Studebaker body shell and drive train. He had been named president in late July 1956, and to have only a month to design and develop a 1957 Packard would have been a near impossibility. In their article on the decision to build the 1957 and 1958 Packards, Ebert and Pamphilis concluded that, since discussion was underway at S-P by March 1956 to consolidate production in South Bend, some development work on a Studebaker-based Packard had to have begun around that time.

Evidence suggests that the 1957 Packards were developed in South Bend and not at the Packard styling studios in Detroit. At the time, S-P styling was being directed by William Schmidt, vice-president for styling at S-P, who oversaw both the Packard styling studio led by Richard Teague and the Studebaker studio led by Duncan McRae. Although, as V-P for styling of all of S-P, Schmidt made the presentation of the 1957 Packards to dealers at their August 28, 1956, meeting, he was not the stylist responsible

Immediately after becoming president of Studebaker-Packard, Churchill had to make a decision on whether to offer a line of 1957 Packards. The result was the Packard Clipper, based on the Studebaker President Classic 120-inch wheelbase body and chassis. Powering the 1957 Packards was the supercharged 289-cubic-inch Studebaker V8.

for the cars. Neither was Richard Teague, who had been head of the Packard styling efforts until the closing of the Packard facilities in Detroit. In an oral history of Schmidt, recorded in 1984, he makes no mention of the 1957 Packards.[12]

According to Teague, Duncan McRae was assigned the job of creating the 1957 Packards, although Teague recalled going to South Bend several times to help with the development of the cars. Teague concluded that it was logical that McRae was given the job because the 1957 Packard was based primarily on the Studebaker body shell.[13]

By June of 1956, it appears the mechanical configuration of the 1957 Packards had been set. Following a June 8 and 9 group meeting with Curtiss-Wright, which included Roy Hurley, George Brodie, vice-president for coordinating operations, sent a memo to Nance that stated, in part: "The balance of the meeting was devoted to consideration of the automotive, truck and parts programs at Packard and Studebaker. The Packard group spent the evening of June 8 resolving a proposed program which I understand would eliminate the Packard Clipper and provide for the production of the 1957 Packard and Executive models at Studebaker, using the 289 cu. in. Studebaker engine supercharged."[14]

Therefore, by June 25, 1956, when Packard production ended in Detroit, planning for a Packard based on Studebaker components was well underway, which means that by the time the decision to proceed with a Packard for 1957 was made by the Board at its August 20, 1956, meeting, Churchill had something viable with which to work. His big challenge, though, was to sell the anxious Packard Dealer Council on the idea.

Prototypes of the 1957 Packard were shown to the Packard Division National Dealer Council members on August 28, 1956, in South Bend. By this time, of course, Packard production had been ended in Detroit and it was an accepted fact that all S-P production would be consolidated into the South Bend plants. As a result, the anxiety level of the Packard dealers was high regarding whether or not there would even be a Packard automobile for 1957, and what the future of their franchises would be. Thus, the management and diplomatic skills of Harold Churchill in dealing with a difficult situation were given a major test in his meeting with the Packard Dealer Council.

In his remarks to the Packard Dealer Council, Churchill gave insights into his decisions to build a 1957 Packard and to build it based on Studebaker components. Following are some of Churchill's comments:

> We come down to the situation that you saw this morning [the dealers had seen the prototype of the 1957 Packard], what we believe to be a realistic resolution of our problem of how to perpetuate Packard.
>
> We explored the possibilities of moving manufacturing. Tools for '56 Packards are in existence, and we have carefully surveyed the possibility and expense of setting up those tools in our consolidated plants, and arrived at a conclusion that on the basis of the 6.5 million dollars involved in setting up those facilities, that it was not a wise business move to do that.
>
> First of all, the present '56 Packard body, being wider than the facilities in South Bend are capable of taking, means that we would have had to go through our consolidated manufacturing operation and widen out all of our spray booths, bake ovens, final lines, and other related facilities related to those jobs, which would have meant a serious curtailment of Studebaker-Packard manufacture of automobiles and a later 1957 model announcement.
>
> We have further decided, realistically, that first and foremost, we must have some way of perpetuating the Packard name in an interim period until we could come out with our '58 line of Studebakers and Packards which, I can tell you, provisions for tooling are made. Engineering is going on at the moment on our '58 models.
>
> In my opinion and in the opinion of my associates ... if the Packard name were dropped out of the business for one year, it would be almost an impossible job to ever revive that grand, old name which is one of our biggest assets.[15]

The minutes of the September 10, 1956, Board meeting note that Churchill told the Board that he had met with the Packard Dealer Council to announce the program for the 1957 Packard. He said that while the Packard dealers were not enthusiastic, they did appreciate the forthrightness of the corporation in presenting its problems to them, and many of the Packard dealers indicated that they would go along with the dualing program (i.e., the dualing of Studebaker and Packard franchises in the same dealerships).

To say the Packard dealers were not enthusiastic about the Packard program for 1957 was an understatement. After the Packard Dealer Council had an opportunity to discuss the 1957 Packards without management present, R.E. Bickelhaupt, a Clinton, Iowa, Packard dealer, read a statement to Churchill and management on behalf of the Dealer Council which stated: "The members of the Council all did not like the '57 Packard Clipper as presented, but will go along a hundred percent to make it a success, with the understanding that early in the Fall of '58 we will have cars with the Packard name comparable to the fine Patrician...."[16]

The station wagon was added to the 1957 Packard Clipper line at the urging of the Packard National Dealer Council, whose members wanted more than just a four-door sedan to sell for the 1957 model year. The Packard Clipper Station Wagon was built on the Studebaker 116.5-inch wheelbase.

As presented to the dealers, the only model shown was a four-door 1957 Packard Clipper sedan. Considerable discussion occurred at the meeting where the dealers pressed Churchill to include in the Packard line more models, specifically a four-door station wagon and a model based on the Golden Hawk. Churchill responded that the suggestions were excellent and would get the complete investigation of the marketing group and sales department.[17] In the end, a second model of 1957 Packard Clipper was offered — the four-door station wagon. However, the model based on the Golden Hawk had to wait until the 1958 model year, when the Packard Hawk was introduced. Although, as Churchill told the Board, the dealers were not enthusiastic, a number of the dealers did comment they were going out of the meeting with an open mind and were prepared to sell the 1957 Packard and make money on them.[18]

Further indication that the decision to build the 1957 Packard was a sound one can be seen in the data shown in the S-P Board minutes of December 20, 1957, by A.J. Porta, vice-president of finance. Porta estimated the company's break-even point was 103,000 vehicles for the 1958 model year, but would be 123,000 units if the relatively expensive (and high profit margin) Packard and Studebaker President Classic lines were eliminated. Ultimately, though, controversial styling and the depressed auto market in a recession year were a disaster for 1958 model year Packard production, with only 2622 units built leading to discontinuance of the brand.

It is worth noting that Porta's estimates for a break-even point for S-P production in its single domestic plant in South Bend are consistent with estimates of economists studying the technology and structure of the auto industry in the 1950s and 1960s. The industry is characterized by significant economies of scale (i.e., a decline in costs per unit over a large number of units produced as costs of development and tooling are spread over a larger quantity of units). As discussed in Chapter 2, Bain estimated that in the 1950s an integrated producer such as Studebaker-Packard would have needed in the range of 100,000 to 150,000 units per year to break even, with added economies of scale and profits obtainable at even higher levels of output.[19] Edwards and White calculated that economies of scale continued to be achieved in a single assembly plant through 200,000 to 250,000 units.[20] Porta's estimates, therefore, are consistent with other estimates of levels of operation required for profitable results and continued economies of scale, and also are consistent with the S-P experience with the Lark, which became profitable with output levels achieved in 1959.

Also lending credibility to the argument that the decision to produce the 1957 Packards was rational from an economic standpoint are data provided to the Board in attachments to the March 20, 1957, Board meeting minutes. Although comprehensive and detailed information over a long period of time on the profits made on individual Studebaker-Packard models has yet to be discovered, that attachment gives a rare insight into the company's gross profit per vehicle. The gross profit per 1957 Packard was reported at $382.55, or 146.3 percent of the average gross profit on Studebaker cars. As a premium line of vehicles, then, at levels of output achieved in 1957, Packard, on a per-unit basis, generated substantial profit margins for the Studebaker-Packard Corporation.

The notion that the decision to build the 1957 Packards, and their successor 1958 models, was a rational one from a corporate standpoint is important in terms of the view suggested by some commentators that the 1957 Packards were built to meet franchise requirements to avoid lawsuits by Packard dealers who would have had no cars to sell if the Packard line was discontinued.[21] It is true that a decline had occurred in the Packard dealer organization by early 1956. Board minutes show that the company lost dealers responsible for five percent of Packard and Clipper car sales in January and February 1956 alone. To strengthen the dealer organization, in April 1956, management reported to the Board that a plan was being developed to dual Studebaker and Packard dealers. The plan was not immediately implemented because at that time there was a lack of a definitive program for continuing in the automobile business.[22]

With the conclusion of the Curtiss-Wright agreement, the emergence of Churchill as president of Studebaker-Packard, and the decision to produce the 1957 Packard, the dualing program was implemented. At the time of the Studebaker-Packard merger in 1954, the company claimed it had about 4000 dealers.[23] When the dualing program began, the number of Studebaker and Packard dealerships had declined significantly. As of September 1, 1956, the company had 1,360 dealers selling Studebakers but not Packards, 686 dealers selling Packards but not Studebakers, and 732 dealers handling both, for a total of 2,778 dealers. There were 414 dealer locations where an exclusive

Studebaker and an exclusive Packard dealer existed and where the sales potential would not justify both dealers handling the full line of S-P products. Therefore, some dealers would have to be terminated to eliminate these so-called "conflict points." The company anticipated there would be legal issues associated with those terminations, and about 60 dealers did threaten suit or demanded that the company repurchase their inventories. The company set up a reserve of $250,000 to cover those contingencies. Actual claims did not exceed that amount.[24]

The size of the dealer organization of S-P continued to decline throughout the 1957 and 1958 model years. By the October 31, 1957, Board meeting, for example, the Board was informed the dealer force had declined to 2,050. Strengthening the dealer organization was one of the challenges that Churchill was to face throughout his term as president of the company. Introduction of the Lark compact car helped rebuild the dealer organization for a time. In examining the evidence and data available, therefore, while the dealer organization appears to have been one of the considerations in the decision to build the 1957 and 1958 Packards, there were other, more important factors at work, which leads to the conclusion that the decision to continue the Packard line for 1957 and 1958 was economically rational from a corporate finance as well as product offering viewpoint.

Besides the decision to build the 1957 Packard and coping with the challenges in the dealer organization, Churchill was confronted with the need to reduce costs at S-P quickly and significantly. It is in the area of cost control that he indicated Curtiss-Wright made its most significant contribution to S-P. For example, in South Bend, S-P had aging multi-story plants. According to Churchill, some in management felt successful production of autos could not be achieved in multi-story operations (i.e., some believed that single-story plants were needed for efficiency). Churchill believed differently and implemented cost control systems he considered solidly conceived that were suggested by Curtiss-Wright. A major contribution to cost control by C-W was improved management of manufacturing inventories to reduce inventory carrying cost to preserve working capital.[25]

Upon becoming president, Churchill undertook an immediate program to reduce overhead at S-P. He asked management to go through the plant and give him recommendations on capital investments which would give returns in 3 months, 6 months, 9 months, 12 months, and longer time periods. He observed that it was surprising what happened in terms of payback with minimal investment. One of the most significant areas of cost saving that Churchill initiated was vacating one floor of the S-P body manufacturing building by moving the paint spray booths and other equipment onto the roof of an adjacent single-story building, which saved the direct and indirect labor costs of handling bodies between floors. The result was a quick return on the capital invested in relocating that equipment.[26]

Integrating production of Packard into South Bend operations, implementing significant cost control measures, and establishing a working relationship with both Curtiss-Wright and stockholders would have been challenge enough for anyone just assuming the presidency of Studebaker-Packard Corporation. However, the biggest challenge of all had to be development of products the public would buy. In terms of the basic product and its specifications, Churchill believed S-P was in good condition.

Top: The 1958 Packard Hawk occupied the top of the Studebaker-Packard model offerings for 1958. Featuring unique but controversial front-end styling and based on the Golden Hawk, it was not received well in the marketplace. Only 588 were built. *Bottom:* Faced with sharply declining sales for Packards in 1958, Churchill decided to free up corporate resources to emphasize the compact Lark in 1959. After 59 years, the last Packard built was a 1958 four-door sedan similar to the one above, on July 25, 1958. Only 1200 Packard four-door sedans were produced for the 1958 model year.

Top: The 1958 Packard hardtop was built on the same body shell as the 1958 Studebaker hardtops — a design unique to the 1958 model year. Production of the 1958 Packard hardtops was only 675 units. *Bottom:* Production of the 1958 Packard station wagons was a minuscule 159 units, making them the rarest of the last representatives of the Packard nameplate. Note that the taillight assembly on the 1958 (and 1957) Packard sedans and station wagons was the same as for the 1956 Clippers.

In styling, though, he recognized there were problems because the styling had become obsolete in a buyers' market where customers were conditioned to make purchases on the basis of obsolescence. Studebaker-Packard simply did not have the finances to address the styling obsolescence problem. Therefore, Churchill believed one of his major tasks was to work toward better product acceptance through facelifts, changes in performance, etc.[27]

Whereas Nance tried to make S-P into a fourth major United States auto producer of the nature of General Motors, Ford, and Chrysler, Churchill and C-W's Hurley agreed that S-P would have to exploit profitable niches in the market. In remarks to automotive and financial editors in New York City on September 5, 1956, Churchill articulated the focused and niche types of markets that S-P would concentrate on during his presidency as follows:

> The market we are aiming at is selective. It consists of buyers who want soundly designed and engineered, high quality distinctive automobiles, and who want them at competitive prices. They prefer not to buy a car identical with a million other cars produced in a given year.[28]

As part of his strategy, Churchill saw S-P's opportunity in the mass market for a cheap, stripped-down car that could be sold for less than the Big Three charged for their basic cars.[29] Churchill had come to Studebaker in 1926, as it sought to break into the low-priced market with the Erskine and Rockne and then had tremendous success with the 1939 Champion. Also, during the mid-1950s, American Motors Corporation, formed through the 1954 merger of Nash and Hudson, was having significant success with its compact Rambler. Consumer acceptance of the Rambler had pushed AMC production from 99,774 units in 1954 to 194,175 in 1955 and then by 1958 to 217,338. (Ultimately, AMC sold almost a half million Ramblers per year in the early 1960s.)[30]

Taking over as president of S-P in late summer of 1956 meant Churchill had very little influence on the company's line of 1957 cars, other than arranging for continuance of the Packard. His desire, though, for an economy car in the S-P model range did become manifested in the development of the Studebaker Scotsman. At the April 5, 1957, Board meeting Churchill reported that the corporation would introduce an economy "Champion" model as a two-door sedan and two-door station wagon. (When introduced, the Scotsman line also had a four-door sedan.)

Planning for the "Economy Champion" or Scotsman model had begun in January 1957. In a January 24, 1957, memo to Churchill, Chief Engineer Eugene Hardig gave an indication that Curtiss-Wright was involved in S-P product planning and gave the rationale for the Studebaker model that became the Scotsman as follows:

> At a joint meeting of Studebaker-Packard and Curtiss-Wright Product Planning Committees, it was decided that the Studebaker Champion Custom 2 and 4 door sedan be stripped of product items, thereby enabling the sales department to offer their model at a greatly reduced price for fleet operation as well as offer a new car to prospective buyers of one year old used cars.

In that memo Hardig went on to explain that a targeted $150 reduction in manufacturing costs for the stripped-down model was proving difficult to achieve. However, the reduction in manufacturing costs ultimately did occur, and the car, devoid of chrome except

Top: The 1957 Studebaker President Classic was the top of the Studebaker sedan line. Built on the 120.5-inch wheelbase, its body shell also served as the basis for the 1957 Packard Clipper sedan. The body shell traced its origins back to the sedan styling introduced in the 1953 model year. *Bottom:* The Studebaker Custom four-door sedans were the lowest-priced standard sedans for 1957, but were available as either the 259-cubic-inch Commander V8 or the 185-cubic-inch Champion L-head six.

Introduced late in the 1957 model year, the Scotsman represented Churchill's effort to test the market for low-priced economy cars. Originally introduced at a price of $1776, the 1957 Scotsman was actively promoted by Studebaker as the economy leader among all full-sized competitive cars. The Scotsman shared the same body shell as the Commanders and Champions on the 116.5-inch wheelbase but was definitely a stripped-down vehicle and was available only as the 185-cubic-inch six-cylinder with standard transmission. Shown here is a 1958 Scotsman station wagon.

for bumpers, having a very austere interior, and named the Scotsman, made its debut on May 28, 1957. Powered by Studebaker's 185-cubic-inch, 6-cylinder, 101-horsepower engine, and offered only with a manual transmission, the full-sized Scotsman was priced at $1776, which the company claimed was over $200 less than the lowest-priced cars of the Big Three.[31]

Churchill's intuitive belief in the future of economy cars paid off. At the June 20, 1957, Board meeting he reported that the original schedule of production for the Scotsman of 6000 units had been increased to 9300 units and that the company expected to have none on hand at the end of the model year.

The Scotsman continued as a market success in the recession-plagued 1958 model year even though auto industry sales were down 30 percent. The Scotsman, which had a taxicab and pickup truck added to the line for 1958, accounted for about 40 percent (over 20,000 units) of S-P's 1958 output.

Hurley of Curtiss-Wright summed up expectations for the market in that recession year of 1958 in comments at the November 15, 1957, S-P Board meeting. He stated he had complete confidence in the managing officers of the corporation but that a tight

Top: The massive fiberglass grill for the 1958 Studebaker Transtar trucks was a continuation of styling introduced in 1957. *Bottom:* Encouraged by the success of the Scotsman automobile, Studebaker expanded its truck offerings in the spring of 1958 by resurrecting basic styling of its R series of trucks originally introduced for the 1949 model year for the Scotsman pickup. Priced at $1595, the Scotsman pickup was the lowest-priced U.S.–built pickup truck that year. Shown here with the first Scotsman pickup coming off the S-P truck assembly line are Allen E. Fitzpatrick (behind the wheel), manager of S-P truck and fleet sales, and Novak Pasajlich, truck assembly manager.

The 1949 R Series Studebaker truck was both popular and a market success as well as having a basic body design and grill treatment that were reintroduced for the 1958 model year in the Scotsman pickup (AACA Library and Research Center).

money situation, stock market uncertainty, the introduction of Ford's Edsel car, and industry-wide sales problems were "illustrative of some of the handicaps under which the corporation has been laboring of late in its efforts to achieve profitable operating rates."

Even though the Scotsman was a very successful addition to the Studebaker model line, in 1958, things became markedly worse for S-P. Before the crisis that enveloped that company and challenged Harold Churchill's management skills to the limit is discussed, some comment is in order about the line of cars the company offered in 1957 and 1958 in addition to the Scotsman.

The 1957 and 1958 Studebaker lines were mild facelifts of the 1956 model, which had been a major facelift of a design originally introduced in 1953. The 1957 and 1958 Studebaker V-8 engines had larger cubic inch displacements than, but were based on, engines introduced in 1951. The Studebaker 6-cylinder engine continued to be based on the pre–World War II designs. These six- and eight-cylinder engines in various forms were used by Studebaker through the 1964 model year. The basic body shell, although facelifted several more times, was used by Studebaker until the end of automobile production in 1966. (Appendices A and B document in picture form the transformation of these body shells through time. Appendix C gives some basic specifications of the 1953 through 1966 Studebaker-Packard products. The results of road tests on Churchill-era S-P products are discussed in Chapter 7.)

Studebaker did cultivate a performance image in 1956 through 1958 in its Hawk line. The 1956 Studebaker Golden Hawk had a Packard V-8 engine while the three other Hawk models in 1956 had Studebaker six and V-8 engines. Although dramatically facelifted, the Hawk line was based on the 1953 Studebaker Starliner and Starlight sport coupes. The 1957 and 1958 Hawk model offerings were reduced to two — the Golden Hawk and Silver Hawk. With Packard engine production discontinued, in order to maintain a performance image for the Hawks in 1957, the Golden Hawk featured the Studebaker 289-cubic-inch V-8 with a McCulloch supercharger. The Silver Hawks were available with either an unsupercharged V-8 or a six-cylinder engine.

The Studebaker-Packard product line was enhanced at this time through an arrangement to distribute Mercedes-Benz products in the United States. In April 1957, Curtiss-Wright, working with S-P and using connections it had with Daimler-Benz,

The big news at Studebaker in 1957 and 1958 was the Golden Hawk, in which the Packard engine of 1956 had been replaced with a 289-cubic-inch Studebaker V8 with a McCulloch supercharger to give it 275 horsepower. Except for minor trim, the Hawk line was virtually unchanged for 1958. The 1957 and 1958 Golden Hawks utilized the pillarless Studebaker sport coupe body. This 1958 Golden Hawk, in a factory photograph taken at the Studebaker-Packard proving grounds outside of South Bend, has wheel covers that differed from the production models.

Top: The 1958 Studebakers and Packards were the first ones for which Harold Churchill had full control over all models in the line. Churchill is pictured here with a 1958 Studebaker President in front of the company administration building in South Bend (Richard Quinn). *Bottom:* The Champion 6-cylinder 2-door sedan was the lowest-priced car of the standard Studebaker models for 1958.

A.G. of Germany, worked out the agreement giving Studebaker-Packard exclusive rights to import the Mercedes-Benz line of passenger cars and trucks into North America. Larger Studebaker-Packard dealers were selected to handle the Mercedes-Benz line of upper-middle through high-priced luxury class automobiles, which certainly expanded the S-P offerings.[32]

Through Curtiss-Wright, Studebaker-Packard was urged to increase its product line and boost its volume by investigating possible imported automobiles to market in the United States. At the July 25, 1957, Board meeting, Churchill announced that the corporation had been studying the possibility of acquiring the distribution and assembly rights to the Goggomobil, a small German car manufactured by Hans Glas G.M.B.H., Isaria, Machinenfabrik, Dingolfing, West Germany. The directors' meeting was recessed for a brief time to enable the viewing of two Goggomobil models.

Roy Hurley of Curtiss-Wright briefed the Board Meeting on the negotiations that had been held with Hans Glas G.M.B.H. He forecast that sales of the Goggomobil could be expected to reach 150,000 and offered the most possibilities for S-P in the small car field. Hurley said the sedan could be sold in the U.S. for $1000 and the convertible for $1400. The Board authorized negotiations to continue with Hans Glas to acquire exclusive rights to distribute and manufacture the Goggomobil.

The Studebaker Starlight hardtops for the regular Studebaker sedan line were a model unique to the 1958 model year. Shown here is a President Starlight.

The rest of the Goggomobil story as it relates to Studebaker-Packard borders on the humorous. In a memo to Churchill dated August 7, 1957, M.P. deBlumenthal, Chief Research Engineer for S-P, reported on the experience his staff had in driving two Goggomobils from New York City, where they had been shown to the Board, to South Bend, a distance of 725 miles. The convertible had especially poor performance with the spark plugs having to be cleaned five times and the carburetor cleaned once, the clutch was grabbing, the engine flooded, at idle the engine was rough and ran on only two of its four cylinders, and the headlights continually flickered on and off. The sedan performed quite well until 35 miles from South Bend when the engine locked up. The convertible averaged 23.3 miles per gallon of gasoline and the sedan averaged 33.2 m.p.g.

Churchill told the Board on September 16, 1957, that Hans Glas would not be able to provide the quantity of Goggomobils forecast at the July 25, 1957, meeting and that only 18,000 units would be available for 1958. Furthermore, because the Goggomobils were basically hand-finished, the manufacturing processes of Hans Glas were not adaptable to the S-P facilities. Given these performance and availability problems, it is not surprising that the Goggomobil idea was dropped by Studebaker-Packard.

Through 1957 and 1958, S-P was faced with sales and production continuing to decline (see Table 2). As a result, S-P was not even close to its break-even levels in 1957 and 1958. With sales of 9300 units in 1957 and over 20,000 units in 1958, the Scotsman was a success, but the increased sales it contributed did not offset declines in the rest of the line. By November 1957, the crisis was at hand. Studebaker-Packard Corporation was on the verge of bankruptcy and the challenges Harold Churchill faced in 1956 were eclipsed by the challenges he faced in the 12 months between November 1957 and November 1958.

4
The Lark Miracle

"Through dedication and loyalty of these people [Studebaker employees] the Lark was done. Couldn't have been done without it, because it was done in a very short space of time by people that were believers in the philosophy of it and unquenchable zeal to see it succeed, from the dealer body right through the sweeper out in the foundry."[1]

Reflecting on the development of the Lark, the above quotation is how Harold E. Churchill explained the success of the compact Lark by Studebaker, introduced for the 1959 model year. The comment by Churchill is consistent with the modest nature of the man whose character, ability, and personal commitment energized the Studebaker-Packard Corporation to achieve for the 1959 model year what many skeptics from the media to financiers believed was an impossibility.

Churchill, who was affectionately known as "Church" by many, if not most, in the Studebaker organization, appears to have been deeply respected and liked within the company. Before describing the development of the Lark, a discussion of how some Studebaker people viewed Churchill as a leader will enhance an understanding of his ability to rally the company behind the extraordinary effort needed to develop the Lark in a short period of time.

The comments summarized here are from a sampling of interviews taken from the Indiana University Oral History Project. A common theme throughout these interviews was expressed by John M. Piechowiak, a chief steward for United Auto Workers Local 5 at Studebaker. Piechowiak stated that Churchill probably tried as hard as anybody could to save the company with the resources he had. Frank Rosenbaum, who worked a variety of jobs in the plant from the final assembly line to a salaried position, noted that Churchill was particularly respected for his engineering ability. That sentiment was echoed by Theodore Zenzinger, who ultimately became administrative assistant to Gordon Grundy after Studebaker production was consolidated in Hamilton, Ontario, in 1964. Zenzinger stated Churchill was a good president who came up through engineering and was a good businessman. Frank Sitarz, who worked in several auto and truck plant jobs from 1933 to 1963, related how Churchill enjoyed mingling with the workers. Sitarz recalled that after Churchill resigned as president of S-P, but still had administrative responsibilities, he came by and shook hands with strikers and exchanged morning greetings during the U.A.W. strike in 1962. According to Sitarz, "He's

[Churchill] down to earth. He knew the job from the ground up. He'd walk through the plant and see just what went on there ... and he knew it all." Although these few comments about Churchill are at best anecdotal, they are evidence he had the ability to motivate and inspire his people.

The ability to be a visionary and to motivate was a critical asset at Studebaker in 1957 and 1958. Harold Churchill had the vision that Studebaker needed to enter and find a niche for itself in the compact car field if it was to have a chance to survive. His vision was consistent with his experiences with economy cars including the 1939 Studebaker Champion and the recent success of the Scotsman, as well as a realization that by the late 1950s, small imports were selling about half a million units a year in the U.S. That vision had to be translated into action which required the commitment of the Board of Directors, employees, bankers, and stockholders.

The October 31, 1957, Board meeting minutes show Churchill announced that product planning for 1959 included proposals for three models. The 1959 line, though, could not be an entirely new car because the tooling costs would be prohibitive. Then, at the February 24, 1958, Board meeting, Churchill outlined the possible programs for the 1959 model year as follows:

1. Reduce the number of models in the S-P line from 18 in the 1958 model year to 14, principally by dropping the Packard line. With a Packard line the tooling bill would have been an estimated $4.2 million. Without the Packard it would be $3.25 million. Under this program, changes to the Studebaker line would have included new front sheet metal, fins, tail lamps, cowls, hard and soft trim, and new instruments.
2. Produce a small car under one of the two following programs:
    * Plan A: Build a 108.5-inch wheelbase car in two- and four-door sedan models. A station wagon could also be added. (Note: the 1958 Studebaker-Packard line was built on 116.5-inch and 120.5-inch wheelbases.) Under this plan the Silver and Golden Hawks were to be retained without any sheet metal changes. Tooling costs were estimated at $5.843 million, of which $4.513 million was for sheet metal. Estimated break-even level of output for Plan A was 121,000 units per year.
    * Plan B: Build a small car on a 108.5-inch wheelbase in a two-door and four-door model with a station wagon on the 116.5-inch wheelbase and the Hawks and a four-door sedan on the 120.5-inch wheelbase. Tooling costs for Plan B would be $7.287 million. Estimated break-even level of output for Plan B was 115,000 units per year.

Churchill asked for and received from the Board a preliminary tooling appropriation of $400,000 for a small car at the February 24, 1958, meeting.

At a special meeting of the Board held on March 14, 1958, Churchill reported on a meeting of the steering committee of the company's banks and insurance companies, held on March 4, 1958, at which he informed the steering committee that the corporation was going forward with the plan for small cars. However, for most of the spring and summer of 1958, the banks and insurance companies remained skeptical about the possibility of success for the small car program. In fact, the minutes for that March 14, 1958, Board meeting report the steering committee asked for a report showing what the asset realization would be if S-P were liquidated. In reflecting on the situation, Churchill later stated he was sure many of the 21 banks and 3 insurance companies with which S-P was working did not believe the small car program would succeed. Characteristic, though, of his determination at the time, he said that, in spite of hot words flowing with regard to how solid his estimates were, "I don't think I ever backed up from one of them, and we made it."[2]

By the April 24, 1958, Board meeting, Churchill was confident that production could begin on the small car by October 1, 1958. Therefore, he asked for and received an additional appropriation of $4,865,061 for 1959 model tooling and plant equipment and rearrangement. In his request for this appropriation, Churchill noted that as a result of savings associated with placing all tooling orders with one vendor, instead of several vendors as had been done in the past, a savings of over $450,000 would be achieved. In the interview, Churchill acknowledged a major risk was being taken by placing all the tooling with one firm, the Budd Company. To quote Churchill's own description of the situation from his oral history interview:

> Our manufacturing people and the purchasing people almost died when I told them we were going to put all the dies in one shop. This is unheard of in the industry, but it had advantages ... with respect to shrinking time. Before the dies were shipped out of the die shops they would have all been through the tryout process ... the tools came in ... and the pieces that came out of the dies went together just like they were made to fit.[3]

In neither the Board meeting, where placing all the tooling with one vendor was announced, nor in the oral history interview of Churchill, did he fully explain why he made that critical decision, which was, after all, a gamble, as his staff realized. Therefore, we can only speculate on the reasons for taking that risk. It is possible that Churchill was remembering the problems associated with the launch of the 1953 Studebakers, when sheet metal parts did not fit when they came down the assembly line, and he did not wish to repeat those problems with the Lark. Given that Studebaker, in 1958, had only one chance left to stay in the automobile business, Churchill may have felt that taking a chance on one vendor was better than taking a chance that the tooling would give the company problems and delay production of the Lark.

So what happened in 1953 that may have made an impression on Churchill? He had just become vice-president of engineering, and it is inconceivable that the events associated with the launch of the 1953 models would not have influenced his thinking. Working as part of the Raymond Loewy organization, stylist Robert Bourke created a styling sensation with the 1953 Studebaker Starliner coupes. A manufacturing issue developed, however, because the standard Studebaker line of sedans had to be made to have the same general styling cues as the coupes. As a result, the company had to build two different lines of cars at the same time. Most of the sheet metal for the coupes was different from the sheet metal for the standard Studebaker sedans.

Serious production delays were encountered as the assembly plant attempted to process all those different parts. Production delays occurred due to bottlenecks, which caused the company to have to install a new conveyor belt system. Important sales were lost as a result of the chaos that was occurring in the plant. The calamity reached a climax when the components for the first coupe body moved down the assembly line and did not fit. The coupe body then had to be partially re-engineered in a crash and expensive program.[4] The magnitude of this disaster is apparent when examining two statements by Harold Vance, then board chair and president of the company. In the *Studebaker Corporation Annual Report for 1952*, Vance said the following:

> In January 1953, the new models, called the "Studebaker Centennial Models of 1953," were put on display, first to our dealers and later to the general public. We are happy to report that the reception accorded the new models, both here and abroad, has been even beyond our expectations and seems to be more than equal to the acceptance of our first postwar cars in 1946.

The problem, of course, was that because of the production problems, the enthusiastic public was not able to buy the beautiful new Studebaker coupes designed by Bob Bourke. By the time regular production could be resumed, quality and fit and finish problems also plagued the 1953 Studebakers, which further cooled consumer enthusiasm for the cars. Thus, in the *Studebaker Corporation Annual Report for 1953*, Vance was forced to report:

> In January 1953, a new line of Studebaker passenger cars was introduced. It involved extensive retooling. Unusual difficulties were encountered with the new tools in suppliers' plants, as well as in our own plants, which seriously reduced production and greatly increased costs during the early part of 1953.

Given this rather sobering experience in bringing out the 1953 Studebakers, one can hardly blame Churchill, faced with bringing out a new model just five years later, for taking the risk that placing all the tooling at one vendor (which was the Budd Company) would improve fit and finish and avoid production problems.

So overall, plans for bringing out the small car that was to become the Lark were moving in a positive direction during the spring of 1958. There was one problem, though. Studebaker-Packard Corporation did not have the funds and resources to bring the small car program to fruition.

The dire circumstances of Studebaker-Packard became apparent at a special meeting of the Board of Directors on November 15, 1957. Churchill announced that the special meeting had been called at the suggestion of Roy Hurley of Curtiss-Wright in order that the Board could be advised of recent developments. A.J. Porta, vice-president of finance, had the task of reporting on serious sales and financial problems of the company.

Minutes of the November 15, 1957, Board meeting show Porta reminding the Board that a September 16, 1957, sales forecast by Sydney Skillman, vice-president for sales, for the 1958 model year was for 135,000 units. However, there had been a sharp drop-off of actual orders since September 16, with the consequence that Porta reported the corporation was faced with a serious overproduction and inventory problem. As of October 31, 1957, orders had been received for approximately seven thousand 1958 units, but production of 1958 vehicles totaled 11,500 units. As a result of the sharp drop in orders, the assembly line speed was reduced from 60 units per hour to 35 units per hour. Porta forecast that if the trends existing in November 1957 continued for the rest of the model year, only 80,000 units would be sold, but the break-even point was 103,000. Therefore, significant financial losses could be expected. Churchill stated that as a result of cutting back production schedules there could be adverse effects on dealer and public morale, but he hoped that a stepped-up advertising campaign would help offset those effects. In fact, an aggressive advertising campaign was launched on December 8, 1957, with 5 million copies of a Sunday supplement magazine, devoted exclusively to Studebaker, Packard, and Mercedes-Benz cars, included in five newspapers. Churchill also stated that the production cutback to 35 cars an hour and a four-day week was as far as the corporation dared to go in slowing down its rate of production short of shutting down altogether. In March 1958, Churchill had the unhappy task of reporting to the board that the hoped-for return from the advertising campaign resulted in a temporary increase in orders from the factory by the dealers, but no increase in the rate of retail sales.[5] The news was only to become worse.

At a special Board meeting held on May 8, 1958, A.J. Porta reported on the serious sales and financial position of S-P. Sales of the Studebaker-Packard plus Mercedes-Benz vehicles for the first three months of 1958 totaled 14,951, compared to 23,798 in the same period in 1957. The net loss of the corporation for January, February, and March of 1958 was $6.3 million, compared to $2.5 million in 1957. Working capital was declining at the rate of $1.3 million per month, the corporate cash position was becoming tenuous, and the company had $54.7 million in debt. In response to the situation, the Board began consideration of a financial reorganization of the company. By the June 18, 1958, Board meeting the details of the plan were being completed and the refinancing plan was approved.

On September 4, 1958, Harold Churchill signed a letter accompanying a proxy statement to the shareholders of Studebaker-Packard Corporation outlining the details of the proposed refinancing plan. The plan is summarized as follows:

1. The $54.7 million of debt to the banks and insurance companies was to be converted into:
   a. $16.5 million of 15-year secured notes; and
   b. $16.5 million of preferred stock, convertible into 5.5 million shares of common stock at $3 per share after two years.
2. New agreements were reached with Daimler-Benz for the organization of a new wholly-owned subsidiary of the company to take over the distribution of the Mercedes-Benz cars.
3. The advisory agreement with the Curtiss-Wright Corporation and the option for C-W to purchase 5 million shares of S-P stock at $5 per share were terminated. Also, C-W agreed to purchase for $2 million the equity interest S-P had in its Chippewa Avenue plant in South Bend and the Utica, Michigan, plant that had been under long-term lease to C-W.
4. The company was prepared to sell other (unspecified) properties.
5. A diversification plan to bring new earnings into the company and make use of its tax loss carryover in excess of $100 million was developed. The plan authorized

additional shares of common stock (to be determined by the Board of Directors) and the issuance of $25 million par value of second preferred stock.

6. Abraham M. Sonnabend, president of Hotel Corporation of America and president and chairperson of Botany Mills, was brought onto the Board as a director to head the acquisitions and diversification program.
7. Two other persons were named to the Board of Directors: Clarence Francis, formerly president and chairperson of General Foods Corporation, and Edward H. Litchfield, chancellor of the University of Pittsburgh, and former dean of the School of Business Administration at Cornell University.

The refinancing plan was complex and requires some explanation. *Business Week* magazine described the refinancing plan at Studebaker-Packard as a means of handling the debt problems of the company. The banks were owed $29.7 million and insurance companies $25 million for a total of $54.7 million. Of that total debt, $21.7 million was "forgiven." The balance of $33 million was split into two parts: $16.5 million was continued as loans bearing 5 percent interest and secured by virtually every piece of property and equipment that Studebaker-Packard owned. The other $16.5 million was transformed into preferred stock convertible after January 1961 into common stock. If the holders, on conversion of the preferred stock into common stock, were able to sell the common stock for $7 per share or more, they would recoup the $21.7 million that was "forgiven."[6] As things turned out, S-P's fortunes improved enough that the banks recovered their loans and the "forgiven" amount by a substantial margin.

In asking for stockholder approval of the plan, Churchill noted attempts to reach a break-even point and efforts to find a strong company with which to merge had not been successful. He also expressed disappointment that Curtiss-Wright had not exercised the option to purchase S-P stock. Churchill's comments to the shareholders were direct and to the point, as follows: "Without this plan the chance of restoring real value to your stock is practically nonexistent. With this Plan we have a new chance to rehabilitate the business and earning power of the Company and give value to the shareholder's investment.... The Refinancing Plan makes it possible to carry out the new car program. Without such a plan and the readjustment of debt it provides for, it would be very doubtful whether we could carry out such a program.... With the consummation of the plan, there is a chance of developing value for the shareholders and, I believe, it is a good chance."[7]

In an October 15, 1958, news release, S-P was able to announce that its shareholders had approved the refinancing plan by an overwhelming vote of 98 percent in favor. In the news release, Churchill elaborated on details of the marketing plan for what Studebaker called its "New Dimension in Motoring, The Lark by Studebaker," which was to go on sale on November 14, 1958. He stated: "We have every confidence the Lark will demonstrate in 1959 that Studebaker-Packard has come up with the right car at the right time. As the motoring public becomes aware that it can purchase a smaller, economical car with large car roominess and comfort, we expect the Lark to have a strong sales impact in the areas previously dominated by imported cars. The Lark also will appeal to large numbers of buyers who no longer want larger and larger cars with greater horsepower."[8]

Parking the 1959 Silver Hawk and Lark next to each other shows the Hawk influence on the front-end styling of the Lark. The Hawk line almost was dropped, but under pressure from dealers, Churchill agreed to keep the car as part of Studebaker's offerings. Hawks for 1959 were confined to the pillared-coupe Silver Hawk available with either the 169-cubic-inch six-cylinder engine or 259 c.i.d. V8.

The development, production planning, and introduction of the Lark went quickly and smoothly by automotive industry standards. However, there still were some very real challenges that had to be confronted to have the car in dealer showrooms in November 1958. Not the least of the challenges was to make the Lark look like an all-new car while utilizing many existing mechanical and body parts. Churchill carefully oversaw the styling and mechanical development of the Lark. His involvement in the Lark project is evident in the reports he gave to the Board of Directors throughout 1958. While Churchill supervised the project, the challenge of implementing development of the Lark went to chief engineer Eugene Hardig and chief stylist Duncan McRae. The styling of the Lark was a completely in-house affair, with McRae being assisted by several other designers, including Bill Bonner and Virgil Exner Jr.[9]

Then, just as the Lark was going into production and being introduced to the public, labor problems occurred. Full analysis of labor issues at Studebaker in the era following World War II involves many complexities and is beyond the scope of this book. However, brief mention of the background to the situation in November 1958 is helpful to understanding the environment in which the Lark was introduced.

Labor relations at Studebaker-Packard in 1958 had historical roots going back at least to the Depression of the 1930s. When Harold Vance and Paul Hoffman assumed administrative direction of Studebaker following the company's filing for bankruptcy in 1933, one of their priorities was to maintain labor peace and harmonious relations with the workforce. Studebaker advertising throughout the remainder of the 1930s and into the 1940s often portrayed that harmonious labor relationship, even to the extent of showing advertising with father and son teams working in the Studebaker plant. As late as 1954, Hoffman told the annual shareholders meeting that quality workmanship was based on the attitude of workers in the plant. However, by then he and Vance had already begun to discuss the problem of relatively high labor costs at Studebaker with the Board of Directors. The Board agreed with them that the cause of relatively high labor costs at Studebaker was an excessively high piece rate premium.[10]

The result of the piece rate system was that the Studebaker hourly rate was 22 percent above the industry average. Compounding the problem was low productivity.[11]

Attachments to the minutes of the S-P Board of Directors Meeting of September 16, 1957, show that the total labor hours required to build a standard Studebaker Commander 4-door sedan in October 1956 were 105 hours, and by July 1957, that had been reduced to 99.5 labor hours. It took until 1959 for the labor hours per car to be reduced to fewer than 80.[12]

The labor problems at Studebaker were evident long before the events of 1958. By 1954, with losses escalating at Studebaker, even the United Auto Workers began to be concerned about labor costs and productivity at the company. Walter Reuther, President of the U.A.W., instructed Studebaker Local 5 leadership to work to bring piece rates and production standards at Studebaker into line with the rest of the industry. After negotiations between the company and Local 5, a compromise agreement was reached which reduced wages by 18 percent but gave a continuation of the 40 minutes of personal time (sometimes referred to as clean-up time) per day to labor as well as increased vacation pay. The agreement was contentious, and initially the union membership turned it down by a 3 to 1 margin. After a public relations campaign by management pointing out that, on average, Studebaker wages were 18 percent higher than its competitors and work standards were 20 percent below the industry norms, another vote was taken; the agreement passed by an 8 to 1 margin and a strike was averted.[13]

Following the merger of Studebaker and Packard, labor relations became acrimonious in 1955. Nance had little sympathy with the historic labor traditions at Studebaker. He attempted to impose new work standards in the plant, which resulted in a 36-day strike in 1955. Even after the strike was settled, serious labor relations problems remained, and a series of 85 wildcat strikes broke out. The existing contract with U.A.W. Local 5 expired in July and negotiations were conducted, but a seven-day wildcat strike occurred in September 1955. Finally, a new contract was approved in January 1956, which had a 21-cent-per-hour raise, but rest and relief and personal time was reduced from 40 to 24 minutes. Workers gained some improvement in pension and insurance contributions but plant-wide seniority and bumping rights were eliminated.[14] Nance was able to report to the stockholders in the S-P *Annual report for 1955* that a substantial reduction in manufacturing costs had been achieved in South Bend.

As discussed earlier, fundamentally, Churchill maintained good relations with the labor force. But clearly the labor relations atmosphere in which he took over the presidency of the company was not the best. He was aware that Studebaker's labor costs still were greater than industry norms. He admitted it took considerable diplomacy to bring labor standards at S-P in line with the rest of the industry. By 1958, that had been achieved.[15]

At the September 25, 1958, Board meeting, Clifford MacMillan, vice-president for industrial relations, reported that negotiations were ongoing with the United Auto Workers Local 5 on a new contract. The goal of S-P was to have no major increase in labor costs. MacMillan did not anticipate there would be a strike. His prophecy turned out to be wrong. Almost exactly at the time the Lark was introduced to the market, the

U.A.W. did strike Studebaker from November 23 to 27, 1958. In an Indiana University Oral History Project interview, MacMillan related that Studebaker was trying to get some concessions from the union on idle time and obtaining more productivity. It was his view that the union did not think S-P would take a strike, but it did. Of course, it was a critical time because the Lark was turning out to be a market success and the company needed to build cars to meet the demand. So, in MacMillan's words, "We hustled around for 3 days, and we finally got an accommodation." The U.A.W. demanded an hourly pay increase of six to eight cents retroactive to September 1, 1958. The company had offered a two-cent hourly pay increase for each calendar quarter in which the company sold at least 30,000 units.[16] The final settlement was that skilled employees received a 16-cent-per-hour increase and regular hourly rated employees received a 7-cent-per-hour raise starting December 2, 1958. However, 5 cents of the 7-cent increase for regular workers came from money S-P had paid into a supplemental unemployment benefits fund.[17]

The Larks that Studebaker introduced to the market in the fall of 1958 had a distinctly different look to them than the 1956 through 1958 Studebakers. They were shorter but had the same basic body shells, which gave them relatively large interior space. The Lark four- and two-door sedans and two-door hardtop models were built on a 108.5-inch wheelbase. The station wagon and the Econ-O-miler taxicab were built on a 113-inch wheelbase. The 108.5-inch wheelbase cars and the station wagon had the same basic body shell as the 1958 and earlier models that had been built on the 116.5-inch wheelbase. The Econ-O-miler taxis on the 113-inch wheelbase had the same body

Selling the Lark to the mass market required enlarging and upgrading the dealer network. Dealers were encouraged to upgrade and modernize their facilities along the lines of the Elizabeth, New Jersey, dealer shown here.

shells as the earlier Studebakers built on the 120.5-inch wheelbase. The engines available for 1959 were limited to the 169-cubic-inch 6-cylinder and 259-cubic-inch V8. The Silver Hawk for 1959 was the only Hawk offered, and it was available with the same engines as the Lark. The 289-cubic-inch V8 was not an option for the 1959 model year. Further specifications on the Larks and Hawks can be found in Appendix C. How the Larks and Hawks performed is covered in a survey of road tests on the cars in Chapter 7.

To develop, design, engineer, and build the Lark were challenges that the company was successful in facing. Once built, though, the Lark had to be sold. Franchised Studebaker dealers were the venue through which the Lark was to be retailed. The problem for Studebaker was that its dealer organization was weak. Churchill claimed that the Studebaker dealers could break even on half the volume that was necessary for the plant to break even. In addition, the dealers were old chronologically. He claimed they were very loyal, but because they did not need the same volume as the factory, they had little motivation to market cars aggressively.[18]

Sydney Skillman, vice-president for marketing and sales, reported to a special meeting of the Board on May 8, 1958, that even with conservative estimates of sales for the 1959 Model X (the internal name it was given prior to choosing the "Lark" nameplate), there was a need to improve the effectiveness of the dealer organization. To accomplish this, the minutes of that meeting show Skillman claimed there would have to be dualing with other makes — especially with Big Three dealers. Two of the directors present, Russell Forgan and Royall Victor, vigorously supported the dualing plan, with Victor pointing out S-P was committed to its creditors to a more vigorous dualing program. In support of the need for a stronger dealer organization, at the same meeting Churchill noted that in 1953 the average Studebaker dealer sold 5.2 cars per month, but in 1958 it was only 2.1 cars per month. By the September 25, 1958, Board meeting, Skillman reported encouraging progress in signing new dealers, particularly in major cities. At the October 21, 1958, Board meeting Skillman reported S-P had 2,271 dealers, up from 1,993 on June 30, 1958. Therefore, launch of the Lark was handled by a growing dealer organization.

At the June 18 and July 24, 1958, Board meetings, considerable discussion occurred regarding the advertising agency being used by S-P. Churchill and Skillman recommended appointing a new advertising agency to obtain a new viewpoint in advertising matters with the launch of the new model. The new agency was D'Arcy Advertising Company, which replaced Burke, Dowling, Adams, Inc. While there is a level of subjectivity in assessing the effectiveness of advertising, a comparison of a 1958 magazine ad for Studebaker with a 1959 magazine ad for Larks (see the accompanying advertisements) demonstrates the quite different approach taken by D'Arcy as it promoted the new compact. The 1959 ad shows the Lark in an upbeat lifestyle setting, while from the subjective viewpoint of this author, the 1958 advertising was dull and stodgy and failed to inspire enthusiasm. Although Churchill told the board he was not critical of the Burke, Dowling, Adams results, his intuition was correct that a new approach to advertising was needed to promote the Lark.

In bringing out the Lark, Harold Churchill was taking a major risk. The S-P corporate assets were meager. Risks were taken in placing all tooling with one firm. Major

Above and page 66: In promoting and advertising the Lark, the switch to the D'Arcy Advertising Company from the Burke, Dowling, Adams, Inc. agency resulted in more lifestyle-oriented and fresh advertising for 1959 than the somewhat more formal advertising of 1957 and 1958.

marketing (dealer and advertising) issues had to be confronted. Labor problems were encountered. However, the Lark had a smooth and very successful launch. By the end of the 1959 model year, Studebaker had built 131,078 Larks, 7,788 Silver Hawks, 8,823 trucks, and was working on an order for 5,000 military trucks.[19] As shown in Table 2, significant profits were earned in 1959, as S-P exceeded its break-even level of output

by a substantial margin. On November 14, 1958, Churchill reported to the Board that output was being increased from 54 to 60 units an hour and that on January 2, 1959, it was to increase to 70 per hour and that the plant was operating nine hours per day for five days and eight hours on Saturday. By the April 23, 1959, shareholders meeting, Churchill could report that output had been raised to 84 units per hour.

Tuesday, May 12, 1959, must have been a day of considerable gratification, and perhaps even vindication for Harold Churchill. On that day the 100,000th Lark rolled off the South Bend assembly line. Churchill personally delivered the car to its new own-

HAROLD E. CHURCHILL, Studebaker President, with new Lark 4 Door Sedan.

Above and pages 68 and 69: The Lark by Studebaker was introduced to the public through a three-page advertisement in major magazines in November 1958. The first page of the ad is probably the most famous picture of Harold Churchill as he stands next to the car he conceived and brought to the market.

ers, Mr. and Mrs. Frank Herzog of Florin, California. At a civic luncheon preceding delivery, Churchill said that Studebaker was "on the threshold of the best first year sales record of any automobile introduced to the postwar American scene."[20] However, in spite of all the success the Lark was having, as early as the February 16, 1959, Board meeting Churchill anticipated some shrinkage in corporate backlog and said a second shift was not under consideration.

YOUR NEW DIMENSION IN MOTORING BORN IN SOUTH BEND

BY HAROLD E. CHURCHILL

Like millions of others, you have probably been looking to Detroit for a new kind of car—something that strikes a smart, sensible balance between the ⅝ size foreign imports and the oversize U.S. makes. ➤ Among 1959 models, already announced or about to be, you will at last find one such car. ➤ It is the newest concept in automobiles—a whole new dimension in motoring—brought to you, happily, by the oldest name in the industry. ➤ It comes to you not from abroad, not from Detroit . . . but *out of South Bend—by Studebaker.* ➤ And not surprising—for only an independent manufacturer, flexible in operation and centralized in management, could move this quickly to meet the needs and tastes of the times. ➤ It is the only car of its kind. It is smart, sensible, smooth, solid and spirited. It is as fresh and full of life as the Indiana countryside where it was conceived and is being made today. ➤ This new car is full six-passenger size inside. It has comfortable big-car width and headroom and footroom, all of it cradled within a wheel base nearly equal to the largest selling car of the day. ➤ But outside, it is almost 3 feet shorter than most of the so-called "low-priced" three models. Unnecessary nonfunctional overhang has been eliminated. As a result, the car handles with exceptional ease, parks without effort, corners beautifully. ➤ In styling, it is smart and simple, even classic, and completely individual, in a friendly, happy way. It is not a utility car, a sports car or a show-off car, but a perfectly balanced design that incorporates the best virtues of all. The interiors are simple but tasteful, with fine pleated fabric and vinyl upholstery. Their fashion rightness has been commended by Harper's Bazaar. ➤ In power (you can have a six or an eight) this car is far more than adequate—is, in fact, wonderfully spirited and lively, but not wastefully excessive. It operates with amazing economy, needs regular gasoline only, and delivers more than 30 m.p.g. in many cases. ➤ All this for prices starting under $2,000. We think you'll agree with us, it's the most rewarding car value available today. ➤ At any rate, when it comes your way this week (on display at your Studebaker Dealer's), try it, won't you? You knew it had to happen. You've been wanting it to happen. And when you drive this one—you'll be glad it did.

By the way, the name of the car is The Lark by Studebaker. ➤

Even as the Lark was a market success in 1959, Studebaker-Packard continued to look for automotive products that could supplement its product lines in dealer showrooms. The Mercedes-Benz line was doing moderately well with 12,308 units sold in 1959, according to the company's *Annual Report for 1959*. However, the Mercedes cars were not a volume product. Another opportunity presented itself in 1959 through what was then the Daimler-Benz Auto Union subsidiary. S-P obtained the distribution rights for Auto Union-DKW vehicles. The distinguishing feature of the Auto Union-DKW line at that time was its 3-cylinder, 2-stroke engine with front-wheel drive. Sales

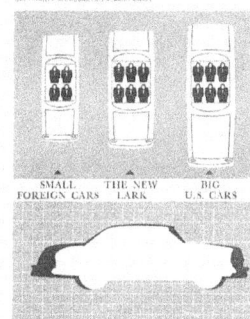

of the Auto Union-DKW vehicles, handled through the S-P Mercedes-Benz Sales, Inc. subsidiary, languished for several years. Whereas sales of 16,000 or more DKW units were expected per year, realized unit sales initially were only about 4000 units annually. The 2-cycle engine (which required mixing of oil with the gasoline) and a number of quality issues seemed to be significant reasons why the DKW vehicles did not become well established in the U.S. market.[21] Board minutes from February 7, 1963, indicate

Above: The 1959 Lark Station Wagon was available in a 2-door version built on the 113-inch wheelbase (AACA Library and Research Center). *Left:* Harold Churchill often was seen walking through the plant to observe operations and greet workers. In this picture he had a right to be smiling as he stood along the Lark assembly line in 1959 as 84 cars per hour were being built (Richard Quinn).

only about 1000 DKWs were sold in the U.S. in 1963, and beyond what was in inventory, none were on order, effectively ending Studebaker's involvement with Auto Union-DKW.

The success of the Lark in the 1959 model year surely was vindication for Harold Churchill of his view of the segment of the automobile market in which he believed Studebaker should be. Without giving specifics of the Lark design, he told

Top: Production of the 100,000th Lark was cause for great celebration at Studebaker. Harold Churchill is third person from the left. *Bottom:* Among the Lark models offered in 1959 was continuation of the Econ-O-miler Taxi Cab, built on the 113-inch wheelbase. The Econ-O-miler was the only four-door sedan built on the 113-inch wheelbase by Studebaker in 1959 and 1960 (AACA Library and Research Center).

the April 24, 1958, annual shareholders meeting that Studebaker-Packard was planning a different type of car for 1959 that the American public had been asking for. He admitted in his remarks at that meeting that "the Scotsman, when it was introduced, was intended to plumb and measure this expanding market for such a basic type automobile." He stated that the success of the Scotsman indicated that the demand for automobiles was changing in the direction of lower-cost, well-made transportation that retains elements of full-sized passenger space while offering economical operating costs and permanence of design. The initial success of the Lark confirmed that his view of future trends in the industry was correct. However, even as the Lark enjoyed outstanding success, clouds began to form on the horizon.

5
Evolution of the Lark

Even before the November 1958 official public introduction of the Lark in dealer showrooms, it was clear it would be a success. Sydney Skillman reported to the Board on September 25, 1958, that the company had 24,480 orders for the new cars, double the year earlier at the same time, and orders for 1,119 new trucks, up from 693 the year before. Churchill knew, though, that the Lark, developed in record time and on its way to being a market success, was about to face stiff competition as the Big Three prepared to introduce their compact cars. He realized that Studebaker would have to stay a step ahead of the competition if the Lark was to have long-term success.

Minutes of the November 14, 1958, Board meeting state that Churchill told the Board that Ford and General Motors would be entering the small-car field within a year. To maintain volume, he envisioned Studebaker would have to emphasize its fleet and truck programs. He indicated that the engineering and styling departments already were devoting a major part of their time to 1960 product plans. Included in those plans was adding a soft-top convertible to the Lark line. Churchill estimated the tooling budget for the 1960 line would be between $5 million and $6 million.

Churchill put considerable emphasis on the truck program in his reports to the Board in late 1958 and early 1959. On January 6, 1959, he announced that the company officers had been directed to prepare an expanded truck program for evaluation by the directors. At the February 16, 1959, Board meeting, A.J. Porta, vice-president for finance, reported that orders for 4000 civilian trucks (military trucks were separate) had been received for production through March. That compared with total civilian truck sales of 4551 in all of 1958. Porta also reported that on the basis of out-of-pocket costs, the break-even point for Studebaker truck production worldwide was 4500 units. Although Porta observed that, at these volumes, the trucks did not help the passenger car business significantly, it is clear that the financial bottom line and cash flow were helped when truck output exceeded the break-even levels. By the June 15, 1959, Board meeting, Porta could report that the truck line was profitable in 1959.

At that June 15, 1959, Board meeting, Churchill showed the directors new models of the proposed ½- and ¾-ton trucks which used Lark sheet metal. Churchill anticipated that this truck (which was introduced as the Studebaker Champ) would cost about $900,000 in tooling. Churchill stated the new line would considerably improve the

The appearance of the basic Lark line was little changed for 1960 except for small changes in trim items. Pictured here is the Lark hardtop for 1960.

The Champ truck, introduced during the 1960 model year, was a clever adaptation of Lark styling to freshen the Studebaker truck offerings (AACA Library and Research Center).

salability of Studebaker trucks, which had been basically unchanged for nine years. At the July 7, 1959, Board meeting the truck program was approved by unanimous vote. The Champ turned out to be another very successful part of Churchill's program. Total Studebaker truck production went from 10,800 in 1959 to 12,300 in 1960 and 14,000 units in 1962.

Development of the Champ truck gives insight into the ability of Studebaker to be both innovative and clever in its product development during the Churchill years. In a 1972 oral history interview of Otis Romine, former truck body engineer at Studebaker-Packard Corporation, conducted by Loren E. Pennington and published in a 2010 series of articles in *Turning Wheels*, a publication of the Studebaker Drivers Club, Romine documents the story of how the Champ pickup truck bed was upgraded for the 1961 model year.

In the interview, Romine acknowledged that Studebaker trucks were being outdistanced by the competition by the late 1950s. For example, Studebaker had entered the decade of the 1950s with a very solid record in the postwar sales of trucks. Annual sales of Studebaker trucks in 1947, 1948, and 1949 exceeded 65,000 units per year. A restyled line of trucks known as the R Series was introduced for the 1949 model year and, although truck sales did trail off somewhat, they were still above 60,000 units in 1952.[1]

As early as December 1955, as head of the Studebaker Division of Studebaker-Packard, Churchill expressed determination to return Studebaker to a more aggressive position in the truck business. Churchill noted that in 1950 Studebaker had captured 4.4 percent of the total truck market and still held 4 percent of the truck market in 1952, but by 1954 had slipped to only 1.35 percent of the market. However, in 1955, Churchill observed that Studebaker could not force dealers to do a truck selling job equal to the one they did on passenger cars. In essence, what Churchill was saying was that the company had to put more emphasis on the value of the truck line to encourage dealers to see the profit potential of selling the trucks.[2]

The question arises, of course, as to why Churchill waited nearly three years after becoming president of Studebaker-Packard to introduce a new truck to the market. One can only speculate on the reason, but it is worthwhile to recall that resources for new product development were scarce at S-P and most of them were going into the development of the Lark, introduced in the fall of 1958 for the 1959 model year. Also, it is evident that Churchill had his hands full in his first couple of years as president in dealing with developing a Packard line to be built in South Bend, handling corporate financial problems, and testing the economy car and truck market with the introduction of the Scotsman sedans and truck.

By the 1958 model year commercial sales of Studebaker trucks were expected to decline to fewer than 9000 units.[3] As a result of this decline, Romine relates that some serious attention began to be paid to the trucks and the potential they had for Studebaker. For the 1960 model year, then, it appears that Churchill was ready to tackle the truck line and was well aware of the profit potential that even marginal increases in truck sales could achieve.

Romine, in the oral interview, stated that a major part of the problem for Studebaker in its marketing of trucks was that the pickup truck bed being used by Studebaker had been introduced as part of the restyled 1949 line of trucks and not changed since then. Very little money was available for redoing the truck line, according to Romine. While modifications could be made from year to year in interior trim and colors, there had not been any money for retooling the trucks. The initial Champ model for 1960 with the Lark sheet metal for the cab (which gave the trucks a refreshing new look) used the old pickup truck bed which, Romine stated, was too narrow for the market demands of the 1960s.

Romine had heard that Dodge was coming out with a new style pickup. He thought that the old Dodge pickup bed might be usable for the Studebaker Champ and give it a newer look and a larger cargo capacity. So, on his own, without authorization to do so, he claims he went to see the Chrysler people to see if the tooling for the old Dodge pickup bed could be purchased and used by Studebaker. Romine was able to get Frank Corcoran, Studebaker truck manager, to approve the project, and after about a half dozen trips to Detroit an agreement was reached. Corcoran convinced management of the wisdom of the project and Studebaker purchased the tooling for the old Dodge pickup bed for $198,000. With some minor tooling changes to the Champ cab, the truck was given a whole new look.[4]

One of the puzzling aspects of Churchill's tenure as president of S-P was his view toward the Hawk line. The Hawks, originally introduced in 1956 as a major facelift of

As the Champ evolved for the 1961 model year, the pickup bed was available in the smooth-sided version — tooling for which Studebaker bought from Dodge (AACA Library and Research Center).

the original 1953 sport coupe design, gained considerable market fame and gave Studebaker a niche sporty-type car. The 1957 and 1958 supercharged Golden Hawk and the unsupercharged Silver Hawk enhanced the sporty and performance image of Studebaker. However, the Hawk was continued for 1959 only as an unsupercharged Silver Hawk. Then, at the January 25, 1959, Board meeting, where $5.5 million in tooling was approved for an expanded Lark line which included a convertible and four-door station wagon, Churchill announced the Hawk line would be discontinued for 1960.

The minutes of a Studebaker-Packard Corporation Dealer Council meeting at South Bend in the summer of 1959 give some insights into both Churchill's and the dealers' reasoning regarding the Hawk. In response to a question from a dealer about the future of the Hawk, Sydney Skillman, vice-president for marketing and sales, responded that the Hawk was not included in the 1960 model plans. He noted that because Hawk sales in 1959 were only 5 percent of the corporation's passenger car sales, keeping the Hawk in the model lineup could not be justified. Also, Skillman stated that because the Hawk was built in limited volume it carried manufacturing penalties compared to the Lark line. From a marketing standpoint, he said that S-P had been unable to advertise and promote the 1959 Hawk separately and distinctly from the Lark, but that, even so, it should have sold better in 1959 than it did.

Following Skillman's comments, the minutes of that Dealer Council meeting reveal that a torrent of comments in support of keeping the Hawk in the model lineup was forthcoming. One dealer from San Francisco said the dealers there would like to see the Hawk as a real sports car with bucket seats, floor shifter, and elimination of the fins. A dealer representing the New York Zone said the dealers there retained many old customers due to the Hawk and wanted the Hawk because it was a hedge against the future in case there was a return in the market away from small cars. A South Bend dealer said he did not know how the company could say it could afford to lose 5 percent of its sales represented by the Hawk. He noted that his dealership sold a lot of 8-cylinder Hawks and wanted an even larger engine than in 1959. (The only V8 available in the Hawk for 1959 was the 259-cubic-inch displacement model.) Another dealer supported the idea of having the 289 engine available. He said the dealers did not much care about the 6-cylinder Hawk, but wanted the larger engine. The dealer representing the Memphis Zone was 100 percent in favor of keeping the Hawk and did not feel that the dealer body could dispose of that model.

One dealer asked Churchill at that Dealer Council meeting whether the Hawk penalized the company in production of the Lark. Churchill responded as follows:

For 1960, the Hawk was continued, but the "Silver" designation was dropped. Silver Hawks built from 1957 through 1959 and the Hawks of 1960 were built using the pillared sport coupe design. For 1960, the 259-cubic-inch V8 and 289-cubic-inch V8 were the engine options available for the Hawks.

The penalties come about in the final assembly. There are 1200 employees on the final line where the Hawk becomes an entity. From trim on through you have about 1200 people involved, and because of lower volume you have to man lines to take care of Hawks when they come through. When Larks come through you have unused labor. Another penalty is present because of the complete lack of interchangeability of certain materials.... There is no penalty on the 259 or 289 engine. If you can raise that 5 percent sufficiently to justify its being in the line, then we'll have to consider continuing the Hawk.... The advertising budget is another penalty you have, because of the lack of family relationship. It's outside the family of the Lark.[5]

The dealers at that Dealer Council meeting continued to push Churchill on the Hawk issue. One dealer related that originally he ordered no Hawks, but the buying public very quickly forced him to stock Hawks. Several dealers even said the price of the Hawk could be raised by as much as $300 and it would still sell. In response, it is clear that Churchill was willing to listen to the dealers and realized the Hawk issue was an important one. He said:

I think this is an important question.... If our judgment [to discontinue the Hawk] was wrong, then time has gone by and there are certain areas where changes cannot now be made. The engine is no problem; trim is no problem. The water has gone over the dam to the extent now that as far as any basic change in tooling is concerned, that is impossible. You were talking about the stick-shift. The stick-shift [on the floor] is out and the bucket seats are out of the question. If we were wrong, we were wrong in our initial decision in this matter. You must know that.... We cannot run counter to such a unanimity of opinion. We had some selfish motivations. We will take a good hard look at this thing and if it's determined we should have the Hawk it will be resolved on the basis of the 289 engine and a change in trim. We cannot make any major changes and the car would not be available until sometime in October. If that decision is satisfactory, I will look to you people to see that these Hawks sell.[6]

Later, at the July 7, 1959, Board meeting, the minutes indicate Churchill reversed the Hawk decision. His reason for continuing the Hawk was twofold. First, he referred to the Dealer Council meeting where the dealers were unanimous in wanting the Hawk in the model lineup. Second, maintaining the Hawk did not require any new tooling. We can only speculate on Churchill's reasons for not emphasizing the Hawks. He clearly was more interested in economy cars — ever since the development of the Champion in 1939. In his view the Hawk may have been only a distraction (sales were only 4507 units in 1960) from the emphasis he wanted to place on the Lark.

As the 1960 Studebaker Larks, Hawks, and trucks were being introduced to the market in the fall of 1959, Harold Churchill could look back on a very successful year for the company with the introduction of the Lark. In remarks to the National Press Club on November 6, 1959, Churchill reflected on the successes of that year. In so doing, he revealed quite explicitly his philosophy on the role of a company like Studebaker-Packard in the automobile industry. He also expressed his view of the strengths S-P could bring to the very competitive automobile market. Quoted below are Churchill's comments on how S-P fit in that market:

... in ours, one of the most competitive of industries, the small company is not prevented from securing profitable consumer acceptance for its product, provided the product is right for the particular market for which it is designed. This is not a theory but a historical fact, as Studebaker-Packard and others can attest.

Studebaker-Packard has what is needed to compete. Our manufacturing costs are competitive; our dealer organization, which is growing both in numbers and in quality, is competitive; and our management organization, we believe, is competitive. Studebaker-Packard suffers from no competitive disadvantages, and, I hope, we will continue to enjoy the styling and engineering advantages which have been typical of the company for so long.

I assume it is not necessary to explain that when I speak of successful competition I do not mean to infer [sic] that Studebaker-Packard intends to divide the total automotive market equally with the so-called "Big Three." Our goal, which we have realized this year, and in most of the previous years of the Company's long history, is a realistic objective, geared to our capacity and our product philosophy. *The Studebaker-Packard passenger cars, its taxis and trucks, are tailored for particular purposes and a particular segment of the entire market* [emphasis added]. The special consumer sections to which we direct our products, and for which we plan, are large enough and receptive enough to make reasonably certain that Studebaker-Packard's rather modest requirements for substantially profitable success can be met. After all, one of the virtues of a small company is its low break-even point and high rate of profits once the break-even is exceeded.[7]

Thus, we see that Churchill, three years after assuming the presidency of Studebaker-Packard, was not wavering from his philosophy of targeting the company's products to specific niches in the market. His comments would seem to reflect a high degree of optimism about the future of Studebaker-Packard.

However, his comments to the Board as early as the November 14, 1958, Board meeting and even comments he made in the oral history interview (see Chapter 8 for details) indicate he was not naive about the prospects for Studebaker-Packard's success in the growing but highly competitive compact car market. Yet, Churchill was not about to give up on S-P as the 1960 automobile market was emerging. The 1960 Larks were designed to compete across a broad spectrum of the compact market.

Most of the tooling costs for the 1960 Larks were for the expanded line of the convertible and a four-door station wagon. The appearance of the 1960 Larks was little changed from 1959. In reporting to the Board on May 4, 1959, Churchill said he had just completed a visit to dealers in twelve sales zones and they were unanimous in saying the Lark should be maintained for 1960 without change. He also pointed out that with the addition of the convertible and four-door station wagon, Studebaker had product coverage unmatched by any of the other compact cars coming on the market for 1960.

As shown in Table 2, the effects of competition from the Ford Falcon, Chevrolet Corvair, and Plymouth Valiant compact offerings of the Big Three were felt by Studebaker. Calendar year worldwide production (of all cars and trucks) declined from 182,300 in 1959 to 134,000 in 1960. From strong profits of $28.5 million in 1959, corporate profits declined to less than a million dollars in 1960.

The planning horizon for new models in the auto industry required that Churchill be vigilant regarding emerging trends. Even as the Lark was enjoying strong success for 1959 and the 1960 models were being prepared, Churchill began to look ahead to the 1961 model year. On May 4, 1959, he presented the Executive Committee of the Board with proposals for the 1961 model year. Those proposals were to leave the basic Lark vehicle unchanged but to make some annual identification changes so that the 1961 Lark would be recognized as a new model. The total cost of bringing out the 1961 line was

Top: Harold Churchill enjoyed driving the cars Studebaker-Packard was building and often took one off the assembly line to drive overnight. Here Churchill is seen driving a 1960 Lark convertible, an addition to the Lark line in 1960, by the gates of the S-P Proving Grounds (Richard Quinn).
Bottom: By expanding the Lark offerings for 1960 to include the convertible and the 4-door station wagon (shown here), the Studebaker Lark line was the most comprehensive line of compact cars offered by any United States automaker in 1960.

estimated at $5.7 million, which included about $2.5 million to modernize the six-cylinder engine.

The major change in the Lark for the 1961 model year was in its engine. Churchill told the Board at its May 4, 1959, meeting that the existing six-cylinder L-head engine used in the Lark (which dated back to the 1939 Champion) needed to be redesigned as an overhead valve engine. Fortunately, the old Packard engine-head line equipment had been kept in storage by S-P after the closing of the Detroit and Utica, Michigan, Packard plants. Churchill told the Board that the old Packard head line could be adapted to make the six-cylinder Studebaker overhead valve engine.

The modest trim and design changes, addition of a Cruiser luxury Lark model on a 113-inch wheelbase (originally introduced as the Lark Econ-O-Miler taxicab in 1959), and the new overhead valve six-cylinder engine were not enough to improve the competitive position of Studebaker for the 1961 model year. The Hawk, which was continued in 1961 with upgraded interiors and trim including the bucket seats and four-speed on-the-floor shifter that dealers had asked for, did not add significantly to sales, with only 3929 produced. Table 2 in Chapter 3 documents the continued slide in Studebaker

The 1961 Lark featured a mild facelift of the earlier Lark styling. The 1961 Studebakers were the last model year planned under the leadership of Harold Churchill as president of Studebaker-Packard. The big news for 1961 was in the 169-cubic-inch 6-cylinder engine which now was of overhead valve design, was called the Skybolt Six, and had horsepower increased to 112.

The 1961 Lark Regal 4-door sedan on the 108.5-inch wheelbase continued many of the styling cues of the original Lark but was also available with an innovative skytop sunroof at extra cost. With the new OHV Skybolt Six engine, Larks for 1961 were advertised as having *Performability* (AACA Library and Research Center).

worldwide output in the 1961 calendar year to just over 100,000 units (cars and trucks), with the company once again losing money.

As the 1959 model year came to a close and the 1960 models were being readied for production and plans were developed for the 1961 line, Churchill began to look even further ahead. He told the May 4, 1959, Board Executive Committee meeting that the company's long-range plans included new drive train configurations and power plant designs.

Churchill's view that a new drive train configuration and power plant were needed was motivated by the realities of the automotive market. Although production of the Lark was maintained at a relatively high rate through most of the 1960 model year, sales were not keeping up. The original handwritten minutes of the Executive Committee of the Board on July 6, 1960, indicate Porta reported that the dealer and factory inventory, plus what was scheduled for production, was 35,400 Studebaker units, or over three and a half months' supply at the rate the cars were selling. Porta also introduced the new S-P vice-president for marketing, Lewis Minkel, who noted the dealer organization needed to be injected with young blood, good salespeople, and good managers.

Top: The Studebaker Lark Cruiser was a new model introduced for the 1961 model year. It was built on the 113-inch wheelbase (previously used only for Lark station wagons and Econ-O-miler taxicabs) and was an attempt to recapture some of the upscale market that had previously been covered by the Studebaker President discontinued after the 1958 model year. *Bottom:* Exterior styling of the 1961 Studebaker Hawk was little changed from its 1959 and 1960 counterparts except for the two-tone effect as a result of the color strip on the fin. Interior appointments were upgraded with contoured bucket seats and an optional 4-speed floor shift.

The competition from the Big Three compacts was taking a toll on the dealer organization. Studebaker was losing many of the dealers it had dualed with when the Lark was introduced for 1959. In 1960 and 1961, Studebaker lost 356 outlets.[8]

Churchill anticipated the day when Studebaker would need a new product to take on the Big Three in the competitive market for compact cars. Therefore, Churchill's May 4, 1959, comment to the Board about the company's long-range plans was a hint of plans for a dramatic new car being planned by Studebaker. By mid–1960, plans for the new Studebaker model, which was to be a four-cylinder car smaller than the Lark, were well advanced.

Harold Johnson, a Studebaker engineer from 1936 to 1964, recalls that initial planning for the four-cylinder engine was done with great secrecy. Johnson did not know of the project until the first block casting reached the experimental machine shop, where he had the responsibility of reporting on the progress of the various components.[9] From the recollections of Johnson and Otto Klausmeyer, superintendent of the Studebaker foundry, it appears that Churchill first revealed plans for the engine to Klausmeyer on a plane trip returning from a Board meeting in New York in early 1960.

In a 1984 interview for the Indiana University Oral History Project, Klausmeyer stated Studebaker actually built 12 of the castings for the four-cylinder engine and machined three of them. According to Johnson, the decision to go ahead with the engine was made at a meeting in Churchill's office on April 19, 1960, with Churchill, Klausmeyer, Porta, Gene Hardig (V.P. for engineering), A.D. Whitmer (manufacturing manager), and C.E. Gerke (manufacturing engineer) in attendance. The engine was to be a 143-cubic-inch displacement flat four-cylinder engine with plans made for a 157 c.i.d. version as well. Indicative of the seemingly impossible tasks the Studebaker people were capable of achieving in remarkably short periods of time, the first of these radically different engines, with block and crank case integral, was running and installed on a dynamometer by October 15, 1960. At the December 5, 1960, meeting of the Executive Committee of the Board, Porta reported the four-cylinder engine had completed a 100-hour test which was the most successful ever with a new engine for Studebaker.

The four-cylinder engine was only part of what was necessary to build the new Studebaker small car. That engine had to be wrapped in a new body. Raymond Loewy, who, along with his industrial design firm, had been involved with Studebaker since the 1930s, was enlisted to help with designing the new small Studebaker. In the oral history interview Churchill confirmed that Loewy was involved at a cost of $25,000. Studebaker historian Richard Quinn found that Churchill had a discussion with Loewy on February 9, 1960. On February 26, the Loewy staff under W.T. Snaith submitted a proposal to develop a concept for the new car at a fee of $25,000. Churchill agreed to proceeding with a proposal in a letter to Loewy dated March 18, 1960, in which he stated the arrangement must maintain the strictest confidence. Quinn believes that Churchill did not want the news to leak out to the general public and probably not even to the Studebaker design team in South Bend, then headed by Randy Faurot, who had taken over as director of styling from Duncan McRae in July 1959.[10]

At this point the precise nature of the arrangements with Loewy becomes unclear. The dating of the letter to Loewy by Churchill on March 18, 1960, was after receipt of a letter from Loewy to Churchill dated March 16, 1960. In the March 16 letter, Loewy

Top and bottom: Churchill realized that Studebaker would have to stay a step ahead of the competition if it was to survive. Shown here is the prototype of the next step in the evolution of the Lark, which would have been a 4-cylinder car on a 100-inch wheelbase and 162-inch length. Lack of financial resources and the departure of Churchill as president ended the project. Would a four-cylinder Lark have been enough to save Studebaker? We will never know, but it is an interesting question to debate (Richard Quinn).

proposed a forward-slanting windshield, for which he listed some possible favorable attributes, including enabling lengthening the hood and easier clearance of the glass from snow and rain. Churchill addressed the forward-slanting windshield idea in a memo to Porta and Hardig on March 18, 1960 (to which the Loewy proposal was attached), in which he stated, "I am not in full agreement with some of the advantages he [Loewy] cites for a slanted windshield."

The prototype of a 1962 six-cylinder or optional V8 Lark on a 108.5-inch wheelbase and having a length of 178 inches shown here demonstrates the larger Studebakers would have shared many body components with the 4-cylinder model. These cars never reached production (Richard Quinn).

Quinn suggests that in-house styling efforts for the small car were going on under the leadership of Randy Faurot at the same time that Loewy was working on the project. The in-house styling was what made its way to the prototype stage. The accompanying four photographs, courtesy of Richard Quinn, show two different models that were proposed — one on a 100-inch wheelbase with the flat four-cylinder engine, and one on the 108.5-inch Lark chassis, but with body parts interchangeable with the 100-inch-wheelbase car. The larger version could have been powered by the existing Studebaker V-8 or OHV Six engines. The interchangeable parts on the two cars included doors, bumpers, and roof section.[11]

It is probable that the two cars shown in the accompanying pictures were the ones that the handwritten minutes (but not the official minutes) say were described to the Executive Committee of the Board by Porta on June 3, 1960. The larger car was described as 178 inches in length and the small car as 162 inches long. Porta also stated that both the 162-inch and 178-inch cars were coming along well in their development. His expectation was that the 6-cylinder engine would be available at introduction time for the 1962 models and the 4-cylinder engine available 30 to 60 days after that. Dr. Edward Litchfield of the Board commented at that June 3, 1960, Board meeting that there was considerable hope for the automobile business of Studebaker in 1961 and 1962 and pointed to the new smaller car with a four-cylinder engine for 1962 as being a particularly positive development.

What happened to this smaller four-cylinder Studebaker and its larger six-cylinder and V8 engine companions? Here the story becomes complex and is interwoven with the declining fortunes of S-P in the market and with changes in management. Conventional wisdom suggests that when Sherwood H. Egbert became president of S-P on February 1, 1961, his decision to go off in another direction to build a performance image car called the Avanti resulted in abandonment of the small-car program.[12] A careful reading of the Board minutes in the last four or five months of 1960, however, suggests that for all practical purposes the small-car project was dead by the November 28, 1960, Board meeting and that Churchill had a role in ending the program that he had promoted with hope and vigor.

To understand what happened at Studebaker-Packard in the last few months of 1960, it is necessary to understand the dynamics of the Board of Directors during that period. That understanding is enhanced by recalling that Harold E. Churchill became president of Studebaker-Packard Corporation in July 1956, but was not elected board chair. For the more than four years from July 1956 to September 1960, there was no board chair of S-P. Churchill did "chair" meetings of the Board, but he had neither the position nor title of board chair.

At the September 2, 1960, special Board meeting, the minutes reveal that the position of board chair was created and Clarence Francis, who had become a Studebaker director in 1958 and had retired earlier as board chair of General Foods Corporation, was elected to the position. He also assumed the position of chief executive officer (CEO), which had been held by Churchill. Churchill, however, retained the position of president. The dynamics of that September 2 Board meeting are particularly interesting in understanding the position and personality of Churchill.

The *New York Times* stated that the election of Francis as CEO in place of Churchill was a result of Board dissatisfaction with lagging sales and differences of opinion over the diversification and acquisition program.[13] Indirectly, Francis addressed that issue in his remarks to the Board at its September 2, 1960, meeting. The transcript of his remarks is found in the handwritten minutes but not in the official minutes. Among his comments were:

I personally look on my job as getting the company organized for growth and progress and then stepping down.... Churchill and I have had frank talks on this matter. I want to commend him. We have a clear understanding that he will be in a staff function. We shall try to work that out for the good of the company.... By working together we can create a better climate for acquisitions — [and] may be able to use our stock to advantage.

Francis went on to say that he created an operating committee consisting of him and several directors including Churchill. He stated his appreciation for the continued valued support of Churchill as a staff officer. The handwritten minutes of that September 2, 1960, Board meeting record that the directors gave Francis's remarks a standing ovation — which may be interpreted as much as a tribute to Churchill as to Francis.

Francis asked Churchill at that September 2, 1960, Board meeting if he had any remarks. Churchill responded that the changes were a desirable move and pledged his full cooperation. Dr. Edward Litchfield, member of the Board, then made a statement that summarizes the objectivity, commitment, and integrity of Harold Churchill: "Through all of this Mr. Churchill's attitude has at all times been even more than could be expected of a person. In my experience it is rare to find a man who is as objective about such a situation as Churchill has been."

As the fall of 1960 wore on, the situation at S-P continued to deteriorate. Handwritten minutes reveal Clarence Francis called a special Board meeting on November 28, 1960, for one purpose — review of the automotive program. Included in the discussion at that meeting was possible liquidation of the automobile business on both a crash and planned basis. Francis stated a crash liquidation would cost $95 million and an orderly liquidation beginning then would cost $10 million to $12 million less. The meeting then went into a comprehensive review of the automotive program by A.J. Porta and Byers Burlingame, vice-president for finance, which is summarized below:

- Porta proposed a facelift for 1962 that would cost in the range of $3.25 million to $3.5 million. Worldwide sales of between 100,000 and 106,000 units would be break-even.
- The cost to tool for the 4-cylinder car and engine alone was estimated to be $18 million to $19 million.
- Byers Burlingame stated total tooling costs for the 4-cylinder car and engine plus the new six- and eight-cylinder car and body would be $24.2 million, which the Board had approved on September 19, 1960. He offered the opinion that losses since then cast doubt on whether this money should be risked.
- If the program for an all-new four-cylinder car and the six- and eight-cylinder car was adopted, the projected volume would be only 115,000 units annually because it was believed the four-cylinder car would merely take sales away from the six-cylinder model because the proposed four-cylinder car looked almost the same as the six and eight.
- Consideration was given to putting the four-cylinder engine in the present, but modified Lark. There would have been a gain of two miles per gallon in fuel economy, but it was projected to generate only 96,000 worldwide sales and a loss of $13 million. Tooling for this plan would have cost $9.75 million.

- Churchill stated that spending $24 million on tooling could not be justified given the disappointing 1961 model introduction. He came out in favor of spending $3.5 million on tooling to give the current models a new appearance.
- Lewis Minkel, vice-president for marketing, stated that for the four-cylinder car to be the basis of S-P's business it would have to sell for under $1600. He also stated that the styling of the four-cylinder car (as shown in the accompanying pictures) was not exciting enough and that it should be restyled.
- The Board approved both $3.5 million for tooling of a facelifted 1962 model and an $8.5 million corporate cost reduction program. The original 1962 tooling program was canceled although development work on the four-cylinder engine was continued.

The dream of Harold Churchill to follow the initial success of the Lark with a still smaller four-cylinder car effectively was dead.

6
Churchill —
Beyond the Presidency

Clarence Francis, in a November 6, 1960, *New York Times* interview, stated: "Probably the greatest service that I could render to Studebaker-Packard would be to be succeeded by a vigorous, capable, younger chief executive officer."[1] There was to be plenty of contentious debate on the S-P Board of Directors before that goal was achieved.

Throughout the minutes (both handwritten and official copies) of Board meetings in the last half of 1960, there is evidence of considerable tension between the overall Board and two of the directors, Abraham Sonnabend and D. Ray Hall. Sonnabend, brought on the Board as part of the 1958 refinancing deal, was interested in diversifying the operations of S-P through acquisition of profitable companies. Hall was on the Board as a result of one of those acquisitions — the Gravely Company, a manufacturer of lawn care equipment of which Hall had been principal owner.

While there is no evidence that Churchill ever had any desire to be board chair, there is adequate evidence that both Sonnabend and Hall coveted that position. For example, it is noted in the handwritten draft of the minutes of the December 19, 1960, Board meeting, that Hall announced he wanted to be chair and that it was a matter of self-preservation to save the company, but that he had no plan of action to offer at that time. Hall also threatened a proxy fight if he was not elected chair. At the same meeting, Sonnabend made a long statement highly critical of the Board but supportive of the team running the automotive division (that would have included Churchill). Sonnabend said the company needed a dictator but that he (Sonnabend) would not be chief executive officer, and that the CEO position should go to Churchill. Sonnabend also suggested a proxy fight was possible and even first offered and then withdrew his resignation.

On December 5, 1960, the Executive Committee of the Studebaker-Packard Board met to consider a proposal presented by Board member Royall Victor that Sherwood H. Egbert, executive vice-president of McCulloch Corporation, manufacturer of a wide range of industrial equipment from chain saws to automotive superchargers, be offered the position of S-P's chief executive officer. Six S-P directors had interviewed the 40-year-old Egbert. He was looking for a new challenge and was considered to be the young, aggressive, highly motivated person desired by Francis. The handwritten minutes of the meeting quote Francis as saying Egbert's title would be president and CEO and that Churchill should be made vice-chair of the board. In reacting to the proposal by Francis, Churchill said: "I would resign as President to become Vice Chairman of the Board. I am interested in the welfare of the Corporation. I am willing to be a consultant if the Board prefers." Francis added, though, that Ray Hall, who could not attend the meeting, was opposed to Egbert because he (Hall) wanted to be board chair and CEO.

At the December 19, 1960, Board meeting, Francis reported that on December 16 Sherwood Egbert withdrew his name from consideration. As already indicated, Hall and Sonnabend were each very eager to assume the position of board chair and CEO of Studebaker-Packard. As a result of their interest, the Board engaged in a lively question-and-answer session with the two men.

After Hall and Sonnabend were excused from the meeting, Churchill and Porta were asked what they would do if Hall were elected. Churchill responded that he would not remain unless he were given tangible responsibilities that were clearly defined. Porta said his decision would depend on what his assignment would be. Asked the same question about what they would do if Sonnabend were elected, both Churchill and Porta said they would stay on if asked to.

During the discussion at that December 19, 1960, Board meeting, Churchill stated he thought Sonnabend was eloquent and could do some good with the dealers. However, in much of the discussion among the Board members, there was emphasis that diversification and acquisitions were needed and were important to turn the fortunes of the Corporation around. The Board finally decided it could not make a decision, that more time was needed to consider the matter, and that it would recess until December 28, 1960.

At the Board meeting on December 28, 1960, the handwritten minutes show Byers Burlingame, vice-president for finance, reported that with projected production of 90,000 worldwide units for 1961, the auto division would operate at a $28 million loss and that in recent days dealer orders had dropped off sharply. Daily production was 280 cars but orders were running at only 100 cars per day. Minkel reported that efforts to bolster the dealer organization had not yielded results. Burlingame offered the opinion that if the deterioration was not stopped in 60 to 90 days there would be no alternative to liquidation. In this gloomy scenario, Churchill stated his opinion that psychological factors are important. Specifically, he noted that corporate events in those past few months had had a negative effect on dealers and that solidifying the management situation at S-P would have a significant positive effect on the dealers.

After the assessment of the deteriorating sales situation, the Board took up the question of a new CEO. Francis announced there were three candidates: Hall, Sonnabend, and Egbert (who had once again placed his name in contention). Board members engaged in a wide-ranging discussion about the three candidates. Churchill made the following statement:

> Egbert showed some instability in reversing his decision twice. I doubt he can help psychologically. It looks to me like Egbert is a compromise resurrected after the December 19 meeting recessed. I seriously question whether Egbert is the solution. There is no question Sonnabend, through his eloquence, could give our dealer organization a boost.

Porta also threw his support behind Sonnabend. However, other directors were concerned that creditors were not in favor of Sonnabend. Most of the directors were impressed with Egbert's youth and his apparent willingness to accept a challenge and make a commitment to the community as well. Churchill then stated: "If Egbert is to be elected, of course I will resign as President. I don't want to prejudice the decision. I don't want to serve as Vice Chairman [one of Francis's proposals]. I will continue as a director until the next annual meeting if the Board so desires."

Russell Forgan, who was the director who called Churchill in July 1956 to ask him to be president of S-P, paid a tribute to Churchill and Porta, saying they had given everything in them to the company, but luck had been against them. Consistent with what appears to have been overall positive views of Churchill on the part of the directors, Francis said one alternative was to make Churchill the CEO, which he (Francis) preferred to Sonnabend or Hall. Then, Forgan and Morris Strauss (another director) both asked Churchill if he would accept the CEO position if Egbert were elected board chair. Churchill's response was clear: "No, I will not accept the Chief Executive's spot." He went on to say he was willing to continue as a consultant.[2]

With a vote of 8 directors for Egbert, two against (Sonnabend and Hall), and two abstentions (Churchill and Porta), Egbert was elected president and chief executive officer of Studebaker-Packard Corporation. As a result, Sonnabend resigned and Hall threatened a proxy fight (which did not materialize).[3] On December 29, 1960, just one day after he resigned from the Studebaker-Packard Board, Sonnabend sold all of his stock in the company.[4]

Sherwood H. Egbert assumed the position of president and CEO of Studebaker-Packard Corporation on February 1, 1961. Clarence Francis continued on as board chair. The handwritten minutes of the February 6, 1961, Board meeting contain Egbert's statement of appreciation with the management of S-P for its cooperation in helping with the managerial transition. He specifically singled out Churchill for praise, who was helping him as a consultant, particularly in the area of assessing acquisitions.

At the February 6, 1961, Board meeting, the Board's personnel committee reported Churchill asked to be terminated as an employee and continue as a consultant, at a rate that was up to management to approve, effective March 1, 1961. Directors Francis, Hall, and Strauss all spoke highly of Churchill with Francis, in particular, calling him a dedicated man. The Board's handwritten minutes state the decision was to give Churchill $64,500 termination pay (however, the official typed copy of the minutes states $56,250) plus "normal" consulting rates and a $1500 per month consulting fee. The Board's vote was unanimous approval.

Churchill, nearly 20 years after these events, observed that he stayed on as a director of Studebaker-Packard and then Studebaker Corporation, as the firm was called after the Packard name was dropped in 1962, until 1968, when Studebaker merged with Worthington Corporation to form Studebaker-Worthington. He stated that his skills were used primarily in the evaluation of prospective acquisitions by the company.[5]

By the time Harold Churchill retired from the Board in 1968, the Studebaker Corporation *Annual Report for 1967* listed six continuing divisions of the company, as follows:

Onan Engine/Generator Division
Gravely Tractors Division

Top: When Sherwood Egbert became president of Studebaker-Packard in 1961, he initiated a program to facelift the Lark. The 1962 Cruiser shown here is the result of that facelift. The 1962 Studebaker line met with moderate success in the market. *Bottom:* Churchill never put much development effort into the Hawk and kept it in the model lineup only under pressure from dealers. Egbert, however, had Brooks Stevens rework the car into the Gran Turismo Hawk for the 1962, 1963, and 1964 model years. The 1964 G.T. Hawk pictured here was the last model year for the Hawks (both photographs, AACA Library and Research Center.)

Top: The 1963 Avanti represented the fulfillment of the vision of Sherwood Egbert for Studebaker products, which differed dramatically from that of Harold Churchill. Instead of a 4-cylinder compact car, Egbert initiated the development of the luxury sports coupe, the Avanti. (AACA Library and Research Center). *Bottom:* The 1963 Studebaker sedans had an all-new roof line and center (B) pillar, but appeared almost unchanged from the 1962 models because the front-end and rear-end styling was almost identical to that of the 1962s. Pictured here is a 1963 Cruiser with a child and an original Studebaker junior wagon sold by the Studebaker Brothers Manufacturing Company in the late 19th century.

Clarke Floor Machinery Division
Schaefer Commercial Refrigeration Division
STP (Chemical Compounds) Division (motor oil additives)
Big Four Automotive Equipment Division (tire changing equipment)

Studebaker had acquired other companies over the years, but had disposed of some operations, including the Franklin Appliance Division and the CTL Missile Space Technology Division.

Analyses of Studebaker under the leadership of Sherwood Egbert, Egbert's health problems, and under the leadership of Byers Burlingame as president and Randolph Guthrie as board chair after November 1963, are discussed in Chapter 8. Discussion of the modest success of the 1962 Lark and Gran Turismo Hawk facelifts, the unfortunate and disappointing experience with the fiberglass-bodied Avanti performance image car

After the move of all Studebaker assembly operations to Canada, the 1965 models carried styling virtually identical to that introduced for the 1964 model year. Churchill, as a director and consultant, had the responsibility of determining whose engines would replace the South Bend–built engines after the 1964 model year. The 1965 Daytona sports sedan pictured here differed from the 1964 Daytonas in that the 1965 version added a vinyl top but utilized the basic two-door (pillared) sedan body instead of the pillarless style of 1964 Daytona hardtops. The 1965 Studebakers used the General Motors McKinnon Industries six and V8 engines recommended by Churchill (AACA Library and Research Center).

The 1966 Studebakers, like these Commanders, built in Canada, were the last of the line. The 1966 Studebakers were available with either a 194-cubic-inch or 230-cubic-inch six-cylinder engine or 283-cubic-inch V8 engine. The engines were built by McKinnon Industries, a General Motors subsidiary in Canada. The last Studebaker automobile came off the Hamilton, Ontario, assembly line in March 1966.

of 1963, the sales deterioration in 1963, the closing of the South Bend plants at the end of 1963, the transfer of production to Canada, and final ending of all Studebaker automotive production in March 1966, are covered in Chapter 8 as well. However, the involvement of Harold Churchill in the company during the 1961–1968 period does warrant further discussion here.

Although Churchill did not support the election of Egbert as president of S-P, it is clear he was making a professional and not personal judgment at the time. All evidence indicates the professional relationship of Churchill and Egbert was excellent. At the February 28, 1961, Board of Directors meeting, when Egbert presented his plans to the Board for a restyled Hawk and facelifted 1962 Lark line and completely restyled 1964 cars, he asked for comments from the Board. Churchill responded that he agreed with the program and noted that negative talk over the previous four years had hurt the company. He stated, "Egbert's program is sound. With the cost reduction program and what we are doing with the '62 model we are making the best job if we go ahead."

Although his responsibilities were primarily in helping with analysis of possible corporate acquisitions by Studebaker, Harold Churchill made one final, but significant, contribution to the engineering and development of Studebaker automotive products. Churchill was assigned the responsibility, in late 1963, of determining whether or not it was feasible to continue Studebaker automobile production in the Canadian plant in Hamilton, Ontario, if production was ended in South Bend. Minutes of several subsequent Board of Directors meetings reveal the role Churchill played in helping the transition to Canadian production. He reported at a special meeting of the Board on December 1, 1963, that his preliminary studies indicated such a move in production would be feasible. At the next special meeting of the Board on December 12, 1963, it was evident Churchill's abilities continued to have the confidence of management and the Board. He reported he had had discussions with Henry Ford II about providing 6- or 8-cylinder Ford engines as substitutes for Studebaker engines for Studebakers produced in Canada. (Production at the levels obtained in Canada — see Table 2 in Chapter 3 — would not have justified continued operation of Studebaker's foundry and engine plant in South Bend.) At the January 3, 1964, Board meeting, Churchill reported that extensive redesign of the Lark would be required to use the Canadian-produced Ford engines, but that Chevrolet engines appeared to be practical substitutes for the Studebaker engines. Churchill's assessment of the Chevrolet engines proved accurate, and Burlingame, who had become president of Studebaker following the resignation of Egbert in November 1963, reported to the Board at its January 17, 1964, meeting that General Motors had agreed to furnish the engines for the Canadian-made cars. Technically, the engines were not Chevrolet engines, but were made by GM's McKinnon Industries subsidiary in St. Catherine, Ontario. The engines were supplied as a 194-cubic-inch displacement six, a 230 c.i.d. six, and a 283 c.i.d. V-8.[6]

7
Churchill Era Studebaker-Packard Products: An Assessment

"The market we are aiming at is selective. It consists of buyers who want soundly designed and engineered, high quality distinctive automobiles."[1] These remarks by Harold Churchill to the Automotive and Financial Editors Press Conference on September 5, 1956, shortly after he became president of Studebaker-Packard, give some insight into what Churchill's objectives were for S-P products.

Harold E. Churchill was president of Studebaker-Packard Corporation from July 1956 to February 1, 1961. During that period of time, five model years of S-P products were introduced for 1957, 1958, 1959, 1960, and 1961. While he was not directly responsible for most of the 1957 models, they were built during his administration and he did influence the introduction of the 1957 Packards and Studebaker Scotsman. The question that must be raised, then, is: were the Studebaker-Packard products produced during the Churchill era "soundly designed and engineered, high quality" vehicles? How did the media view the cars? What was the public reaction to the products? How did they compare in terms of quality and performance with the competition?

Here we examine these questions by looking at media reports on the Studebaker-Packard products from 1957 through 1961. The source of the information presented here is primarily test reports from automobile enthusiast magazines of the late 1950s and 1960s plus some reports from the consumer advocacy magazine *Consumer Reports*. No pretense is made that the assessment of the Studebaker-Packard products presented here is a scientific analysis. What is presented are the comments of the media, subject to whatever biases and assumptions the media may have had toward or against S-P products. As such, the material summarized in this chapter reflects the kinds of information the general public was reading about Studebakers and Packards during the Churchill presidency of the company. What can be assumed from this material is that the automobile-buying public was influenced to some extent by the findings and comments of the media about Studebaker-Packard products. No attempt has been made to summarize recent articles about the 1957–1961 Studebaker-Packard products in vintage automobile enthusiast magazines. The use of media contemporary to when the cars were built and on the market is viewed as being more relevant to the fortunes of the company in the late 1950s and early 1960s, and, by extension, to the career of Harold Churchill as president of Studebaker-Packard.

The approach taken here is to discuss each model year separately beginning with 1957. While the test reports and media comments summarized cover representative Studebakers and Packards in the various model years, no attempt is made to show every test report on every individual model of the two makes. Covered and discussed are representative models as reported on by selected sources in the media.

Studebaker-Packard Products for 1957

One of the first challenges confronting Harold Churchill when he became president of Studebaker-Packard was what to do about the Packard product line. All automotive production of S-P was being consolidated into South Bend, and the Packard plants in Detroit had been closed. We begin the assessment of the 1957 model year, therefore, with a look at the 1957 Packards.

Motor Life magazine in its February 1957 issue gave a brief description of the 1957 Packard Clipper four-door Town Sedan and Country Sedan station wagon. Recognizing that the new Packards were based on Studebaker bodies and chassis, *Motor Life* nevertheless called the "Packardizing" of the cars a minor miracle in view of the short period of time allowed for the redesign and preparation for production. *Motor Life* did say that the 1957 Packards were not likely to cause a great stampede among car buyers because the competition had poured too much into its new products. However, the article concluded on the high note that the 1957 Packards were a significant indication that the firm was far from throwing in the towel, which *Motor Life* said might be the best news of the whole year.

In a follow-up road test of a 1957 Packard Clipper Town Sedan in its May 1957 issue, *Motor Life* concluded the car is a good one with performance, fuel economy,

While acknowledging that the South Bend–built Packards were not of the same tradition as Packards of previous years, the media nevertheless rated them as pretty good performing cars.

roadability, and handling equal to most of its direct competitors in the medium-priced field. *Motor Life* did find that the Clipper suffered somewhat in the ride and general comfort category when compared with the competition. Acceleration from 0 to 60 miles per hour was in the range of 10.2 to 10.5 seconds. In their test a speed of 110 miles per hour was recorded, but top speed was not checked. *Motor Life* concluded that, although not cut from the traditional Packard cloth, the 1957 Packards were sound cars that should be attractive to discerning buyers.

Joe H. Wherry, in the March 1957 issue of *Motor Trend* magazine, reported on a "Drivescription" of the 1957 Packards. Wherry introduced the article with the interesting question of: "What manner of car is this that is slated to perpetuate one of the industry's most historic names? Is it just a more luxurious Studebaker or is it a distinctive make in its own right?"

Road tests often examine the acceleration of cars from 0 to 60 miles per hour. In the *Motor Trend* tests, the 1957 Packard four door Town Sedan did zero to sixty in 11.6 seconds and the Country Sedan station wagon did it in 11.0 seconds. (Note that these times for 0 to 60 m.p.h. were slightly slower than achieved in the *Motor Life* road test.) Both cars, of course, were equipped with the McCulloch supercharger. Wherry attributed the better acceleration of the station wagon to its having a better weight distribution front and rear than the four-door sedan. Both cars exceeded 100 miles per hour easily on the track at the Studebaker Proving Grounds outside of South Bend. Wherry also found that both models provided adequate acceleration in city traffic, giving zero to thirty miles per hour in 4.1 seconds.

Wherry's Drivescription of the two 1957 Packards went to great lengths to discuss the luxury touches of the interiors, with particular comments about the instrument panel's having preserved the Packard identity (it was nearly identical to the 1956 Packards and Clippers). In his conclusion to the *Motor Trend* article, Wherry stated that the use of a common body shell by Studebaker and Packard should not be of concern to car buyers because it is a common practice in the industry to use one body shell over two or three different nameplates. He noted that the Packard stylists performed an arduous task in an incredibly short period of time and gave the car a Packard-like grille and rear quarter panels with the net result being a car readily distinguishable from Studebakers. He stated that the driver who wishes something off the beaten path should closely examine and drive the new Packard Clipper. Wherry also observed that the quality of craftsmanship of the cars was excellent.

Consumer Reports was not as kind to the 1957 Packard Clippers as *Motor Life* and *Motor Trend*. In its April 1957 Annual Automobile Issue, *Consumer Reports* classified the Packards as upper-medium-priced cars and said there was little relationship between the 1957 Packard Clippers and previous Packards. It described the Packard Clipper as a supercharged and redecorated, six inches longer Studebaker President Classic with no substantially superior ride, handling, or structure. It summed up its view of the car by saying the Packard Clipper picture was clouded by below-par steering and handling and narrow seating. It is interesting to note that whereas *Motor Life* and *Motor Trend* found the handling characteristics of the 1957 Packards quite acceptable, *Consumer Reports* was critical of the handling of the cars. *Consumer Reports* classified the probable trade-in value of the 1957 Packard Clippers as below average.

The addition of the McCulloch supercharger to the Studebaker 289-cubic-inch V8 engine for use in the Golden Hawk was the big news out of South Bend in 1957. The 1956 Golden Hawk with the Packard 352-cubic-inch engine generated 275 horsepower. For 1957, though, the Packard engine no longer was available, with the result that the supercharger was employed to get the horsepower of the Studebaker 289 engine up to 275. The unsupercharged version of the 289 engine in a Silver Hawk with a four-barrel carburetor generated 225 horsepower. *Speed Age* magazine in its May 1957 issue classified the 1957 Golden Hawk as one of the industry's hot cars for 1957. *Speed Age* writer Bob Veith did a comparison test of what he called Detroit's "hot trio"—the Chevrolet Corvette, Ford Thunderbird, and Studebaker Golden Hawk. (Of course, technically, the Golden Hawk was not a Detroit product, but that point seems to have been lost on the *Speed Age* editors.)

Veith began his assessment of the three cars by saying all of them were virtual bombs loaded with power. He also noted that none of the three was technically what he considered a pure sports car. The Golden Hawk was designed for family-car comfort with sports-car performance. The Thunderbird looked like a sports car, had sports-car performance, but had a soft ride. His comment on the Corvette was that it was designed to appeal to sports-car enthusiasts.

Veith observed that the supercharger definitely gave the Golden Hawk a tremendous boost on acceleration. In acceleration runs, the Hawk was the fastest of the three cars from 0 to 40 miles per hour at 3.79 seconds. The Corvette, with a 283 V8, did 0 to 40 mph in 4.24 seconds, and the Thunderbird, with a 312 V8, did it in 5.45 seconds. For 0 to 60 mph, the Corvette did it in 6.93 seconds, the Hawk in 7.46 seconds, and the Thunderbird in 8.49 seconds. However, the Hawk ran out of supercharger boost at about 90 mph and ended up being the slowest of the three cars from 0 to 100 mph at 23.73 seconds (the Corvette did 0 to 100 in 17.69 seconds and the Thunderbird in 22.19 seconds.)

Veith was critical of the Hawk's handling due to a light rear end with much of the car's weight concentrated on the front end. He was disappointed in the overall handling of the Hawk: he found the body leaned considerably in tight turns and the steering wheel felt sluggish. He did observe that handling of the 1957 Golden Hawk was better than handling of the 1956 model due to the front end's actually being lighter than the 1956 with the large Packard engine. The availability of the Twin Traction non-slip differential also improved handling of the 1957 over the 1956 model. He found that the Hawk's brakes were the best of the three cars tested. Veith said the craftsmanship on the Golden Hawk was something for Studebaker to boast about.

In summing up the test of the three cars, the Corvette, Thunderbird, and Golden Hawk, Veith said all three were a credit to American styling and engineering and he could not recommend one over another. The Corvette was the most like a true sports car; the Thunderbird was what he called an "in-betweener" that had both sports-car features and passenger-car comfort; the Golden Hawk, he said, had the challenge of being both a family car and having to appeal to sports-car enthusiasts.

Motor Life magazine in its August 1957 issue tested the 1957 Golden Hawk. In describing the Golden Hawk, *Motor Life* was consistent with the findings of *Speed Age*. *Motor Life* said that Studebaker's calling the Hawk a family sports car was probably a

The 1957 Studebaker Commanders and Champions found more than their share of criticism from the automotive media for problems such as the narrow bodies and poor roadability and handling.

good description of it. In commenting on the sportiness of Golden Hawk styling, *Motor Life* said the car was a definite attention-getter and found that groups of curious onlookers gathered around the test car every time it was parked.

The *Motor Life* analysis of the performance of the Golden Hawk was consistent with that found by *Speed Age* magazine in its test. Top speed was found to be at least 115 miles per hour. Zero to sixty mph was achieved in 9.1 seconds, which was somewhat slower than the acceleration achieved in the *Speed Age* test. Handling characteristics was the area that *Motor Life* was most critical of with the Hawk. It observed that steering was considerably improved over the 1956 Golden Hawk, but was still too slow for maximum maneuverability. However, *Motor Life* found that the Hawk offered a much smoother ride than the typical sports car.

The instrument panel of the Golden Hawk came in for particular praise by *Motor Life*, which called the dash near-classic in design with a tachometer, vacuum gauge, speedometer, and full complement of other necessary instruments. In conclusion, *Motor Life* said the Golden Hawk was a car best suited to the enthusiast-type car buyer, especially if the family had two or three children. For about the same price as a Corvette, Thunderbird, or Jaguar, the Golden Hawk offered many of the same advantages as those cars without the drawbacks of constrained space.

Consumer Reports, in its April 1957 Annual Automobile issue, did not test any of the Studebaker Hawks in 1957 in detail. However, it did make some observations on the three Hawk models — the Golden Hawk, the Silver Hawk V8, and the Silver Hawk 6-cylinder. Its casual observation and expectation was that, even though the Golden Hawk's supercharged Studebaker engine was much lighter than the Packard engine used in 1956, the Golden Hawk would remain below the best sports cars in handling.

Consumer Reports, in that April 1957 issue, did analyze the regular line of 1957 Studebakers. In the category of low-priced cars, *Consumer Reports* rated the Chevrolet model 210 with the 283-cubic-inch engine and Powerglide automatic transmission as the "Best-Buy." Rated as "acceptable" in the low-priced category were the Studebaker Commander Deluxe V8, President V8 (on the 116.5-inch wheelbase), and the Studebaker Champion Deluxe 6, in that order. Unfortunately for Studebaker, its three cars were rated at the very bottom of the *Consumer Reports* low-priced acceptable list, behind Chevrolet, Ford, Plymouth, Rambler, and Dodge.

Consumer Reports was particularly critical of the inside dimensions of the Studebaker low-priced cars. Headroom was found to be good, as was vision, and entry into the cars was convenient. However, the narrow body made them the least roomy American-made cars for 1957. The major criticism of the three low-priced Studebakers by *Consumer Reports* was with regard to handling. Steering was found to lack road sense and was numb in and near the straight-ahead position. On curves, corners, and off-the-crown of blacktop roads, the Studebaker V8s required undue effort to keep them on course. To quote *Consumer Reports*: "The result is a car very burdensome to drive, and which requires undue concentration to steer." The magazine's road testers found that in terms of ride quality, Studebaker's resistance to twisting and shake was below average, and the ride on ripples and small bumps was extremely harsh, but the cars rode well over large bumps.

Consumer Reports did like the better-than-average fuel mileage of the Commander V8 with the 259-cubic-inch engine. The President with the 289 engine was found to have more powerful performance, but at the expense of gas mileage The Champion 6 was found to be quiet at idle speeds, but roaring upon acceleration. The use of overdrive gave the Champion very good gas mileage. However, the Champion was subject to the same faults as the other Studebaker low-priced cars with respect to handling. Overall, on those low-priced Studebakers, *Consumer Reports* concluded that the bad points outweighed the good points, with probable trade-in value average to below average.

Among lower-medium-priced cars, the 1957 Studebaker President Classic V8 (120.5-inch wheelbase) was at the bottom of the *Consumer Reports* "acceptable" list in April 1957, behind such makes as Oldsmobile, DeSoto, Dodge, Mercury, Pontiac, Buick, Nash, and Hudson. The things that *Consumer Reports* liked about the President Classic included the powerful and quiet-running 289-cubic-inch V8 engine, its very adequate brakes with anti-fade drums, its luxurious interior appointments, comfortably high front seats, and plenty of rear headroom. However, the criticisms leveled at the low-priced Studebakers continued to be a problem with the President Classic. The structural rigidity of the car and its body shake received pointed criticism. Riding qualities and handling were found to be problematic, which *Consumer Reports* called a disabling factor in a car with some attractive features. Probable trade-in value was expected to be average.

Studebaker-Packard Products for 1958

The 1958 Studebaker-Packard product line was very similar to that for 1957. Significant changes to the cars included a lower roof line, the addition of hardtops to the sedan line of cars, very prominent fins on the rear fenders of the sedans, extension of the Packard models to include the Hawk and hardtop in addition to the four-door sedan and the station wagon, and the somewhat awkward-looking quad headlight pods. The economy Scotsman was the biggest seller for the 1958 model year, which was to be the last year of full-sized sedan production for Studebaker and the end of Packard output.

The 1958 Packard Hawk appears to have been of particular interest to the automotive enthusiast magazines. At least three magazines road-tested the Packard Hawk — *Motor Life*, *Motor Trend*, and *Speed Age*. The headlines of the articles give insights into how the automotive press was viewing the new breed of Packards coming out of South Bend as a result of the consolidation of Studebaker-Packard production there. The June 1958 issue of *Motor Life* had the following headline: "Gone forever are the marks of its greatest era — but Packard retains a name for styling, quality and mighty performance." Similar in concept to the *Motor Life* assessment was that written by *Speed Age*'s Donald Warren, who stated: "Behind its shark mouth, Packard's sportster is a variation on Studebaker's Hawk theme. But it matches performance with luxury reminiscent of Packard's golden days." *Hot Rod Magazine*'s Technical Editor Ray Brock summed up in the May 1958 issue: "A supercharged four-passenger coupe with handling and brakes that top the '58 crop." All three magazines acknowledged that the Packard Hawk was a powerful and distinctive automobile.

The *Motor Life* article on the Packard Hawk stated that the car had a closer kinship to the Studebaker Golden Hawk than to previous Packards. *Motor Life* was impressed with improvements that had been made to the handling characteristics of the Packard Hawk compared to the 1956 Studebaker Golden Hawks. *Motor Life* noted that the 1957 Golden Hawk, with a lighter Studebaker engine, had improved handling compared to the 1956 Golden Hawk with the heavy Packard engine. The 1958 Packard Hawk was found to have even better handling with less body lean and a more secure feel than the 1957 Golden Hawk. The improvements were credited to a lower center of gravity due to revisions to the front and rear suspensions. The Packard Hawk was a half inch lower than earlier Hawks due to a change to a one-piece drive shaft and use of 14-inch wheels instead of 15-inch wheels. A larger diameter stabilizer bar was also used on the Packard Hawk than was used on earlier Hawks, as were four-inch-longer rear springs, which reduced rear-end squat during fast starts and front-end dive when braking. The June 1958 *Motor Life* road test of the Packard Hawk resulted in acceleration times of 0 to 60 miles per hour of 9.2 seconds.

Motor Life described the interior of the Packard Hawk as lush, with top-quality leather used throughout. The instrument panel in the Packard Hawk, and all Studebaker Hawks, was described as the best instrumentation being used in an American-built car. The quality of the car was found to be excellent, with body parts, including the fiberglass hood and front end parts, fitting properly and covered with an excellent paint job.

Donald Warren in the May 1958 issue of *Speed Age* began the article on the road test of the Packard Hawk by calling it a "must-see" for car-shoppers looking for top performance coupled with high comfort. The completely leather-lined interior reminded Warren of Europe's finest cars. The rear seat, divided by a folding armrest, was found to be comfortable for two passengers. However, Warren did not like the strip of matching leather-like plastic along the top outer edge of the doors. The instrument panel, with its Stewart-Warner gauges, came in for praise by Warren.

Automotive enthusiast magazines were fascinated with the 1958 Packard Hawk which, in general, received favorable reviews in spite of the controversial styling.

In the acceleration tests, Warren found the Packard Hawk went from 0 to 60 miles per hour in 9.4 seconds (almost equal to the 9.2 seconds obtained in the *Motor Life* tests). A standing quarter mile was achieved in 17.4 seconds and a top speed of 124 mph was obtained.

The improvements in handling of the Packard Hawk observed by *Motor Life* also were observed in the *Speed Age* road test. That improvement was attributed to the placement of the rear springs outside of the frame side rails and the rear axle's being mounted farther forward on the rear leaf springs. The transverse roll bar on the front was also credited with improving handling. As a result of these improvements, the Hawk, taken around a sharp, flat turn, no longer plowed or leaned crazily as had earlier Hawk models. However, Warren concluded that even though the roadability of the Packard Hawk was of a high order and handling was easy and light, the Hawk could not be considered a sports car. He did note that Studebaker-Packard engineers agreed with this point and stated that the car was one that a driver with a family could handle at speeds above the capabilities of most competitive cars while giving the passengers a comfortable ride.

Ray Brock, in the May 1958 issue of *Hot Rod Magazine*, agreed with the assessment of the Packard Hawk given in the *Motor Life* and *Speed Age* tests of the car. He began his article by stating that Studebaker-Packard should revive the old Packard slogan of

"Ask the man who owns one" because a talk with someone who owned a Packard Hawk might be quite revealing. Brock characterized the Packard Hawk as not a true sports car, but a car with a certain amount of sports-car styling and handling qualities.

Steering control of the Packard Hawk was rated by Brock as not too fast but better than average for American cars. The power brakes on the Hawk were found to be the best of any 1958 car *Hot Rod Magazine* had tested. Acceleration results in the car tested by Brock were 0 to 60 miles per hour in 9.2 seconds and the quarter mile in 17.5 seconds—virtually identical to the results in the *Speed Age* magazine tests. As was true in the other two road tests of the Packard Hawk reported on here, handling was found by Brock to be quite balanced, with the car staying level through corners.

In perhaps a diplomatic but subtle comment on the front-end styling of the Packard Hawk, Brock said he would leave styling opinions up to the potential customer because buying a car was a matter of personal taste. But Brock did say that the Packard Hawk is a fine car. He found the Packard Hawk to be neither the most powerful nor the fastest car available, but it had superb handling and brakes with a smooth ride and he loved the leather interior.

Comprehensive road tests on the regular 1958 Packard line of sedans—the four-door model, the hardtop and the station wagon—were not conducted by the magazines. However, in the January 1958 *Motor Trend*, Joe Wherry did a quick "First Feel Behind the Wheel" of Packard sedans. Wherry complimented Studebaker-Packard chief stylist Duncan McRae for achieving much in the styling of the 1958 Packards with remarkably little in the use of new dies. Wherry called it a facelift, but more than had been expected for the 1958 Packards. He found that the most attractive of the sedans was the two-door hardtop.

In driving the Packard hardtop, which was a hand-built prototype, Wherry complained that it was a bit stiff, but was capable of 0 to 60 miles per hour in 11.9 seconds. Given that the 1958 Packard sedans no longer had the supercharger (as did the 1957 sedans), this performance was considered quite good. Wherry stated that the cornering ability of the 1958 Packard hardtop was much improved over past years, the seating was comfortable, and rear legroom was competitive with the industry and even better than some of the higher-priced prestige cars. Wherry did observe that the 1958 Packards did not convey the prestige of earlier Packards, but he quoted S-P officials who reportedly stated that the cars were not of the prestige class, but offered distinction and quality craftsmanship.

Consumer Reports magazine, in its June 1958 issue which covered station wagons, carried an assessment of the 1958 Packard station wagon. The assessment was hardly flattering. *Consumer Reports* observed that the Packard body was the same as the Studebaker Provincial station wagon, which had gone unaltered since being introduced in 1953. However, *Consumer Reports* did say that the body was solidly built and had the best height inside and at the rear opening of the station wagons tested. The ride was found to be harsh and the handling and steering were found to be indifferent.

The three road tests of the Packard Hawk reported here and the brief road test of the Packard sedans in *Motor Trend* were basically favorable and conveyed that the persons testing the cars were impressed with them. It is interesting to note that the Packard Hawk road tests all appeared late in the model year (May and June of 1958) and probably far too late to have had any major impact on the sales of the cars. In fact, the articles appeared after the decision had been made by Studebaker-Packard to discontinue the Packard line after the 1958 model year. Only 588 units of the Packard Hawk, for example, were sold. One can only speculate whether the favorable road tests, had they appeared earlier in the year, would have led to more Packards being ordered and built in 1958.

The Packards, of course, were at the top of the line for Studebaker-Packard in 1958. What about the other vehicles the company built that year? What did the automotive media have to say about the Studebaker Champion, Commander, and Scotsman? Several of the automotive magazines did test those models.

The November 1957 issue of *Motor Trend* magazine carried an article by Joe H. Wherry that gave a comprehensive overview of the 1958 Studebaker and Packard line. The article noted that most of the S-P line had been lowered by two inches in the sedan due to new floor pan and roof sheet metal stampings, the use of a one-piece drive shaft which enabled a lowering of the transmission tunnel, and use of 14-inch wheels on all models except the Scotsman. Wherry found it significant that the lowering was accomplished without any sacrifice in interior space, even in headroom.

Wherry stated that in the years immediately preceding 1958, Studebakers had not quite met the competition in roadability and preciseness of handling. He found significant improvements in the handling of the 1958 Silver Hawk, Champion, and Commander models that he drove. A new anti-sway bar and asymmetrical placement of the rear axle on the semi-elliptic leaf springs reduced rear-end squat on fast starts and nose diving on stops.

For its July 1958 issue, *Motor Life* magazine did a complete road test of a 1958 Studebaker Commander four-door sedan V8. The car was characterized as displaying quiet but strong capabilities. The Commander sedan was built on the 116.5-inch wheelbase, had a 259-cubic-inch V8 engine and the S-P Flightomatic automatic transmission. The *Motor Life* test drivers made an interesting observation about the Commander and the Studebaker-Packard cars in general in the opening paragraph of their article. Following is an excerpt from that first paragraph:

> The first impression from behind the wheel of Studebaker's middle-priced Commander is the thought that here is a product of a design philosophy quite different from the one practiced in the Motor City [Detroit]. Granted, the car is loaded with concessions to the fin, dual headlamps and the like, but the Commander's basic austerity is in direct contrast to the chromed and gimmicked entries of the bigger manufacturers. It's a contrast from which S-P's ideas do not always suffer.

Motor Life's writers went on to say that they marveled at the ingenuity of Studebaker engineers in keeping their product up to date. After discussing the lowered profile of the car, the article turned to an analysis of the Commander's performance. Acceleration was quite good for the 259-cubic-inch V8 with 0 to 60 miles per hour being accomplished in 13.5 seconds. An interesting observation in the article was that on the road, the test car demonstrated remarkable steering ability (an area of considerable criticism on the 1957 models). The car did not have power steering, but the lack of it was hardly noticed by the *Motor Life* test drivers.

The interior of the Commander was found to be austere by the *Motor Life* test drivers. Instruments and controls were described as simple and the upholstery was unornamented. While the styling was described as acceptable, with the new fins blending in well with the fenders, criticism was leveled at the podded dual headlights, which *Motor Life* said were rather awkward attachments that looked like they were made from a do-it-yourself kit. Overall, *Motor Life* seemed to be cautiously complimentary to the 1958 Commander. They did not lavish a large amount of praise on the car but said that, although it did not have all the polish of the Big Three products, it was basically a sound and conservative car which based its sales appeal on a search for quality and craftsmanship.

The June 1958 issue of *Car Life* magazine featured another road test of a 1958 Studebaker Commander sedan. Among *Car Life*'s observations were the narrowness of the Studebaker body compared to the competition. The Commander, with a seat width of 56 inches, was about three inches narrower than the Chevrolet Biscayne, Plymouth Savoy, Ford Custom 300, and Rambler Rebel. The Commander also was found to be a couple of hundred pounds lighter than its competition, which gave its smaller 259-cubic-inch V8 engine nearly as good performance as the competitors, including the 283-cubic-inch Chevrolet V8, 318-cubic-inch Plymouth V8, and Ford's 292-cubic-inch V8. The Commander was found to compare favorably with the Rambler Rebel with a 250-cubic-inch V8. *Car Life* viewed the Studebaker as a compromise for those who wanted sufficient performance but also wanted good gasoline mileage.

Car Life's view of the Studebaker styling was similar to that of *Motor Life*. *Car Life* said the fins on the Commander looked like an integral part of the car's design, but the dual headlight pods were described as inharmonious with the styling of the car.

The *Car Life* assessment of the 1958 Commander's handling and riding comfort was the same as that of *Motor Life*. That is, the ride and handling of the car were improved considerably over earlier years due to the new anti-sway bar and new rear spring configuration. Steering, though, was found to be problematic, requiring more turning of the wheel to get a given change of direction of the car. *Car Life* did not report on acceleration statistics of the Commander.

In the July 1958 issue of *Car Life*, the Studebaker Commander was compared with other cars that the magazine had road tested in 1958. *Car Life* used a five-check rating system so that a 5.0 rating would be highest. The Studebaker was given a 3.9 check rating compared to 4.3 for the Rambler, 4.3 for the Plymouth, 4.1 for Ford and 4.5 for Chevrolet. The only area where the Studebaker Commander rated five checks was in fuel economy, which was the best among all U.S.-built V8s. Lowest ratings of three checks were given to roadability and value per dollar. Styling, interior design, and riding comfort were given four checks.

Studebaker's economy car, the 1958 Scotsman, was tested and compared with the 1958 Rambler American by *Popular Mechanics* magazine for its August 1958 issue. Art Railton, the *Popular Mechanics* auto editor, opened his description of the Scotsman by saying: "It's a plain Jane—a dull, unexciting machine. It has no glamour and knows it.... It's a car that will work hard at little expense while asking no preferential treatment. You'll get no frills on it, but no thrills with it." The contrast between Railton's comments on the Scotsman and his opening comments on the Rambler American are striking. Of the Rambler American he said: "Although without frills, it is stylish and has no air of self denial. Priced under $2000, it doesn't look as though every penny has been pinched out of it. It may be a workhorse, but it retains the chic look so necessary to attract buyers." It is probably an understatement to say that Railton obviously did not see the Scotsman as the style and fashion leader of the 1958 automobile industry!

Popular Mechanics, in preparing the August 1958 article, asked hundreds of Scotsman owners why they bought the car. Almost half (49 percent) said they bought it for economy of operation and another 27 percent said they bought it for the initial low price. Consistent with these data was another statistic — that 54.9 percent of the owners said the economy of operation and upkeep was what they liked the most about the car. Even though a significant majority of Scotsman owners liked its economy of operation, the largest single complaint, by 16.9 percent of the owners surveyed by *Popular Mechanics*, was that the gas mileage was not good enough.

By comparison, the feature that *Popular Mechanics* found 58 percent of Rambler American owners liked the most was handling ease. Economy of operation was mentioned by 42 percent of Rambler American owners as a positive feature of the car. The most complained-about factor on the Rambler was water leaks, mentioned by 13.7 percent of the owners, and 10.7 percent of them said the car did not give good enough gas mileage.

On the gas mileage issue, *Popular Mechanics* found the Scotsman obtained 13.4 miles per gallon (mpg) in an urban traffic route, 24.3 mpg at a steady 50 miles per hour, and 28.7 mpg at a steady 30 miles per hour. Comparative results for the Rambler American showed it to be considerably more fuel efficient than the Scotsman with 18.2 mpg in traffic, 27 mpg at a steady 50 miles per hour, and 34 mpg at a steady 30 miles per hour. Neither car had blinding acceleration, with the Scotsman taking 24 seconds to go 0 to 60 mph and the Rambler taking 19 seconds.

For its June 1958 issue, *Consumer Reports* presented a report on the auto industry's 1958 station wagons. Among low-priced 6-cylinder station wagons, the Studebaker Scotsman rated last, below the Ford Ranch Wagon, Chevrolet Yeoman, Plymouth Suburban, and Rambler Cross Country. The Scotsman interior was described as neither attractive nor durable. The 185-cubic-inch 6-cylinder engine was found to have adequate power but had a high noise level. Riding qualities were rated satisfactory, but a typical complaint of *Consumer Reports* about Studebaker-Packard products was that the steering was imprecise. However, at the basic transportation-per-dollar level, the Scotsman was judged to be a good buy for the really budget-minded consumer.

Among low-priced 8-cylinder station wagons, the 1958 Studebaker Commander V8 Provincial was rated last in acceptability, below the Chevrolet V8 Yeoman, Ford V8 Ranch Wagon, Plymouth V8 Suburban, and Rambler V8 Super Cross Country. The Studebaker Commander wagon was found to suffer from the disadvantage of being nose-heavy, a peculiar ride that was better on bad roads than on smooth ones, and imprecise steering and poor handling. Positive features of the Studebaker were said by *Consumers Reports* to be good brakes, good height dimensions, and compact outer dimensions. Trade-in value was rated as below average.

Perhaps the most fascinating article written about the 1958 Studebakers was done by Bob Fendell in the March 1958 issue of *Car Life* magazine. Fendell titled his article "The Perfect Family Car." He prefaced his article with the statement that he wished

The 1958 Studebaker Provincial Station Wagon had the unhappy distinction of being rated by *Consumer Reports* as last in acceptability among American-made station wagons.

someone would design a car built for family use that was economical, comfortable, rugged, and roomy. He then went on to say that such a car was being built by Studebaker-Packard Corporation in the form of the Econ-O-miler taxicab — but it was not for sale to the general public because it was strictly for the taxi trade. The Econ-O-miler had the front and rear sheet metal of the Scotsman, but was built on the 120.5-inch wheelbase — the same wheelbase as the President and the Packard four-door sedans.

Fendell described the Econ-O-miler as being built to take 24-hour-a-day use while providing comfort for the driver or any backseat customer. It had special heavy-duty seat springs with foam rubber padding. The springs were heavy duty, but the variable ratio front springing that S-P used on its 1958 cars gave the Econ-O-miler a good ride. The extra-large doors on the extended wheelbase made getting in and out fairly easy. Legroom at 43 inches in both the front and rear was compared favorably to any production car shorter than a limousine. The washable all-vinyl upholstery and headliner were seen as a real plus for families with children. The 185-cubic-inch six-cylinder engine with 101 horsepower was viewed by Fendell as providing adequate power with good fuel economy.

Fendell gave the car a road test unique to the automotive media. He loaded the car with his three children, ages 2, 7, and 10, his wife, and his mother-in-law as test gauges. Ice cream cones were provided to all the passengers. The test route included New York City driving and some poor New Jersey country roads. Fendell reported that the Econ-O-miler checked out quite well. His wife liked the fact that ice cream cone drippings on the seat were easily wiped up with a handkerchief and also liked the fact that a rear door warning light came on when the 10-year-old experimentally opened the door as the car began to move. The ultimate compliment came from Fendell's mother-in-law, who said the car rode as solid as a Pierce-Arrow!

Although not available to the general public, the 1958 Studebaker Econ-O-miler taxicab on the 120.5-inch wheelbase and carrying basic Scotsman trim was called the ideal family car by one automotive writer.

Fendell found the car handled well in traffic, was easy to park, got to 50 miles per hour in about 12 seconds and stopped very positively, even after four panic stops were made attempting to get the brakes to fade. He found the car took sharp curves faster and better than the Studebaker President.

Overall, Fendell found the Econ-O-miler to be an ideal family car that his family liked. He speculated that Studebaker-Packard was not realizing the potential such a car could have in the market because of its ability to take the punishment of sustained family use. He believed that ultimately what he saw as the perfect family car would have to reach the market.

Whether a Studebaker 120.5-inch wheelbase sedan based on the rugged engineering but somewhat austere design of the Econ-O-miler would have been a market success is something about which we can only speculate. It is worth noting, however, that after continuing the Econ-O-miler for the 1959 and 1960 model years on the extended 113-inch Lark wheelbase, Studebaker reintroduced the extended-length family car, albeit a luxury upscale version, in the form of the 1961 Studebaker Lark Cruiser on the 113-inch wheelbase. Beginning with 1962, all Studebaker four-door sedans were built on that wheelbase.

Studebaker-Packard Products for 1959

The Studebaker-Packard Corporation model lineup for 1959 was greatly simplified when compared to the 1957 and 1958 offerings. The Packard line was gone. There was only one Hawk model — the Silver Hawk available with either a 169-cubic-inch 6-cylinder engine or a 259-cubic-inch V8. The Lark line was basically simple, with the same engine choices as for the Hawk available on the four-door, two-door, hardtop, and station wagon. The 1959 Lark was the result of the vision of Harold Churchill as he saw the fairly good market response to the Scotsman, the increasing popularity of the American Motors Ramblers, and the rising sales of smaller imported cars. The Lark was also a major risk for Studebaker-Packard as it struggled for survival. As they rolled off the assembly line and reached the automobile buying public, what were the 1959 Larks and Silver Hawks like? Because the Lark, although not an "all-new car," was a new and dramatically different product for Studebaker-Packard, many automotive magazines were eager to road test it.

First, though, the 1959 Silver Hawk is analyzed. With the Golden Hawk and its supercharger now absent from the Studebaker Hawk line, only the Silver Hawk pillared sport coupe was available. Clearly, Churchill's intention was to narrow the Studebaker product line and to emphasize economy cars over performance cars such as the Golden Hawk. *Motor Life* magazine tested the Silver Hawk for its December 1958 issue and made special note of the change in the engines available. *Motor Life* put a positive spin on the smaller engines now offered on the Hawk; it was pointed out that with the 289-cubic-inch V8 being dropped from the product line and the 259-cubic-inch V8 being the only V8 available, the Hawk's horsepower declined from 210 to 180, but now both the V8 and the six ran on regular gasoline, which the magazine considered a major selling point. The 6-cylinder model was the 169-cubic-inch engine used on the Lark, and represented an engine downsizing from the 185-cubic-inch engine used in earlier 6-cylinder Hawks.

Silver Hawks for 1959 received moderately favorable reaction in enthusiast magazine road tests, even though they were only available with the 169-cubic-inch 6-cylinder engine or 259-cubic-inch V8 (AACA Library and Research Center).

Brakes, transmission, and drive line were found to be similar to the 1958 Silver Hawk. However, the ride was judged by *Motor Life* to be improved considerably over 1958 as a result of redesigned variable-rate front springs which offered a softer ride. Cornering and travel over severe bumps was improved due to extra coils added to the front springs. Sway bars and finned brake drums were features found on the V8 but not on the 6-cylinder Hawks.

The real interest of *Motor Life* and the other automotive magazines was to test the Lark. The road tests reported in the December 1958 *Motor Life* included both a 6-cylinder Lark two-door sedan with standard transmission and a V8 Lark hardtop with the Flightomatic automatic transmission. *Motor Life* liked the spaciousness of the Lark, which it found exceptionally roomy for a compact car. The Larks were found to give a smooth ride up to 65 miles per hour but tended to pitch and wallow at higher speeds over rough pavement.

The V8 Lark Regal Hardtop that *Motor Life* tested had what the magazine's testers considered a nicer and more luxurious interior than the basic 6-cylinder two-door sedan, although they did say both cars looked sharp and "well-dressed" and not like the austere 1957 and 1958 Scotsman. Acceleration of the V8 hardtop was 0 to 60 miles per hour in 10.3 seconds, However, *Motor Life* found that cornering of the Lark was not very good because it was a softly sprung over-the-road car with no pretense of being engineered and designed for racing or high-speed cornering. In cornering, the body leaned, the tires screeched, and the rear end tended to break loose. At a steady 40 miles per hour, the Lark V8 gave 22 miles per gallon, and at 60 mph it gave 17.5 mpg. *Motor Life* did not perform a gas mileage test on the 6-cylinder model but estimated it would give in the range of 21 to 24 mpg.

Al Berger, in a December 1958 article for *Speed Age* magazine, called the 1959 Studebaker Lark the "Biggest 'Little' Car in the World." He noted that although the Lark was shorter than the Rambler American, the Lark was the only small car on either side of the ocean to offer genuine comfortable seating for six adults while offering an excellent ride, good handling, and performance superior to other cars its size and in its price range. Although it was only 175 inches long, Berger said that in seating, luggage space, speed, pickup, and riding comfort, the Lark was a big car.

The 6-cylinder sedan tested by *Speed Age* accelerated from 0 to 60 miles per hour in 18.9 seconds, while the Lark hardtop equipped with the 259-cubic-inch V8 with overdrive transmission went from 0 to 60 mph in 10.5 seconds and reached a top speed of 105 mph. Berger's conclusion on the Lark was that it was neat and had clean lines. He said that South Bend's designers and engineers had turned into automotive magicians in bringing out the compact but roomy Lark.

Ray Brock tested the 1959 Lark Hardtop with the 259-cubic-inch V8 that had the power pack four-barrel carburetor, which increased horsepower to 195 (compared to 180 horsepower on the standard 259 V8 with the two-barrel carburetor), and was equipped with the Flightomatic automatic transmission, for the January 1959 issue of *Hot Rod Magazine*. Brock found the brakes and standard steering so effective on the V8 Lark that he recommended against spending the money on power brakes or steering.

A common observation of people testing the Lark was about its roominess. Brock's comments were no exception. He was impressed with the headroom and comfortable steering wheel position. In driving the V8 Lark, Brock found that the faster he drove it the steadier it seemed to get on the highway. It did not wallow or roll on the roller-coaster desert roads when driven there, and in the city the ride was termed excellent. However, as had been the case with a number of the Studebaker products reported on in this chapter, Brock found fault with the Lark's handling on sharp, twisting curves. Acceleration results achieved by *Hot Rod Magazine* were similar to those found by *Speed Age*, with 0 to 60 mph taking 10.7 seconds. Brock's conclusion was that the Lark was a good compact car.

Introduction of the Lark compact car by Studebaker gave rise to a natural comparison of the car with the compact Rambler American being built by American Motors Corporation. *Motor Trend* and *Car Life* compared the two cars directly in their test reports. Basic specifications for the Lark and Rambler American are given in Table 3.

Table 3
1959 Studebaker Lark vs. 1959 Rambler American
Basic Specifications

	Lark Flathead 6-cylinder	Lark OHV-V8 Flathead 6-cyl.	Rambler American
Cubic Inch Displacement	169	259	195
Brake Horsepower	90	180	90
Wheelbase	108.5 inches	108.5 inches	100 inches
Length	175 inches	175 inches	178.3 inches

Jim Whipple compared the Lark and Rambler American in the December 1958 issue of *Car Life* magazine. Overall, the Lark came out the winner. In the *Car Life* scale of five checks being best, the Lark had an overall rating of 4.2 checks, while the American rated 3.9 checks. Whipple found the Lark's strongest points were its performance, particularly the V8 model, which went 0 to 60 in 10.5 seconds. The six-cylinder Lark was found by Whipple to have adequate performance, particularly when equipped with overdrive. The economy of the Lark also rated five checks, with good fuel economy in the 6-cylinder cars and the V8 rated as giving the best combination of performance and fuel economy on the American road. Weakest point for the Lark, according to Whipple, was its roadability and handling, which he rated as about average for American cars.

Whipple gave the AMC Rambler American five checks for excellent economy and performance. However, the areas where the American was rated low included riding comfort because of a choppy ride, interior design because it was too narrow, and roadability because it tended to bounce on rough roads. So, at least according to *Car Life* and Jim Whipple, the Studebaker Lark was rated the best buy in a U.S. economy car for the 1959 model year.

Although *Car Life* magazine declared the Lark a best buy over the Rambler American, when Charles Nerpel and Bill Callahan tested the two cars for *Motor Trend* magazine for its December 1958 issue, they did not attempt to rate one of the cars as better than the other. They simply compared the cars side-by-side and let the readers make up their own minds.

Studebaker's fortunes in terms of media perception began to improve with the introduction of the 1959 Lark. However, automotive writers continued to be critical of the handling and steering and noise levels of the cars. Pictured here is the bottom-of-the-line 1959 basic Lark 2-door sedan (AACA Library and Research Center).

Nerpel and Callahan achieved fuel economy of 18 miles per gallon at a steady 50 miles per hour in the 6-cylinder Lark, but shifting into overdrive raised the gas mileage at that speed to 20 mpg in the *Motor Trend* test car. The 1959 Lark V8 gave more impressive fuel mileage results than the 6-cylinder in the *Motor Trend* tests. The 259-cubic-inch V8 gave consistent gas mileage of between 19.5 mpg and 22 mpg. The Rambler American did better than the Lark 6 at a steady 50 miles per hour, getting 21.4 miles per gallon with the 3-speed standard transmission and 24 mpg with overdrive.

Zero to 60 miles per hour was achieved in 10 seconds with the Lark V8 equipped with standard transmission, whereas the Lark with automatic transmission did 0 to 60 mph in 12 seconds and the 6-cylinder took 18 seconds. The Rambler American took 19.3 seconds to reach 60 miles per hour. The *Motor Trend* test drivers found the American and Lark steering very easy, light and responsive. Likewise, the brakes on both cars were found to be more than adequate.

The automotive enthusiast magazines that tested the Lark, therefore, were quite impressed with the car and were complimentary to Studebaker for what had been achieved with the compact Studebaker. *Consumer Reports*, however, was not nearly as impressed with the car. For its February 1959 issue, *Consumer Reports* tested a four-door 6-cylinder Lark Deluxe (the standard model — Regal was the name for the Lark with a higher trim level) with automatic transmission.

Consumer Reports did like the roomy interior dimensions of the Lark and stated that it compared favorably with the Rambler 6 (a larger car than the Rambler American) and was much more roomy than the Rambler American. The Lark's interior was described as having, for a compact car, a surprising number of generous and thoroughly usable dimensions. Once seated inside the Lark, though, something that *Consumer Reports* did not like was how noisy the car was. The engine noise level was high due to the use of an air cleaner without a silencer. It was noted that the upscale Lark Regal models did have silencers, but *Consumer Reports* consultants reported that the noise level still was bothersome. The test car was found to be far noisier than either the Rambler 6 or the Rambler American.

The straight-line riding qualities of the Lark were said by *Consumer Reports* to be unqualifiedly good and even remarkable for a car as lightweight and with as short a wheelbase as the Lark. Steering on the Lark was said to be sufficiently quick but not very sensitive with a less-than-desirable feel of the road for small directional changes and on hard turns. Steering responsiveness on both the Rambler American and the larger Rambler 6 was described as better than on the Lark. The Lark tended to lean excessively on corners, even at normal speeds. On winding or crowned roads, that tendency to lean was said to be tiring for the passengers.

Fuel mileage attained on the Lark by *Consumer Reports* was disappointing. *Consumer Reports* compared the Lark with Chevrolet, Ford, and Plymouth V8s. The Chevrolet BelAir V8 achieved 16.4 miles per gallon at a steady 60 miles per hour; the Ford Fairlane V8 got 15.3 mpg (worst of the group); the Plymouth Belvedere V8 got 16.7 mpg; and the 6-cylinder Lark got 16 mpg. In day-to-day city traffic driving, the Lark did do better by averaging 13.4 mpg compared to the Chevrolet V8's 12.0 mpg, the Ford V8's 14.0 mpg, and the Plymouth V8's 13.0 mpg. Yet it must be kept in mind that here the compact Lark 6 was being compared to full-sized V8s, and in the opinion of *Consumer Reports* did not give comparatively impressive fuel mileage.

Consumer Reports summed up its test of the Lark by observing that it had three distinct failings — noise, poor fuel mileage, and disappointing handling. In conclusion, *Consumer Reports* made the following less than ringing endorsement or complimentary conclusion about the Lark: "If such shortcomings don't bother you — and CU [Consumers Union, which publishes the magazine] feels that you *should* be bothered by them, for the sake of your own driving pleasure and comfort, and of your pocketbook — then you can concentrate on totting up the Lark's many good points: its seating and excellent forward vision; its easy access, easy-to-housekeep interior (no step-down); its good heater; its time tested engine and powerful brakes; its very good ride; and its simplicity and compact size."

Thus far, the test reports on the 1959 Lark summarized here have been from the automotive media. As such, they represent third-party analysis of the car. The question arises, then, what was Studebaker finding out about the Lark on its own? In a rare document found among the Harold E. Churchill Papers at the Studebaker National Museum Archives, a report was found on a study done by the D'Arcy Advertising Agency (the agency Studebaker hired to do the advertising for the Lark) on Lark owners. While there is no date on the study, the opening statement in the report suggests it was early in the 1959 model year. That statement reads: "At its present stage of Lark's marketing development, the principal opportunities for research to contribute to market planning exist in the study of Lark owners and people who have been physically exposed to the Lark."[2] D'Arcy conducted the study in five metropolitan areas: New York, Chicago, Los Angeles, Atlanta, and Houston. The interviews of 496 Lark owners were conducted by telephone. Following are the results of the responses to three questions that D'Arcy considered important regarding the decision of people to buy a car:

1. How did you happen to be in the market for a new car at this time?
2. What was it that first got you interested in looking at the Lark?
3. How did you decide to buy the Lark rather than any of the other American-made cars you might have bought?

From the answers to these questions, D'Arcy distilled five major reasons for purchase of the Lark which, the ad agency said, should guide the marketing focus of Studebaker in the future:

1. Size was mentioned by 75 percent of respondents.
2. Economy was mentioned by 61 percent of respondents.
3. Appearance was mentioned by 31 percent of respondents.
4. Advertising was mentioned by 27 percent of respondents.
5. Studebaker's reputation was mentioned by 27 percent of respondents.

Among the other key things that D'Arcy discovered are the following[3]:

1. The size of the Lark as a factor in purchasing the car did not vary significantly by family size and was the dominant reason for purchase among small, medium, and large families. However, economy of operation had more appeal to larger families than to smaller ones. The Studebaker reputation was substantially more important to one- and two-member households than to larger families. D'Arcy hypothesized that smaller families have fewer real needs to influence their decisions and can, therefore, give more considerations to quality. The appearance and styling of the Lark appealed with equal strength to all family size groups. Advertising as a reason for purchase was stronger among larger families.
2. The size of the Lark was found to have its greatest appeal to low-volume drivers. Low-volume driving was assumed to involve a high percentage of in-traffic driving where the Lark's maneuverability and parking ease would have more appeal than to drivers whose major driving was long-distance trips on the open highway. Economy of operation as a reason for purchase, though, was substantially higher among high-volume drivers. The Studebaker reputation had equal strength among all driving volume groups. The appearance of the Lark was strongest in appeal to middle-volume drivers who drove 8,000 to 12,000 miles per year. Response to Lark advertising appeared to be somewhat stronger among low-volume and high-volume drivers than those in the middle range. D'Arcy said this

finding was not surprising because the advertising appeals to date had been made in terms of size and economy, which were documented as having the strongest influence on light and heavy drivers.

3. Among people who had owned a Studebaker in the past, the company's reputation ranked very high as a reason for purchase — equal to economy of operation and second only to the size of the car. Studebaker's reputation had a negligible impact on those who had not previously owned a Studebaker.

4. The size of the Lark was found to appeal to business and pleasure drivers about equally. Economy had slightly more appeal to drivers using the car for business. The Studebaker reputation had its greatest influence on those who use the car for business. Lark styling, though, had its greatest appeal to pleasure drivers. The response to advertising was about equal for business and pleasure users.

5. The size of the Lark was stronger in its appeal to older people than to younger age groups, but economy of operation was more important to the younger age groups. The Studebaker reputation was important among older Lark owners. Lark styling had substantially greater appeal among younger age groups. Advertising appealed to all age groups equally.

6. The size of the Lark was slightly more important as the reason for purchasing the Lark among higher-income families than among lower-income families. D'Arcy suggested that this finding may have been due to higher-income groups having more second-car families. Economy of operation had its strongest appeal to lower-income groups. The Studebaker reputation was equally strong among all groups. The Lark styling was strongest in its appeal to the upper-income groups. Advertising had approximately equal impact on all income groups.

In its conclusion to the report on the survey of Lark owners, D'Arcy said that a surprisingly high number of Lark purchasers shopped only for a Lark. Among those who previously had not owned a Studebaker, 28.6 percent shopped only for a Lark. Among former owners of late-model Studebakers (1954 or later), 49.4 percent shopped only for a Lark.[4]

The D'Arcy study sheds light on the overall appeal of the Lark in 1959. Because of the circumstances in which Studebaker found itself at the end of the 1958 model year, the introduction of the Lark was an extremely important step for the company to take. It was very much a "make-it or break-it" situation. While the details in the D'Arcy study are interesting, it does appear that the Lark generally had a strong level of appeal to the full spectrum of ownership groups — often for varying reasons among the groups, but widespread, nevertheless. Also, the results of the study suggest that, in spite of the problems Studebaker was having financially, the Studebaker name still had positive market value.

Studebaker-Packard Products for 1960

The 1960 model year was one in which only the most minor appearance changes were made for the Lark and the Hawk. The big news for those two Studebaker models was the addition of a four-door station wagon and convertible to the Lark line and the return of the 289-cubic-inch V8 as an option on the Hawk (which now was simply called "Hawk" and no longer was referred to as the Silver Hawk). Another new product for 1960 from South Bend was the introduction of the Champ truck.

When assessing the 1960 Studebaker Lark, the big issue with the 1960s models was how they compared with not only the Ramblers, but also with the new compact cars introduced by the Detroit Big Three, including the Ford Falcon, the Chevrolet Corvair, and the Plymouth Valiant. While it is not the purpose here to engage in extended descriptions of the Big Three compact cars, some basic, but summary, comparative data from the tests of these cars by the automotive media will be presented to contrast them with the Lark.

Table 4
1960 Compact Cars Basic Specifications

Make and Model	Engine Size Cubic Inches	Horsepower	Wheelbase*	Length*
Chevrolet Corvair 6	140	80	108	180
Ford Falcon 6	144	90	109.5	181
Plymouth Valiant 6	170	101	106.5	184
Rambler American Super 6	196	90	100	178.5
Rambler American Custom 6	196	125	100	178.5
Rambler 6	196	127	108	189.5
Rambler Rebel V8	250	200	108	189.5
Studebaker Lark 6	169	90	108.5	175
Studebaker Lark V8	259	180	108.5	175

*Wheelbase and Length dimensions in inches
Source: *Consumer Reports*, April 1960

The mechanical specifications and the dimensions of the Studebaker Lark for 1960 were the same as in 1959. The Lark specifications are shown in Table 4 in comparison to the other compact cars available in 1960. In commenting on the styling of these compact cars, Bill Callahan, in an article in the December 1959 issue of *Motor Trend* magazine, noted that the Lark, Rambler American, and Rambler were changed only modestly from the 1959s. The Plymouth Valiant he described as having a distinctly European flair, the Ford Falcon as having styling that was completely different from previous Fords, and the Chevrolet Corvair as representing a completely new concept with its rear-mounted engine.

On interior space, Callahan said the Lark, Falcon, Rambler 6, and Valiant offered the greatest comfort on long trips, but the Corvair had the advantage of a totally flat floor because the rear-engine design eliminated the transmission hump. In getting specific on the 1960 Lark, *Motor Trend* said its interior was functional in appearance, appointment, and design, and was a genuine five-seater automobile and even a six-seater if the middle passenger in the front seat straddled the hump. The Lark upholstery was described as rugged but not fancy. Its body design, Callahan said, looked muscular and with the V8 was the performance champ of the compact car group. The six-cylinder Lark, he said, required little maintenance, and repairs were inexpensive and infrequent.

In its February 1960 issue, *Motor Life* magazine did a more comprehensive comparison of the several compact cars than was true of the *Motor Trend* article. The actual road test of the Lark was less than complimentary to the car. In observing that the 6-cylinder Lark was powered by the old Champion L-head engine, *Motor Life* said that its economy rating was average but was below par for performance and a more modern engine was overdue for the Lark.

Motor Life was particularly, and surprisingly, critical of the interior of the 1960 Lark. Whereas most test reports of the Larks were impressed with the roominess of the interior, *Motor Life* was extremely critical in stating that redesigning the front seat to give more legroom in the back did not make getting in and out of the Lark back seat any easier, and that it was awkward because the back door, a holdover from earlier Studebakers, was not wide enough. The padded dash was described as useless as a safety feature because it was only about a quarter-inch thick. However, some good words were used in describing the Lark as having an intelligent relation of exterior dimensions to interior space, which promotes passenger comfort even on long trips.

Motor Life found the 1960 Lark handled well at slow speeds and had excellent parking maneuverability, but steering effort was too stiff at slow speeds. The steering effort became easier at highway speeds. Cornering was reasonably good, but tight turns induced tire squeal and leaning. The ride of the Lark was said to be equal to that of many American large cars.

One of the problems found on the 1959 Larks by *Consumer Reports* was the noisy engine. *Motor Life* said that problem was virtually eliminated in 1960 through improved engine mounts and use of a new air cleaner on the engine. One surprise in the Lark road test by *Motor Life* was the improvement in the gas mileage for the Lark 6, with average mileage jumping from 16.1 miles per gallon in 1959 to 21.1 mpg on the 1960 Lark. The improvement in gas mileage was attributed to a new carburetor and modified cylinder-head combustion design. *Motor Life* observed that the old design of the Lark's Champion engine achieved fuel consumption only average for the compact class.

The *Motor Life* acceleration tests of the several compact cars gave the following results for the 0 to 60 miles per hour test: the 1960 Lark 6 was the slowest of the compacts with a time of 20 seconds; the Corvair did it in 18.2 seconds; the Falcon took 17.2 seconds; the Valiant took 16.7 seconds; the Rambler 6 did it in 16 seconds, as did the Rambler American. Handling of the Corvair was viewed as good with little of the oversteer characteristic of rear-engined cars; the Falcon had exceptional cornering ability; roadability of the Valiant was good, but the driving feel was described as heavy for a compact car; a soft suspension caused the Rambler American to suffer in cornering; the bigger Rambler 6 was found to have handling as a major weak point; the Lark was said to be nose-heavy, especially with the V8 engine, giving it a sluggish driving feel. The 1960 Lark riding qualities were described by *Motor Life* as being on the firm side compared to the Falcon and Valiant, which were labeled the most comfortable of the compacts.

Jim Whipple, writing in the February 1960 issue of *Car Life* magazine, did a brief comparison of the Rambler American, the Rambler 6, and the Lark (the three compact cars he called the "old pros") with the new compacts of the Big Three. He noted that the Rambler Rebel V8 and the Lark V8 would leave the other compacts trailing behind, but acknowledged that comparing the V8s with the sixes of the other compacts was not really fair. From a passenger compartment comfort standpoint, he said Rambler and Lark had a bit more to offer than Corvair, Falcon, and Valiant, especially in seating width and higher seating arrangements.

Whipple, in the February 1960 *Car Life* road test of the 1960 Lark, remarked that with a convertible and four-door station wagon, the Studebaker Lark was the first of the compacts to offer a full lineup of models. In Whipple's opinion, the Lark 6 and Lark V8, while sharing the same bodies, were quite different cars. The V8s were real "go" cars, to use his words, that were good at high-speed passing, were hot hill climbers, and right out front at traffic lights. The V8 gave excellent performance with any of the three transmission options: manual three-speed, overdrive, and the Flightomatic automatic.

Whipple said the Lark he really liked the most was what he referred to as the "spunky" little six. He put 500 miles on it for the road test and enjoyed every minute of it. The car he tested was equipped with the overdrive transmission. Consistent with the findings of the *Motor Life* test of the 1960 Lark 6, Whipple liked the quiet operation of the car due to the new air cleaner, which eliminated the hiss of the 1959 models. The Lark's handling took some getting used to because in straight-ahead driving and in taking gentle curves the front wheels could be turned a given amount with very little effort on the steering wheel. When cutting the wheels hard left or right, though, as in a sharp right-angle turn, more effort was required to cause the same degree of turn in the front wheels. In conclusion, Whipple said the 1960 Lark 6 was not a sports car, but possessed outstanding qualities. It was well-built, attractive with lots of passenger comfort, practical, easy to drive and should be considered by anyone desiring to purchase a compact car.

A significant observation in reading the test reports on the 1960 Lark is, in general, how consistent the reports are in observing the same basic strengths and weaknesses of the car. For example, many of the comments in the April 1960 issue of *Consumer Reports* are similar to those reported in other magazines summarized here. *Consumer Reports* liked the interior dimensions of the Lark and noted they were better than the Big Three compacts. *Consumer Reports* found the ride of the Lark to be good, with none of the other compacts on the market riding better and most riding worse, and, consistent with other test reports, said the steering was good in terms of effort but was vague and lacked road sense. The Lark 6 was rated about midway between the Big Three compacts and the Rambler 6. The Lark V8 was rated by *Consumer Reports* as giving very credible gas mileage for an 8-cylinder car. An area of criticism about the Lark's body integrity was that it was more subject to squeaks and rattles than in the Big Three and American Motors compacts, all of which had unibody construction, as opposed to the Lark's body-on-frame construction.

In rankings, the Rambler 6, Valiant, Ford Falcon, Rambler American, and Rambler Rebel V8 were ranked as better buys by *Consumer Reports* than the Lark 6 and V8. However, the Larks were rated above the Chevrolet Corvair, which the magazine classified as a sports sedan, but got low marks as a family sedan.

By far the most glowing report on the Lark was in the June 1960 issue of *Cars* magazine, which rated the Lark the best overall buy of all American cars. The primary

With the addition of the 1960 Lark Convertible to its product line, Studebaker was said to be entering the luxury compact market.

reason for such a high rating, according to the magazine, was that they believed the Lark would do anything and go anywhere the larger cars would, but do it more economically. Also, *Cars* magazine was impressed with the wide range of models offered by the Lark. The Lark styling was viewed as designed for both the contemporary 1960 market and the future. The *Cars* staff was impressed that the bugs in the 1959 Lark had been worked out in the 1960 model.

One of the new models introduced by Studebaker for the 1960 model year was the Lark convertible. Chuck Nerpel, in a road test of the car for *Motor Trend* in its June 1960 issue, said that with the Lark VIII Convertible, Studebaker was introducing a new class of cars — the luxury compact. Basic Larks could be purchased for under $2000 in 1960, but the Lark VIII Convertible, completely outfitted with the power-pack engine (which, with a 4-barrel carburetor, raised horsepower from 180 to 195), automatic transmission, power steering and brakes, limited-slip differential, radio, heater, reclining seats, adjustable headrests, bumper guards, wheel discs, whitewall tires, plus the added overall costs on what he called a veritable jewel box compact convertible, brought the price to about $3500.

Nerpel found acceleration of the Lark convertible somewhat sluggish, with 0 to 60 miles per hour achieved in 14.9 seconds. He attributed this to the car's being equipped with so many accessories that were power-draining and to a heavier X-member frame necessary to support a convertible with rigidity. He liked the Lark convertible's brakes and found the car's steering light and quick in congested city traffic. He found the car gave driving thrills and overall lively performance which, he claimed, was the beginning of a new class of touring car, the luxury compact.

Another new Studebaker model for 1960 was the Champ pickup truck, which combined some of the Lark front-end styling with traditional Studebaker truck features. Joe Wherry tested a 1960 Studebaker Champ ½-ton pickup with an 8-foot truck bed for the August 1960 issue of *Cars* magazine. Although Wherry had hoped the factory would provide a Champ with either the 259 V8 or the 289 V8, what was offered to him was a truck with the 245-cubic-inch L-head 6-cylinder engine with 118 horsepower. It turned out that Wherry was extremely impressed with the power and acceleration of the 245-cubic-inch engine. Zero to 60 miles per hour was achieved in 16.5 seconds, but the truck also had excellent lugging power.

The *Cars* magazine test of the Champ pickup revealed excellent quality of workmanship. Features that Wherry liked included the sliding rear-of-cab window panels and the chromed grille, stainless steel side trim, and foam-based upholstery of the somewhat upscale version in the Champ that was driven. Interior space of the driver's cabin of the Champ was almost identical to that of the Lark front seat compartment. The ride of the Champ was found to be good and the heavy-duty leaf springs provided good control. The conclusion on the Champ was that it was fun and lively to drive.

Studebaker-Packard Products for 1961

One of the critiques of the 1959 and 1960 Larks had been that the old 169 cubic inch L-head engine had become outdated compared to the overhead valve engines of the competition. That criticism was remedied in the 1961 Larks with the introduction of the overhead valve design to the 169-cubic-inch engine, which boosted its horsepower from 90 h.p. to 112 h.p. Therefore, the really big news in 1961 from Studebaker-Packard was in the engineering. Lark styling underwent a modest facelift for 1961 and the Hawk began to take on some features that would cause it to evolve into more of a grand touring vehicle in the future.

Yet the model year 1961 was a pivotal one for the career of Harold Churchill. He was replaced as chief executive officer at Studebaker-Packard Corporation at the very beginning of the 1961 model year by board chair Clarence Francis. Then, about midway in the model year, on February 1, 1961, Churchill stepped aside as president and Sherwood Egbert took over as president and CEO. Therefore, the 1961 model year was the last one for which Churchill had a direct influence on the design and marketing of Studebaker cars and trucks. What the automotive testing media had to say about the cars that represented Churchill's final effort as head of the company is the topic of this section.

In 1961, the Studebaker Hawk finally received some attention from the company after being somewhat neglected in the 1959 and 1960 model years. The Hawk was, in 1961 as in the previous model years since 1956, the top-of-the line Studebaker passenger car. Although the 1961 Hawk had no sheet metal changes and the same engine configuration as the 1960 model with the 289-cubic-inch V8 engine, there were some important developments that began to move the car back into the category of a family sport coupe touring car. One important development with the Hawk was the availability of a four-speed, all-syncromesh floor stick shift transmission, which when combined with the bucket seats gave the car's interior a sportier look and feel. The addition of these features meant that Studebaker was responding to the request of dealers who, even before the introduction of the 1960 Hawks, were asking for the floor shifter and bucket seats.[5]

In a June 1961 road test for *Motor Life* magazine, Chuck Nerpel said the Hawk had to be driven to be appreciated. He said that even though the weight distribution was 55 percent on the front and 45 percent on the rear, the power steering and brakes, a firm suspension, and anti-roll stability gave the car excellent steering characteristics. The road test of the Hawk by Nerpel covered territory containing everything from 11,000-foot snow-covered mountains to Death Valley heat. The roads traveled had many changes in road conditions and the quick steering combined with the floor-mounted shift lever enabled shifting up or down to suit the needs of acceleration and downhill engine braking.

Nerpel liked the Hawk's brakes, which enabled it to stop quickly and repeatedly. He was critical of the position of the seat back on the bucket seat, which he said gave discomfort due to its having too much of a straight-up angle. As was true in several road tests of earlier Hawks, the array of real instruments on the instrument panel were cause for rejoicing by Nerpel.

The Hawk that Nerpel tested for *Motor Life* had the optional four-barrel carburetor, which boosted horsepower to 225. Acceleration from 0 to 60 miles per hour took 11.4 seconds. Gasoline mileage was not phenomenal and averaged between 16 and 17 mpg on the highway and 13.5 mpg in city driving. He concluded by saying that the Hawk was a well-made automobile that shouldn't be overlooked for an honest dollar's worth of real fun driving.

Another road test of the 1961 Hawk occurred for the March 1961 issue of *Cars* magazine by Duncan Maxwell. Not surprisingly, given the reports on the car by Nerpel and reports in prior years, Maxwell especially liked the instrument panel, which he said was the most readable and most functional of any domestic car in 1961. In contrast to the car tested by *Motor Life*, which had the 4-barrel carburetor giving it 225 horsepower, the Hawk tested by Maxwell had the four-speed floor shift transmission and the basic 2-barrel carburetor with the engine delivering 210 horsepower. Even though equipped with only the 2-barrel carburetor engine, Maxwell's achievement of a 0 to 60 miles per hour time of 10.1 seconds was better than what Nerpel was able to get on the car he tested with the four-barrel carburetor.

Roadability and handling of the Hawk were rated as acceptable by Maxwell, but he did say that if somebody wanted a sports car that cornered without lean, then the Hawk was not the car. Leaning on turns, he found, was about average. The four-speed floor shift, though, had a sports-car feel and could be used to downshift easily for best roadability. Maxwell said the car could be driven hundreds of miles a day without driver fatigue. He concluded that the Hawk must be driven to be properly appreciated.

Another road test of the 1961 Hawk was undertaken by *Motor Trend* magazine for its June 1961 issue. Its findings on the Hawk were consistent with those of *Motor Life* and *Cars* magazine. In saying that the Hawk had good performance and roadability,

The only significant change in styling for the 1961 Hawk was modest two-toning of the paint with a strip on the rear fender fins. However, automotive writers approved of the upgrades in performance that a four-speed floor-mounted shifter gave, and they liked the upgraded interiors with bucket seats (AACA Library and Research Center).

Motor Trend declared it a top choice in its price class for driving pleasure accompanied with family utility. The car tested had the standard 289 V8 with 2-barrel carburetor producing 210 horsepower. Acceleration was consistent with that found by *Cars* magazine in its road test at 10.6 seconds for 0 to 60 miles per hour. Steering was rated as adequate but a little slow. *Motor Trend* said the instrument panel was one of the best around and was complimentary on the other aspects of the redesigned interior with the bucket seats and floor-mounted four-speed manual transmission.

In the Lark line for 1961, the big engineering news was the overhead valve six-cylinder engine. The big news in model development was the introduction of the Lark Cruiser on the 113-inch wheelbase. The automotive media, therefore, had plenty to do in testing the 1961 Larks with both the regular Larks with the new OHV engine and the Cruisers receiving attention.

Motor Trend road tested a 1961 Lark Regal hardtop with the new overhead valve 6-cylinder engine and overdrive transmission for its June 1961 issue. The difference in performance between the old flathead 6 and the new OHV six was said to be impressive with the new 6-cylinder engine being the best all-around Lark six that Studebaker had produced. *Motor Trend* stated that the Lark's old flathead six "was clattering, comparatively uneconomical, and very unimpressive in performance. The new engine is none of these, although it is not truly outstanding." The performance in the 0 to 60 miles per hour acceleration tests was 15.2 seconds, which placed the Lark in the moderately good performers of the class of compact cars. A major improvement was acceleration in the 20 to 50 mph range, where earlier Larks were declared to be sluggish and even discouraging to drive. There was no slowing down on hills and passing could be done in far less distance than with earlier Larks. Cornering on the 1961 Lark six was found to be much improved over the 1959 and 1960 Larks, largely because of a sway bar that became standard equipment on the 1961 Lark sixes. Steering was re-engineered with a new recirculating-ball-type steering gear which greatly reduced the steering effort.

Gas mileage on the new engine was in the 18 to 22 miles per gallon range, which was about average for the compact cars tested by *Motor Trend*. Roominess of the 1961 Lark hardtop was above average for the compact class, but the quality of the interior was rated as better than that of other cars in the compact class.

In 1961, Studebaker faced competition in the compact V8 market from a new set of compact cars, which included a trio from General Motors: the Buick Special V8 with a 215-cubic-inch engine; the Oldsmobile F-85 with the 215-cubic-inch V8; and the Pontiac Tempest with the 215-cubic-inch engine. Another compact V8 was the Rambler Custom Classic with a 250-cubic-inch engine. The GM cars, the Rambler, and a Lark Regal and Cruiser were tested against each other by *Motor Trend* magazine for its February 1961 issue.

In the comparison tests of the V8 compact cars, *Motor Trend* said the Lark was the only V8 compact then available in a full line of body types and up to a dozen different power train combinations. The Lark stood out among its competitors because, although the smallest of the compact V8s, it had the biggest engine. One of the Lark test cars was a Regal four-door sedan on the 108.5-inch wheelbase with a 259-cubic-inch V8 and 3-speed manual transmission. The other Lark tested was a Cruiser on a 113-inch wheelbase with the 289-cubic-inch engine and an automatic transmission.

In fuel economy, the two Larks tested by *Motor Trend* had distinctly different results. The smaller Regal gave mileage in the 16 to 20 miles per gallon range with a maximum of 22 mpg in one conservative test run, while the Cruiser was in the 12 to 16 mpg range. In road behavior, the Regal had superior agility in both crowded traffic conditions and tight corners, but its riding quality was judged to be harsh. The longer wheelbase Cruiser provided a smoother ride and steadier handling at highway speeds. Both cars did have a tendency to understeer.

The interiors of both cars were impressive to *Motor Trend*'s road testers. The Regal had 40 inches of rear legroom, which equaled any other car in its class, and the Cruiser had 44 inches of rear legroom, surpassed in American cars only by Cadillac, which had a half inch more. In conclusion, *Motor Trend* said the Lark V8 was the most truly compact car in its field but performed on a par with its competition. The Cruiser was unsurpassed in its class for luxury and comfort and had the hottest engine options of any small car.

Comparative data among the several compact V8s tested by *Motor Trend* included the 0 to 60 miles per hour test: the Buick Special did it in 11.7 seconds with a 3-speed manual transmission and 12.5 seconds with an automatic; the Olds F-85 with a 3-speed manual transmission did it in 11.9 seconds; the Pontiac Tempest with an automatic transmission did it in 11.8 seconds; the Rambler with a 3-speed manual transmission did it in 11.9 seconds and with an automatic transmission in 13.2 seconds; the Lark Regal with 3-speed automatic did it in 10.1 seconds, and the Cruiser with automatic did it in 9.8 seconds. The Larks, therefore, were the fastest of the compact V8 class by a fairly significant margin. The Lark Regal gas mileage figures mentioned earlier were virtually identical to those of the other compact V8s, while the Cruiser, with a much larger engine, was somewhat lower in mpg.

Motor Life and *Car Life* magazines also did road tests on the 1961 Lark Cruiser. Writing for *Motor Life* in its December 1960 issue, Bob Russo described the Cruiser as a luxury compact designed with a bit more quality and considerably more zing than the average compact. Standard on the Lark Cruiser was the 259-cubic-inch engine with the 289 V8 being an option. The car tested by *Motor Life* had the 259 V8 with 2-barrel carburetion and automatic transmission. Zero to 60 acceleration was in 14.1 seconds. Gas mileage was excellent at 25 mpg at a steady 60 miles per hour and 21 to 23 mpg in simulated stop-and-go driving. Compared to the *Motor Trend* test car, this result showed a dramatic difference between the 289 V8 and the 259 V8, with the latter being far more economical to drive. With a longer wheelbase and heavier weight, the *Motor Life* Cruiser surpassed the smaller Larks and most bigger cars in handling qualities and riding comfort, even over washboard roads.

The Lark Cruiser V8 tested by *Car Life* magazine was equipped with the 289 V8 and two-barrel carburetion and automatic transmission. Its 0 to 60 miles per hour acceleration was 10.0 seconds and the normal range of fuel consumption was 15 to 19 miles per gallon, somewhat less than the 259 V8 tested by *Motor Life*. In contrast to both the *Motor Trend* and *Motor Life* experiences with the Lark Cruisers they tested, the quality of the one tested by *Car Life* was rated as only average. Two disconcerting things that happened were that a door handle did not bring the door with it when requested and part of the carpet came loose from its moorings and slid out onto the sidewalk. Also, while big on the inside but being compact on the outside, the Lark had some attributes that *Car Life* considered undesirable. These included a small trunk (commented on, incidentally, by several of the magazines that tested Larks in 1959, 1960, and 1961). A common criticism of Studebaker V8s through the years was their unequal weight distribution with a high proportion of the weight on the front end. The Lark Cruiser was found to have the same weight distribution problem, which compromised road handling, particularly in mountain driving. The riding qualities of the Cruiser, though, were described as soft but well controlled and free from wallowing tendencies.

Among the comparative tests of compact cars that *Motor Trend* did for 1961 was one on the compact station wagons, including the Chevrolet Corvair, Plymouth Valiant and Dodge Lancer (which shared body shells); Ford Falcon and Mercury Comet (which shared basic body shells); the Rambler American; and Buick Special, Olds F-85, and Pontiac Tempest (the three General Motors cars shared basic body shells); and the Studebaker Lark. The tests conducted by *Motor Trend* on these compact station wagons were not the comprehensive road tests, but instead only a summary analysis of the cars.

Motor Trend concluded that the V8 engine option for the Lark would be the wisest choice because its performance was considerably better on the wagon than the six-cylinder engine with almost equal fuel economy. One of the positive features of the 1961 Lark wagon over earlier Lark wagons was the addition of an extra leaf in the rear springs, giving a firmer ride but better cornering and overall stability. The Lark's cargo compartment was rated best of the compacts because, with a 58-inch width and 35-inch height, it was the widest and highest of the compact wagons. The optional front reclining seat in the Lark made it possible to carry some longer cargo items because the seat-back could be dropped back a few inches which would permit cargo nearly two feet longer than the cargo floor to be carried with the tailgate closed.

The "Churchill" Studebaker-Packard Products: Some Perspective

The analysis of the Studebaker-Packard products built during the time that Harold E. Churchill was president of the company necessitated a rather lengthy discussion, but one that produced an interesting timeline of the development of the cars. Here the conclusions regarding the five model years that Churchill was head of S-P give some insights, although at times perhaps speculative, on the reasons for the evolution of the company's product line.

One thing becomes clear: while improvements were made in the quality and engineering of the Studebaker-Packard products over that five-year period, the limited financial resources of Studebaker-Packard constrained what the company could do in terms of the design and engineering of the cars. Styling of the 1961 Larks was not dramatically different from the 1959 Larks and continued the basic body shell from the 1958 and earlier Studebakers. An interesting development for 1961 was the return to the regular passenger car line of what was essentially the earlier Land Cruiser and President Classic (indeed, even the 1957 and 1958 Packard sedan) body shell to the Lark Cruiser. What is remarkable is that in spite of the budgetary constraints existing at Studebaker-Packard, Churchill was able to motivate his stylists and engineers to develop cars that were distinctive in appearance. The facelifts given to the cars over the years demonstrated creativity in styling and interior appointments.

In engineering, perhaps the biggest single development during Churchill's tenure as president was the transformation of the old L-head six-cylinder engine into an overhead valve configuration, yielding far more horsepower for that basic Lark power plant. One engineering issue that Studebaker never did completely resolve was with the handling characteristics of its cars. To be fair, the 1961 products were rated by virtually all the automotive and consumer media as quite improved products compared to the extremely critical comments on the imprecise handling and steering and control of the cars built for 1957. Undoubtedly, Studebaker's lack of financial resources made it difficult to completely re-engineer the front suspension of its cars during that period. Also, the overall excellent performance of the relatively heavy V8s during that period, combined with the financial constraints, rendered the introduction of a completely new line of V8 engines problematic. However, the lack of a lighter V8 engine continued to inhibit the handling of Studebaker-Packard products at least through the Churchill years and on into the 1964 model year.

One of the issues associated with Studebaker-Packard cars during the Churchill era, as well as several years before and continuing all the way to the end of production, was the problem of body rust. None of the test reports summarized here dealt with the rust issue — perhaps because all of the test reports were on brand-new vehicles. In colder climates of the northern states, especially in states where salt is used extensively to clear highways of snow and ice in winter months, it was not uncommon to see Studebakers only two or three years old with considerable body rust. Even though body construction of many competitive makes of cars in that era subjected them to the problem of rust as well, cars built by Studebaker-Packard on the basic Studebaker body shell seemed to be particularly vulnerable. While it is difficult and perhaps even dangerous to extrapolate from anecdotal evidence, this author, who has owned seven South Bend S-P products built between 1957 and 1964, three of which were built in the 1957–1959 period, experienced firsthand what Studebaker aficionados refer to, in less than endearing terms, as the "usual rust." That is, at least rocker panels and front fenders just forward of the front doors rusted out in a relatively short period of time. If editorializing can be forgiven, it has always been a matter of puzzlement why Studebaker did not at least attempt to put inner fender liners on the front fenders and improve the rust preventative treatment of the sheet metal on its cars. Given Churchill's interest in and striving for top quality in the products built under his leadership, the lack of serious attention to the rust problem is mystifying and surely cost Studebaker sales, especially repeat sales, in the so-called rust belt states.

Still, overall, the Studebaker and Packard cars built from 1957 through 1961 should be recognized as worthy, quality automobiles offering reasonable value for the money expended. One of the ironies of the product development during this period is that something considered a liability for Studebaker in 1957 and 1958, i.e., the width of its bodies, turned out to be a strong asset as the Lark came to market. Considered narrow by industry standards when the S-P products were full-sized vehicles, the same basic body shell turned out to be wide and offered exceptional interior space compared to Studebaker's competition in the compact car market.

Perhaps the best way to characterize the product development efforts during the Churchill era is to be impressed with the level of creativity that the stylists and engineers at Studebaker-Packard were able to exercise in the face of budgetary constraints with which the company's competition simply did not have to contend. The test reports on the cars built during the era when Churchill was president of the company reflect a commitment to continuous improvement in the quality of the vehicles coming off the assembly line in South Bend. Given Churchill's vision for the company (a topic to which we return in the following chapter), through his positive thinking and his ability to motivate his staff, who both respected and liked him, some very ingenious and memorable products were developed under very trying circumstances.

8
Harold E. Churchill in Retrospect and Perspective

In assessing Harold E. Churchill's presidency of Studebaker-Packard Corporation, it is appropriate and necessary to put his leadership of the corporation in the perspective of his style and policies compared to his predecessor and successors. From the time of the merger of Studebaker and Packard in 1954 to the ending of Studebaker automobile production in 1966, the corporation had four presidents: James Nance, Harold Churchill, Sherwood Egbert, and Byers Burlingame. Four leaders over a twelve-year period is hardly a sterling record for a corporation that was struggling to stay in business as well as maintain a position as a viable automobile manufacturer. Of those four presidents, Harold Churchill's tenure of 1956 to 1961 was the longest and has been, of course, the primary focus of this book. Before making definitive conclusions about his role in the S-P presidency, however, a brief examination is undertaken of the styles and policies of James Nance, Churchill's immediate predecessor, and Sherwood Egbert and Byers Burlingame, Churchill's successors in the 1961 to 1966 period. Nance is discussed first, followed by sections on Egbert and Burlingame. The final section of this chapter concludes with an overall assessment of Churchill and his policies.

James J. Nance

The first president of the Studebaker-Packard Corporation after the merger of the two firms in 1954 was James J. Nance, a native of Ironton, Ohio, and a 1923 graduate of Ohio Wesleyan University. Nance came to his position at S-P following a career in the appliance industry.[1] Originally, after graduation from college, Nance had planned to become a lawyer like his father. After his father died in his junior year in college, Nance dropped out of school, but returned later and switched from pre-law to business administration because he did not think the family resources would carry him through law school. Following graduation from Ohio Wesleyan University, Nance took some postgraduate courses in business administration at Ohio State University, after which he joined the National Cash Register Company in Dayton, Ohio, in its executive development program.[2] In 1928, he went on to the Frigidaire Division of General Motors, where he directed a $7 million advertising program that helped make Frigidaire a household name. He left Frigidaire in 1940 to join the electronics firm Zenith, served on the War Production Board during World War II, and joined General Electric Corporation in 1945. In 1946 he was named president of the Hotpoint Division of General Electric.[3] It is in his position at Hotpoint that the story of Nance's ultimate association with Packard begins.

Nance's career at Hotpoint had been an outstanding success. In five years, the super salesmanship tactics of Nance had increased sales from about $20 million annually to $200 million. His success at Hotpoint got the attention of Hugh J. Ferry, who had been Packard Motor Car Company treasurer for 23 years, and who took over as the president of Packard in 1949, following the resignation of George T. Christopher. Christopher had become president of Packard in 1942, following the resignation of Max Gilman, who had succeeded longtime Packard president Alvan Macauley in 1939. Macauley then became board chair. Prior to becoming president, Gilman had been a marketing executive who had helped direct the Packard revival during the Depression with the introduction of the Packard "120" medium-priced car.[4]

Christopher and Gilman were distinctly different individuals. Christopher was a production expert and Gilman was a marketing person. Under Christopher, styling did not receive much attention. Christopher appeared to be more eager to get Packard production up to 200,000 cars per year than to offer the public vehicles designed to attract customers to the showroom to make that production goal a reality. In fact, a combination of events following World War II, including a shortage of steel, made attaining that 200,000 level an impossibility. Production of Packard's postwar cars, based on its 1941 Clipper design, was well below Christopher's output goal, at 41,000 units in 1946 and 52,000 units in 1947. Table 1 in Chapter 2 shows that Packard, in its best postwar year, built just over 100,000 units in 1949, and then began to see output decline. Furthermore, Packard was caught without any new car on its drawing boards to capture the imagination of the public at the end of World War II. Its 1948, 1949, and 1950 models were really reworked or facelifted models of the original Packard Clipper design. The Packards of those model years were often referred to as "inverted bathtubs" or "pregnant elephants."[5]

Finally, primarily at the urging of executive engineer William H. Graves, Christopher relented on

James J. Nance left appliance maker Hotpoint to become president of the Packard Motor Car Company in 1952. After the merger, he became president of Studebaker-Packard Corporation. His resignation from Studebaker-Packard in 1956 cleared the way for Harold Churchill to become the company president and chief executive officer.

styling and agreed to a new design for the 1951 model year.[6] The 1951 Packards, restyled by chief stylist John Reinhart, were considered a styling success and received acclamations from automotive industry writers; they even received a Society of Motion Picture Art Directors award for embodying the most advanced concepts of automotive styling.[7] Sales of the redesigned Packards were strong and an improvement over the 1950 models, but output restrictions due to the Korean conflict kept Packard from achieving its full potential in 1951. However, in the meantime, Christopher had resigned in October 1949 and Ferry had taken over as president.[8]

Although heavily steeped in the finances of Packard as its treasurer, Ferry was quoted in *Fortune* magazine as saying, "I just wasn't fit for the job and I knew it." He made the job of finding a successor his first order of business. Ferry believed that Packard, while having ample engineering talent, needed a sales strategist to deal with its challenges. Thus it was that Ferry made his first approach to Nance about taking over the presidency of Packard in 1950. Having heard that Nance was being courted by another firm, General Electric gave him a pep talk about his prospects at GE that made it difficult for him to leave the company at that time. However, by 1952, GE had reorganized its appliance operations and had a new 51-year-old president, Ralph Cordiner. In surveying the situation at GE, the aggressive and ambitious Nance began to believe there might not be opportunities for him to move up the ladder at GE. Ferry heard of the situation and invited Nance to have further talks about Packard.[9]

After a second trip to Detroit and assessing the Packard situation carefully for several months, Nance left GE in May 1952 and joined Packard. Even though it faced some internal problems of complacency among the staff, inability to meet its production goals, and very real challenges in the marketplace, Nance found that, in 1952, Packard certainly was not a corporate basket case. The firm was profitable, had the newly styled 1951 cars available, was debt-free, and had a strong defense business in aircraft engines, which accounted for nearly a third of its revenue.

Nance was described in the media as a hard-working executive who did not regard his job as only an eight-hour-per-day occupation. He was at his desk at eight o'clock in the morning and expected his staff to do the same. He considered himself as being on call twenty-four hours a day. At Packard, those traits were used to implement change. Complacency among the staff was a problem that Nance, with his aggressive personality and management style, confronted early in his time at Packard. He realized that the attitude of some that Packard engineering would always pull the company through was not enough and that aggressive marketing would be necessary if Packard was to be a successful automotive competitor. One of the things that he did immediately for the 1953 model year was to attempt to draw a distinction between the least expensive Packards (then priced at about $2500) and the top-of-the-line models (priced at about $3750). Such a distinction had been lost for Packard in the immediate postwar period. The top-of-the-line 1953 sedans were given the model name of Patricians and were given high levels of trim and equipment to compete directly with Cadillac in the luxury car market. The less expensive, or medium-priced, models were designated Packard Clippers, with the goal (achieved in 1956, but only briefly) of having them called simply "Clippers" made by Packard.[10]

Nance also was concerned about the overall profit position of the company when he took over. Although profitable, it was making about a 6 percent return on sales, which left it vulnerable if prices had to be reduced, for example, by even 5 percent. He pushed for what he called a dynamic pricing strategy to gauge the market to achieve the necessary volume. But he also pushed for greater attention to costs and emphasized the need for the company's vendors to do their part in controlling costs by assisting in the engineering of components that were outsourced. Nance had been successful in reducing costs substantially at Hotpoint and was hoping to achieve the same results at Packard. To accomplish that goal, management structural changes were implemented by Nance and a cost review committee was established which, along with an executive committee, met weekly to review various aspects of company operations. That executive committee, in particular, consisted of several new executives, some brought by Nance from Hotpoint, and some recruited from within the Packard ranks.[11] In general, it can be concluded that the mode of operation Nance brought to Packard was in contrast to the somewhat laid-back methods that had characterized the firm in earlier years.

In his message to shareholders in the *Packard Annual Report for 1952*, dated March 2, 1953, Nance emphasized the new directions he was planning on taking the company. Those directions included the separation of the Packard and Clipper lines which, he claimed, had been a concept enthusiastically embraced by the dealers. He stated 250 new dealers had been signed, which he anticipated would broaden the coverage of the company's products. New emphasis was being placed on the defense business, with the building of a new plant in Utica, Michigan, for the production of jet aircraft engines.

A year later, however, in his message to shareholders in the *Packard 1953 Annual Report*, dated March 1, 1954, things began to look quite different for Nance and his plans for Packard. With the winding down of the Korean conflict, the defense business schedules for Packard were reduced. Sales of automobiles were fluctuating, and the Briggs Manufacturing Company, which had manufactured bodies for Packard for many years, sold the plant where those bodies had been made to Chrysler Corporation. By the end of 1954, sales of Packard and Clipper cars totaled only about 27,000 units, or a third of what they had been in 1953.

The year 1954 saw the merger of Nash and Hudson to form American Motors Corporation and the merger of Kaiser and Willys to form Kaiser Willys Corporation. At the 1953 annual meeting of Packard shareholders, Nance said that 1954 would be a year of adjustment for the automaker with major capital improvements going on while confronting a highly competitive market. Given those market conditions, he said that while Packard was not opposed in principle to a merger, the company had no intention of being absorbed in any type of merger arrangement and would only consider a plan under which the company could enter into an agreement on equal footing.[12]

Only a little more than a year later, on August 17, 1954, stockholders of the Studebaker Corporation and the Packard Motor Car Company voted to form the Studebaker-Packard Corporation by merging those two independent automobile companies. James J. Nance was named president of the newly merged company. The media anticipated what the Nance strategy would be for S-P by noting that the company was a full-line company manufacturing low-priced, medium-priced, and luxury-priced automobiles as well as a line of trucks.[13] In the Studebaker-Packard Corporation *Annual Report 1954*, Nance made his philosophy very clear with the following statement:

> The highly competitive conditions prevailing in the automobile industry for the past 18 months continue, and further support the soundness of the basic philosophy that led your management to adopt the course of producing and marketing a full line of passenger cars in each price class.... The course adopted involves continuing the full line of cars and resulting operating burdens during the earlier phases, until the advantages inherent in design and common tooling of future models can be achieved.

Meanwhile, problems were developing for S-P. In that 1954 *Annual Report*, Nance noted almost in passing that further defense contracts had not been received by the company. Then, the minutes of the December 17, 1954, S-P Board meeting indicate Nance reported that the new 1955 Packards had been very well received by dealers and the press. These were the models with a new V8 Packard engine, new Torsion-Aire suspension system, and new Twin Ultramatic transmission, and that were being built in the Conner Avenue assembly plant now leased from Chrysler, instead of at the old Packard East Grand Boulevard plant. The new V8 engines were being built in a new factory in Utica, Michigan. However, he said production at the Packard Division was disappointing at only about half the anticipated rate due to production problems. Those problems at Packard had not been cleared up by the January 21, 1955, Board meeting, where Nance claimed the production of Packards was approximately thirty days behind schedule as a result of the substantially new automobile being produced in entirely new plants.

Compounding Nance's problems as he tried to get the merged S-P up and running as a going concern was the labor situation in South Bend. At that January 21, 1955, Board meeting, Nance's views toward labor relations became quite clear. The labor cost situation at South Bend was becoming critical in Nance's view. His statement to the Board reflected a hardline position as follows: "The corporation's financial picture is such that it has nothing to give the employees except jobs, and although a strike is not wanted, it would be better to liquidate the assets of the Company than to have them liquidated through impossible production costs."

At the March 18, 1955, Board meeting, he continued to express concern about productivity at the Packard plants and noted overtime was having to be paid to reach scheduled production levels. At the April 18, 1955, Board meeting, the magnitude of the production problems at Packard become evident as a result of data presented on the labor hours required to build the Packard cars. In January 1955, the actual number of labor hours per car was 212, whereas the target had been 148. By April 1955, the situation had improved somewhat with the actual labor hours per Packard car being 152, but the target rate by that time had been 112 labor hours per car. Furthermore, Nance complained that the sales picture for Packard was being complicated by the poor quality of the cars that were being built.

Nance's aggressive style with both marketing and product planning, combined with his basic inexperience in the automobile industry, may have been a factor in the production and cost problems that S-P encountered at Packard in 1955. It can be argued that Packard needed a V8 engine by 1955 — it was late to the market as it was, compared to its competition. Also, the 1951 Reinhart-designed body needed upgrading by the

1955 model year. However, combining in one year a whole new engine being built in a new plant, with a significantly facelifted body design, with a revised Twin-Ultramatic automatic transmission and the completely new Torsion-Aire suspension system, created a manufacturing and quality nightmare. It is unlikely that the production and quality programs of General Motors, Ford, or Chrysler could have been successful with that many major product innovations and production facility revisions in a single year.

Compounding the problems was the situation at the new-to-Packard Conner Avenue assembly plant, where crowded production conditions and a labor force not used to the new plant were contributing to the slow rate of Packard and Clipper output. In brief, Nance had tried to do too much at one time. Costs, which he had endeavored to restrain, were out of control, the company was losing money rapidly, and the quality issues were plaguing the company. In trying to do too much at one time, Nance was perhaps somewhat naïve due to inexperience about the nature of the auto industry and what it takes to bring a new product to production and the market. The product was successful, but Packard was not able to deliver on its production or quality promises to the dealers and the public.

By midyear, the problems at Packard began to take their toll. At the August 19, 1955, Board meeting, Nance stated Packard sales in July had been disappointing and that dealers were asking for rebates. The line schedule for Packard production had been reduced by 1500 units per month because of the slow sales. The sales deterioration continued through the fall of 1955. Even though the production and quality problems at Packard had been fairly well resolved by the time the 1956 models were introduced, a weakening automobile market, combined with the reputation that the poor-quality 1955 Packard and Clipper cars had developed, brought S-P and James Nance's dream of a fourth full-line automobile company to a crisis point.

In Chapter 3, some of the challenges facing Studebaker-Packard in the early months of 1956 were discussed. The end of the full-line philosophy had to be evident even to Nance as he reported to the Board on January 20, 1956, that Packard and Clipper sales were seriously below projections in December 1955 and in January 1956. Furthermore, he had to deliver the news that the banks and insurance companies were reluctant to lend any more money to the corporation. A finance committee of directors, headed by Russell Forgan, was appointed in December 1955, to find $50 million of additional capital for S-P. About $30 million of that was needed for tooling for the planned new body for the 1957 and 1958 products. The body was to be introduced on the Packards for 1957 and then, in 1958, on the Studebakers. The common body shell was designed to continue the full-line concept but share components and tooling to reduce product development and manufacturing costs. This program was key to the styling (based primarily on the Packard Predictor show car shown at auto shows in 1956) with which Nance hoped to regain the acceptance of both Studebaker and Packard products by the public.[14]

In his report to the Board on February 27, 1956, Nance had to acknowledge that the corporation's cash position was such that even if all the bank credit still available to it were taken down, if the tooling program for the 1957 and 1958 cars was undertaken, the company was in danger of not having sufficient cash for day-to-day operations and would have to default on its loan agreements sometime between July and September.

It must have been a bitter pill for Nance to swallow when, at that February 27 meeting, the Board took up the discussion of whether to dispose of the Packard portion of the S-P business. Likewise, it must not have been of any comfort to Nance that the debt-free Packard company he had taken over as president in 1952 now had, according to the 1956 Studebaker-Packard *Annual Report*, nearly $55 million in debt.

Throughout the Board minutes of early 1956, Nance continued to hold out hope that some sort of additional defense business could be procured. However, that possibility began to seem remote. The Defense Secretary under the Eisenhower administration was Charles E. Wilson, who had developed a narrow-based defense procurement policy. As a result of that narrow base, Studebaker and Packard lost defense business estimated by Nance as being worth $426 million.[15]

As the situation at Studebaker-Packard deteriorated, Nance, to his credit, given that his full-line dream was crumbling, made every effort to continue the company in operation. He ordered plant maintenance cut to the bone. All advertising was stopped after June 1956. Expenditures on Packard tooling were suspended in April for as long as two months, in an effort to conserve cash. He did order that word on the suspension of tooling not be allowed to leak out because that news would have been the death knell of the company if suppliers, dealers, and customers had learned of it.[16]

In Chapter 3, the events that occurred in late spring and early summer of 1956, which culminated in the deal with Curtiss-Wright Corporation, were discussed in some detail. That deal provided both cash for S-P to continue operations and the Management Advisory Agreement between Studebaker-Packard and Curtiss-Wright. At the July 26, 1956, Board meeting, when the deal with Curtiss-Wright effectively had been worked out, Nance announced his resignation as president. His resignation was accepted with regret by the Board. It is to Nance's credit that he stayed with Studebaker-Packard as long as he did. Clearly, he had a desire to bring the company into a safe port. *Fortune Magazine*, in its October 1956 edition, stated that in staying at S-P, Nance took most of the blame for the problems of the company. Also, *Fortune* claimed he continued as long as he did at S-P at considerable personal sacrifice because he turned down the presidency of a company nearly three times the size of S-P (that company was not named).[17]

After leaving Studebaker-Packard Corporation, Nance continued in the automobile business for a short time as vice-president in charge of marketing at Ford Motor Company. He advanced to general manager of the Mercury-Edsel-Lincoln Division of Ford but resigned from the company in 1958. He then spent two years, to quote him, "minding my own business," and then, in May 1960, became president of Central National Bank of Cleveland, Ohio.[18] Later he also became head of the First Union Real Estate Investment Trust.

While in Cleveland, he was the founder-chair of the board of Cleveland State University. He helped to make that institution a major urban university. For his efforts the University named its college of business the James J. Nance College of Business Administration.[19]

The Studebaker-Packard Corporation that James J. Nance left in July 1956 was quite a different company from the Packard Motor Company that he joined as president in 1952. The collapse of the full-line concept, the heavy debt, and an aging product line were the legacy that Nance ended up leaving to Harold Churchill, who assumed leadership of the company in the summer of 1956. Nance had had a vision for Studebaker-Packard to become a full-line automotive competitor to the Big Three. He envisioned S-P as the fourth major automobile manufacturer in the United States. He cannot be faulted for lack of vision. If there is criticism to levy at Nance it is that he did not fully grasp the nature of the automobile industry, perhaps failed to fully assess the condition of Studebaker before merging Packard with it, and was overly ambitious regarding the development of the Packard and Clipper lines for the 1955 model year. However, it is necessary to temper any criticism of Nance with the realization that conditions in both the industry and at S-P looked quite different in early 1956 than when he took over Packard in 1952, or even when the merger with Studebaker was consummated. James J. Nance died in 1984 at age 84.

Sherwood H. Egbert

Sherwood Harry Egbert was born in Seattle, Washington, in 1920 and grew up in Easton, Washington. Egbert has been described as energetic, hard-working, and self-confident.[20] His childhood was filled with challenges. His father had scraped a living together from operating a dance hall and café. After a fire burned down the business and the family home, the Egberts had to live in a tent for a while. Egbert recalled having to steal coal from Northern Pacific Railroad cars to provide heat for the family. At age twelve he went to work on a construction gang. He studied engineering for two years at Washington State University on an athletic scholarship (he won fourteen letters in high school and at one time considered going into professional baseball). He quit college after two years to take a construction job. In 1940, when the company he worked for needed an engineer, he applied for and got the job. Later, he worked as an engineer for Boeing, but in 1942, he enlisted in the Marines and became an aviation engineer, served in the South Pacific, and ended up with the rank of major. In 1946, he joined McCulloch Corporation as assistant production manager and was vice-president of that company when he was recruited to be president of Studebaker-Packard Corporation.[21]

Sherwood Egbert was married to Diana Nell Johnson. Together they had five sons, Sherwood James, David Sherwood, Gregory Martin, Robert Paul, and Warren Earl, and two daughters, Nancy Lee and Sherana Eileen.[22]

The situation on the Board of Directors at Studebaker-Packard when Egbert became president and CEO was discussed in Chapter 6. Tensions on the Board had been high and the vote to bring him to S-P was not unanimous. Yet, he accepted the challenge and won the support of Harold Churchill, who had been somewhat skeptical of the decision to hire him. Churchill sent a letter to Studebaker-Packard dealers on January 24, 1961, announcing that Egbert would officially assume his duties as president and chief executive officer on February 1. In that letter, Churchill stated:

> During the last several weeks, he [Egbert] has been participating in briefings on operations.... The selection of Mr. Egbert to head up our organization puts an end to the type of speculation and rumors that had been so prevalent the past few months. During this period, sales of our 1961 models have not been up to our expectation. Let's all put our shoulders to the

wheel to restore sales and profit, both yours and ours, to the position our good products rightfully deserve.... I know that Mr. Egbert can depend upon you to redouble your efforts to increase our sales volume.

Shortly after he took office, Egbert, in a February 23, 1961, letter to shareholders, thanked Churchill and the board for their help in making the transition to leadership easy. In that letter he laid out his plans for the company. Those plans, already put in motion, included ordering the advertising agency to come up with a new and more dynamic advertising campaign; giving dealers renewed confidence in the company's products; and enlisting the help of the National Dealer Council and Raymond Loewy's styling organization to bring the 1962 cars into approval and to the tooling stage. He further indicated S-P would be giving strong consideration to acquisitions that were within the means of the corporation and provide S-P with greater flexibility during times of changing economic trends.

Therefore, very early in his presidency of Studebaker-Packard, Egbert was fulfilling the expectations of the media and former associates that he operated on only one level — full speed ahead. Among his achievements in those first few weeks and months was the redesign of the Studebaker Hawk into the Gran Turismo Hawk for 1962. With the assistance of sports car designer Brooks Stevens, the Hawk was given a major transformation in appearance for the 1962 model year. The transformation of the Hawk took only eighteen weeks and less than a million dollars.[23]

In addition to pushing the development of the 1962 Larks and Hawks forward, Egbert made the bold decision to shut down assembly operations for the 1961 models in mid-June 1961, six weeks earlier than originally planned. His reasoning was that the inventory of 1961 models had to be cleared away if the 1962 cars were to be successful in the marketplace. The strategy worked, and by Labor Day the dealers had very low inventories and were piling up the orders for the 1962 models. While the plant was shut down, he had the workers clean and paint the factories, which had not received that kind of attention for many years.[24]

In an early meeting with the company's top executives, Egbert was very clear in his expectations. He supposedly told the top management team: "I want to work with you as a team. But, if you can't work that way, quit." He did not bring a significant number of new executives with him, but developed a close working relationship with Vice-President for Industrial Relations C.M. MacMillan, Secretary and General Counsel Melvin Milligan, and Vice-President and Controller Byers Burlingame.[25]

Much as Churchill had done in 1956, Egbert also paid attention to the problem of costs. He hired professors from Notre Dame to conduct classes in purchasing and cost accounting. A combination of cost-cutting and good early acceptance of the 1962 models brought S-P to profitable operations by September 1961.[26]

Although his enthusiasm and aggressive style, combined with the renovations and refreshing of the appearance of the inside of the plants, did help build morale at Studebaker-Packard in 1961, the honeymoon came to an end as a result of a 42-day strike by the United Auto Workers union in early 1962. On December 20, 1961, the company made a contract offer to the U.A.W. that included a pay raise of 6 cents an hour or 2.5 percent, whichever was greater, and continuation of a cost-of-living bonus. However, the contract offer also included major changes in relief and wash-up times, premium

Sherwood Egbert saw potential in the Hawk and had Brooks Stevens do a dramatic facelift on it in a very short period of time. The result was the 1962 Gran Turismo Hawk. A prototype, which differs in some minor trim detail from production models, is shown here (AACA Library and Research Center).

pay, and vacation pay calculations. The company argued that it wanted to cut the relief and wash-up time to 25 minutes per day from 39 minutes to be more in line with standards at other auto manufacturers. U.A.W. officials said that the relief and wash-up time were only some of the issues being confronted, which included the amount paid for Saturday and Sunday work and vacation pay issues. The U.A.W. struck the company on January 3, 1962. It appears S-P was preparing for the strike because it had built up a 70-day inventory of cars at the dealerships.[27]

The strike became particularly bitter on January 17, 1962, when some U.A.W. pickets attempted to prevent a car driven by Egbert from leaving the plant property. During the ensuing dispute, Egbert came out of his car, took off his topcoat, and threatened to do battle with the pickets. Ultimately, about a dozen police officers swinging nightsticks cleared a path for Egbert's car, which was being blocked by about 25 pickets.[28] A day later, one of the pickets was arrested for disorderly conduct as a result of the encounter. Egbert was also charged with disorderly conduct, while denying that he had taken off his overcoat.[29] After settlement of the strike, charges against both the employee and Egbert were dropped.[30]

The strike continued until February 11, 1962, when union members voted with an

83 percent approval to accept a new contract that included eliminating five minutes of the wash-up time and a four-cent-per-hour increase in pay plus cost-of-living adjustments. In commenting on the agreement, Egbert expressed hope that the new contract would result in "more efficient utilization of our work force, through co-operation of all parties concerned."[31]

While the strike was occurring, there was another development going on at Studebaker that ultimately was the signature event of the Egbert years at S-P. In much the same way that the introduction of the Lark defined the Churchill era, the development of the Avanti defined the presidency of Sherwood H. Egbert, whose vision for the company's product line was quite different from that of Churchill. Churchill championed the economy family car. Egbert championed the sporty, performance-image car. His initiation of the quick redesign of the Hawk for the 1962 model year was prophetic of the direction he wished to take the company.

On March 9, 1961, Egbert asked Raymond Loewy to return to South Bend and develop something racy and European in appearance for Studebaker in order to bolster what he perceived was Studebaker's sad image. Egbert's concept for Loewy was based on some rough sketches that he (Egbert) had made. Within ten days, Loewy and his staff were at work on the project at a rented house in Palm Springs, California. Loewy's three assistants were John Ebstein, Thomas Kellogg, and Robert Andrews. Within two weeks the Loewy team had a one-eighth model of the proposed new car, and shortly thereafter, Randall Faurot, now head of Studebaker's in-house styling, had his staff developing a full-sized prototype. The car came to be called the Avanti and had a fiberglass body. The fiberglass body enabled the design to be executed as the Loewy team had planned and also reduced the tooling costs. Originally conceived as a two-seater sports car to compete with the Chevrolet Corvette, the Avanti ended up as a four-seater "personal" sports car.[32]

Within six months of the presentation of a full-size clay to the Board of Directors on April 27, 1961, orders went out to suppliers for parts. There was no real money to develop a new chassis and drive train for the Avanti, so chief engineer Gene Hardig and his staff chose the reinforced X-member frame being used on the Lark convertible and the 289-cubic-inch Studebaker V8 engine. The standard Avanti (the R1 model) had the 289 engine, unsupercharged, which developed an estimated 240 horsepower. The R2 model Avanti, with a Paxton supercharger, was estimated to develop about 300 horsepower.[33] The Paxton Company, run by Andy Granatelli, was purchased as a division of Studebaker as part of its diversification program.

By spring of 1962, the Avanti was ready to be shown at the New York International Automobile Show and at the company's annual shareholders' meeting. The car also distinguished itself by setting 29 national stock car records in tests under the auspices of the United States Automobile Club (USAC).[34]

The Avanti was developed as an image car not only to add to Studebaker sales by itself, but also to draw people into Studebaker showrooms who might otherwise not have been there, and who, if they did not buy an Avanti, might drive off in a Lark or a Hawk. Unfortunately, the promise of the Avanti was better than what it delivered. Although orders poured in for the car, Studebaker found out it had orders for a car it could not deliver. The fiberglass bodies were built by the Molded Fiberglass Company

Sherwood H. Egbert (right) became president and CEO of Studebaker-Packard in 1961. He is pictured here with the car for which he is best known, the Avanti, introduced as a performance-oriented personal sports car for 1963. Pictured with him (left) is Raymond Loewy, whose organization designed the body for the Avanti. Unfortunately, manufacturing difficulties slowed Avanti production, resulting in cancellation of customer orders, and the car never had the desired impact on the market position of Studebaker (AACA Library and Research Center).

of Ashtabula, Ohio. Molded Fiberglass could make the body parts, but they had difficulty assembling a completed body in any volume. Studebaker decided to open a second assembly line for the bodies in South Bend in December 1962. However, the unexpected delays in getting the cars into volume production led to orders being canceled, and the momentum generated by the pre-production publicity was lost.[35]

It might well be argued that Egbert's aggressive and somewhat impatient approach to the auto business at Studebaker was both a blessing and a curse. It was a blessing in that a car that became an icon of the 1960s, the Avanti, was developed and brought to market in just over a year's time. The curse was that the rushed schedule probably led to the production problems that plagued the Avanti while it was being produced by Studebaker, with the consequence that the Avanti never achieved its true market potential.

Egbert originally had planned to launch a dramatically new line of cars for the 1964 model year. Loewy was working on designs that would have taken the Avanti themes into the regular line of Studebaker sedans using the existing Lark inner body shell and running gear. Brooks Stevens also had been commissioned to develop prototypes for the standard Studebaker line. However, there was little cash left at Studebaker to implement such a dramatic new line of cars. Whereas Studebaker had started 1962 with about $50 million in cash on hand, the Avanti program had been expensive, the 1963 line was not selling well, and the company was down to about $24 million by January 1963.[36] Egbert argued, though, that the Avanti program cost only $5 million and was worth it for the image-building effect it had on Studebaker. He said: "Put that [the $5 million] against the publicity that went with it and the impact it had on the public and it was money well spent."[37]

By the Board meeting on January 10 and 11, 1963, Egbert had to acknowledge that things were not going well. He emphasized that a prompt decision had to be made as to the future of the automotive business. After considerable debate among the members of the Board, at that meeting and again on February 19, 1963, the Board reaffirmed plans to go ahead with the so-called Avanti II program, which was the Loewy design concept for the regular passenger car line. (Note: this is not to be confused with the Avanti II that later was built by the Avanti Motor Corporation, which purchased the production rights, tooling, and a factory from Studebaker after the shutdown of Studebaker production in South Bend.) To implement this somewhat bold plan for the auto division, additional bank financing would have been required. At the March 1, 1963, Board meeting, it was revealed that the banks wanted to mortgage all of Studebaker's non-automotive assets (which included all the diversified divisions) to finance the Avanti II program. Given the circumstances facing the company and the onerous provisions that would have been required to obtain further loans, the Board agreed to discontinue bank negotiations regarding the Avanti II program. In essence, this ended Egbert's dream of a dramatic new line of cars in much the same way that a lack of financing ended Churchill's dream of a four-cylinder Studebaker.

Randolph H. Guthrie was Board chair by the August 8, 1963, Board meeting. In his report he stated that because of a lack of bank financing for what the Board referred to as Program A (the Avanti II program), the only reasonable alternative was a restyled 1964 model for which there were high hopes. However, Guthrie pointed out the sales picture at Studebaker had continued to deteriorate, and at that time, August 1963, success of and public reaction to the 1964 line could not be foreseen. Therefore, because orderly advanced planning was essential, he recommended that the Board should plan during the following few months as if Studebaker was going out of the automobile business, although no such decision could be made at that time. Egbert, though, continued to be optimistic at that meeting and argued that Studebaker could expect to do as well with the 1964 models as with the introduction of the 1962 models in the fall of 1961. Russell Forgan argued that the problem was the company owed considerably more money in 1963 than it had in 1961, but that, on the other hand, its prospects of continuing without the auto division were better than they were in 1961.

The curtain began to come down on the Egbert tenure as president of Studebaker Corporation by the November 1, 1963, Board of Directors meeting. He reported that sales of the 1964 models were disappointing, that the line speed was being reduced from 60 units per hour to 35 units per hour, and that 1850 workers had been laid off. For Egbert, and Studebaker, this meeting was a critical turning point. The minutes of the November 1, 1963, Board meeting record that for a period of time, the Board met in executive session on the subject of policy disagreements with the President. The Secretary was also instructed to record that Egbert would undergo abdominal surgery. In addition, at this meeting Byers A. Burlingame, vice-president of the corporation, was elected a director effective immediately to serve until the next annual meeting. Burlingame was also given all the powers of the president in the absence of Egbert.

At the November 9, 1963, Board meeting, it was announced that Egbert had undergone surgery and would require a period of convalescence. The Board once again reaffirmed through an amendment to the bylaws of the corporation, that Byers A. Burlingame was elected executive vice-president and was given all the powers of the president in the latter's absence. Egbert was placed on indefinite mandatory leave of absence for health reasons.

At the next Board meeting on November 22, 1963, Burlingame reported that orders for cars had dropped to only 141 units per day and that wholesale sales would probably be only 3000 units for November. He also reported that a task force had been established to accomplish expenditure reductions because expected factory sales of cars would not produce a break-even level of operations. Furthermore, Royall Victor Jr., of Cravath, Swaine & Moore, counsel for the corporation, reported that he had been in extensive negotiations with Sherwood Egbert concerning the proposed resignation of Egbert as President and CEO of Studebaker due to the significant differences that had developed between Egbert and the Board. Victor recommended, and the Board voted unanimously, that the resignation of Egbert as president, CEO, director, and as chair and member of the executive committee be accepted and that he be retained in an advisory capacity until 1971. (Note: in that "advisory" capacity, he was to have no responsibilities to or with the company except to receive a token level of compensation of $10,000 per year unless he accepted full-time employment elsewhere.) In addition, the Board voted unanimously at that meeting to elect Byers A. Burlingame president and chief executive officer of the Studebaker Corporation. The Egbert era had ended.

After leaving Studebaker as its president, Sherwood Egbert returned to Los Angeles, where he opened an office as a consultant in corporate development and industrial management with a specialty in mergers and diversification.[38] He died July 30, 1969, of cancer, at age 49.

Byers A. Burlingame

When Byers A. Burlingame became president and chief executive officer of the Studebaker Corporation in late 1963, he was a distinct contrast to his predecessor, Sherwood H. Egbert. Egbert was young, aggressive, and an outsider to both Studebaker and the automobile industry. Burlingame, born in Oakland, Indiana, was over 20 years the senior of Egbert, having ascended to the presidency of the company at age 63, and was a 38-year veteran of the automobile industry. A U.S. Navy veteran of World War I, Burlingame began his automotive career at Packard in 1925. In 1926, Burlingame became an invoice supervisor at Packard. He had held various financial positions at Packard and Studebaker and became vice-president of finance for Studebaker in 1961. He attended Hanover (Indiana) College and a University of Michigan extension division. Burlingame was married and had two sons and a daughter.[39]

A reading of the Board of Directors minutes of the Studebaker-Packard Corporation, and its successor after 1962 due to the dropping of the Packard name, the Studebaker Corporation, reveals that beginning in 1958, Burlingame frequently was in attendance at Board meetings as comptroller of the corporation. By 1960, Burlingame is listed in the minutes of Board meetings as being in attendance as a vice-president of the corporation and was called upon frequently to make detailed financial reports on the affairs of the corporation and on the cost implications of implementing various programs. Even though A.J. Porta was vice-president for finance of the corporation at the time, Burlingame often was giving detailed analysis and forecasts to the Board in 1960. For example, the handwritten minutes of the November 28, 1960, Board meeting have Burlingame explaining that the action taken at a September 1960 Board meeting to lower prices on the 1961 models resulted in an increase in the company's break-even level from 132,000 units to 140,000 units per year. At that same meeting, Burlingame gave detailed analysis of the cost of tooling up for the four-cylinder car project, which he estimated as $24.3 million, and which ultimately was rejected by the Board. Likewise, at the September 25, 1963, Board meeting, as things began to look rather grim for Studebaker, it was reported that Burlingame, as vice-president of the corporation, was accompanying legal counsel Royall Victor in negotiations with banks over corporate financing issues.

It is clear that Burlingame had a very firm grasp of the finances of Studebaker by the time he was given executive powers in November 1963, and very shortly thereafter made president and CEO. He was a finance person whose primary interest, and it could be argued responsibility, was to preserve the financial interests of the shareholders. Careful reading of reports that Burlingame made to the Board indicate a finance mindset that emphasized cost reduction as opposed to dramatic product development programs.

In his position as acting chief executive, at the November 22, 1963, Board meeting, Burlingame announced that a task force to accomplish expenditure reductions had been established consisting of various top executives. As a result, a

Pictured left to right are Randolph H. Guthrie and Byers A. Burlingame, board chair and president of the Studebaker Corporation after the forced resignation of Sherwood Egbert in 1963. Burlingame made both the 1963 decision to end production in South Bend and move all Studebaker output to Canada and the decision to end Studebaker production once and for all in March 1966.

target of $9 million in reductions had been established, of which $5 million already had been achieved. He also noted that the $9 million in expenditure reductions would not be sufficient to achieve break-even operations on the 65,000-car volume being expected at that point for 1964, and that "it was necessary to seek further economies in order to put the Automotive Division on a sound basis at that level of sales activity." This type of thinking on cost control would be a recurring theme by Burlingame throughout the rest of the history of the Studebaker Automotive Division.

The thinking of Burlingame on the future direction of the Automotive Division begins to be clear in the minutes of the December 1, 1963, Board meeting. Sales were considerably below forecasts, and as a result, the factory was shut down at the time and not scheduled to reopen until December 9, 1963. Burlingame also stated that substantial personnel cutbacks had been made in areas such as home office sales, engineering, promotion, and advertising, and that further cuts would be made in those areas as soon as possible. After Burlingame gave his gloomy report on sales, Churchill reported on a proposal for continued automotive production in the Canadian plant. Churchill said that his preliminary studies indicated that concentrating production in the Canadian plant would be feasible.

Burlingame then stated that conversations had been conducted with the truck manufacturer White Motors and that Churchill would follow up on those. These negotiations, it can be assumed, were related to possible acquisition of Studebaker production facilities by White, because it was also reported at that December 1 Board meeting that other possible approaches for sale or utilization of some or all of the corporation's Automotive Division facilities were discussed. Therefore, it is clear that by December 1, 1963, Burlingame and the Board were very much on track to closing down the South Bend automotive operations. The minutes of the December 12, 1963, Board meeting quote board chair Randolph Guthrie as stating the following: "Dealer orders for new cars had seriously deteriorated and retail sales also had become sluggish [since the December 1, 1963, Board meeting]. At this point, the program for continuing production in Canada, after withdrawal from South Bend, was placed in effect.... One major difficulty would be to cut back on the United States selling cost sufficiently to make money on the Canadian sales volume.... The Chairman indicated that the Corporation expected to solve these problems and to remain permanently in the automotive business through its Canadian operations." Following this statement by Guthrie, the Board unanimously confirmed, ratified and approved the shifting of the corporation's primary base of automotive manufacture to the Hamilton, Ontario, assembly plant and the curtailing of the South Bend automotive operations. Gordon E. Grundy, president of Studebaker of Canada, Limited, was then appointed by the Board as president of the Studebaker Automotive Division. The sequence of events, with the Board ratifying the action after Burlingame had taken it, suggests that Burlingame had the administrative authority as president of Studebaker to close facilities if he deemed it advisable.

There has been speculation among persons interested in the history of Studebaker regarding the true motives of the Board of Directors relative to the closing of the South Bend operations and the move of assembly operations to Canada. That speculation is probably summarized quite well by Stu Chapman, a past-president of the Studebaker Drivers Club, and Studebaker director of advertising and public relations at the Canadian plant from 1964 to 1966. In a June 2008 article in the Studebaker Drivers Club magazine, *Turning Wheels*, Chapman said the following:

> In previous articles I have written, as well as in numerous speeches delivered, I made it abundantly clear that had Studebaker closed up completely in December 1963, they would have faced huge financial penalties for failing to supply dealers with vehicles. Regardless of what some may speculate, the transfer of operations from South Bend to Hamilton was nothing more than a charade that allowed the Corporation to cease automotive operations at the least possible cost.[40]

Concern over obligations to dealers certainly cannot be discounted as one of the motivations for the decision to continue automotive operations in Canada, at least at a minimal level, for a period of time with, perhaps, the idea of eventually phasing out Studebaker automobile production. The move to Canada did result in a gradual decline or attrition in the Studebaker dealer organization from about 2000 dealers at the time of the South Bend closing to only 450 active dealers by the time all production of Studebakers ended in March 1966.[41]

However, exactly what role the dealer obligations played in the decision is not clear from the minutes of Studebaker Corporation Board meetings. It does appear there was at least a nominal commitment by the members of the Board to try to keep Studebaker in the automobile business. Guthrie's statement, quoted above, indicates at least verbal commitment to do so. At the same December 12, 1963, Board meeting, Burlingame stated: "Advertisements were to be run by the Corporation and by Mercedes Benz Sales, Inc. during the week of December 16 in an attempt to develop public confidence in the permanence of the Canadian automotive operation." At a minimum, therefore, there may have been lip service being given to the idea of staying in the automobile business with a "let's wait and see what happens" attitude toward the Canadian production experiment.

As indicated earlier, Burlingame put a great deal of emphasis on controlling costs. This was evident even in the December 9, 1963, corporate Public Relations News Release, sent out under his name, announcing the South Bend closing. In laying out the plans for the future of the Automotive Division, Burlingame stated in that news release that to keep costs to a competitive level, few major styling changes to Studebaker cars were planned during the subsequent few years. He did say that running changes to mechanical and functional aspects of the cars would be made as found to be desirable.

Perhaps the keenest insights we have into Burlingame's thinking regarding the Automotive Division after the move to Canada come in an August 24, 1965, letter that he sent to Gordon E. Grundy, the president of the Studebaker Automotive Division, after the move to Canada. As background to understanding the letter, a word is in order about Gordon E. Grundy. He was a Canadian chartered accountant and had worked for accounting firms before going to work at Studebaker of Canada in 1946. In 1958, he was appointed president of Studebaker of Canada, Limited.[42] Grundy has been portrayed as a strong advocate for Studebaker of Canada and its opportunities to continue the company in the automobile industry. In an interview of Grundy conducted by Loren Pennington, Grundy said he was given to understand that the company would make an all-out effort to remain in business in Canada. In spite of the challenges faced, Grundy made every effort to make the Canadian operation successful.[43]

Richard Quinn, a Studebaker historian and writer of a column for the Studebaker Drivers Club publication, *Turning Wheels*, discovered in 2008 a copy of the letter sent from Burlingame to Grundy in August of 1965, replying to a letter from Grundy of August 19, 1965. Unfortunately, the original letter from Grundy to Burlingame has not been found, but the general nature of that letter can be gleaned from Burlingame's response. Quoted here are some short excerpts from the response of Burlingame in which his penchant for cost control as a requisite for keeping Studebaker in the automobile business becomes very evident:

> ...we must not lose sight of the fact that substantial cost reduction must be instituted for the Automotive Division.... At this point in time I am cautiously optimistic about the short term prospects for the Automotive Division in that I believe it can be profitable for the year 1965.... With [the] substantial decline in dealer orders to date, ... profit projections cannot be attained unless expense reduction is initiated.... It is my fear that the program you espouse would create the very result which we are all trying to avoid — namely a loss operation which ... will not be tolerated.... You suggest a broad program of new dealer appointments coupled with cancellation of inactive dealers ... it is far preferable to use available funds to support active dealers rather than to buy back cars and unneeded parts from inactive dealers.... You suggest a supplementary line of imported vehicles.... Negotiations of a lengthy and serious nature were undertaken unsuccessfully to secure rights on a satisfactory basis to Datsun, Toyota, and Prince. However, the time is not presently appropriate to negotiate for an additional line of cars in view of the priority that must be given to the SASCO [Studebaker Automotive Sales Corporation] reorganization [which Grundy had suggested].... Engineering is over budget and will become seriously so if four additional personnel are transferred in from International as you have requested. When we have Divisions whose very existence is threatened if profitable operations cannot be maintained, we must closely examine the operation of such Division. My responsibility as President of the Corporation permits me to do no less irrespective of my personal desires and wishes.... In the final analysis, plotting the future policy course of the Automotive Division is a question of your judgment or mine. Based on my experience with automotive for over 40 years, I believe that adding expense in promotion and other areas is not going to stimulate sales activity sufficient to warrant the added cost entailed. I have seen this attempted without success for so many years that my mind is firmly made up that the way to weather the current storm is by reducing expenses to try and insure [sic] a solid base of profitable operations from which to build.[44]

In the letter, Burlingame agrees with Grundy that he (Grundy) should be moving forward in the area of 1967 model development, tooling, and styling and asks him to make a proposal as to what should be done and the projected cost. Grundy did have the Dearborn, Michigan, design firm of Marcks, Hazelquist, and Powers, Inc., make proposals for the 1967 and beyond Studebakers. The proposed 1967 styling involved extremely modest trim changes to the body style that had been introduced for the 1964 model year. In another Marcks, Hazelquist, and Powers proposal for beyond 1967, that basic body shell would have received a major facelift that brought back the Hawk styling theme on a sedan body shell.[45] In February 1966, Grundy asked for funds to tool the 1967 model with modest trim changes. The request was for under $30,000, but was denied by management, and Grundy was notified there would be no 1967 Studebakers.[46]

About the same time that the sales of 1966 Studebakers were in a steep decline in late 1965 and early 1966, it appears another problem developed. A deck lid (trunk lid)

After the move of all Studebaker production to Canada, Byers Burlingame, as president of Studebaker, kept the Automotive Division on a very short leash. Very little money was available for product development or promotion. Burlingame saw the Automotive Division in purely financial terms. If it made a profit, it could survive. If it lost money, it had to be closed. However, in spite of the tight budgetary controls on the division, Gordon Grundy, as president of the Automotive Division, was able to implement a very modest facelift on the 1966 Studebakers, as shown in this picture of a 1966 Daytona sports sedan.

die apparently broke. One theory that has been advanced is that the cost of replacing the die might have been the cause for Studebaker to finally shut down after the existing supply of trunk lids was used up. The deck lid is a complex component with several dies needed to produce several different stampings for the deck lid assembly. Therefore, while the failure of a deck lid stamping die may have been a contributing cause to the final decision to end Studebaker production on March 17, 1966, it is doubtful it was the primary reason.[47] Given Burlingame's cost-conscious approach to the business, the decline in car sales combined with losses in the Automotive Division of $300,000 in 1965 and continuing losses in 1966 (see footnote "g" of Table 2 in Chapter 3 for details), it is not surprising that the administrative decision was made to discontinue Studebaker automobile production.

Byers A. Burlingame can be characterized as a risk averter. He saw his primary responsibility as being to the shareholders (owners) of the Studebaker Corporation. His statements and his actions are consistent throughout the portion of his career for which we have a written record, i.e., the minutes of the Board of Directors and his public statements and correspondence. He appears to have seen profitable operations in the Automotive Division as being a function primarily of cost control. Product design, planning, and marketing were not his strong points and, probably, not his main areas of interest in his role as financier and as president of the company.

Burlingame retired as president of Studebaker in 1967. In paying tribute to him in the *Studebaker Corporation Annual Report to Shareholders for 1966*, Randolph H. Guthrie, board chair, said the following:

> Mr. Burlingame assumed the presidency during the dark days of November 1963 and shouldered the responsibilities of (1) discontinuing the then primary business of the Corporation of manufacturing automobiles in South Bend, Indiana; and (2) revitalizing the Corporation's present business. Both of these objectives have now been achieved. From an operating loss of approximately $17 million in 1963, the Corporation has progressed to an operating profit of approximately $8 million in 1964, $10.7 million in 1965 and $16.5 million in 1966. I suggest that this has been one of the truly remarkable corporate recoveries in business annals.

Whatever one might think of Byers Burlingame as an automobile industry executive and his commitment, or lack thereof, to the Studebaker automobile, it is clear that he fulfilled what he viewed as his primary responsibility; that is, he returned a profit to the shareholders of the Studebaker Corporation. Byers A. Burlingame died in 1970 at age 70.

Harold E. Churchill

He was a teacher, engineer, division head, corporate president, and consultant. How, then, do we assess the career of Harold E. Churchill? In the Introduction to this book the question was raised whether Churchill was a successful president of the Studebaker-Packard Corporation.

Certainly, after a 43-year career with Studebaker, it must be concluded he had a deep commitment to and a significant impact on the company. When he assumed the presidency of S-P in 1956, he undertook what might have been the most difficult challenge in the United States automobile industry at the time. It certainly was the biggest challenge of his career. He said he would give it his best — and he did.

Whether it was accepting the assistance of Curtiss-Wright Corporation's Roy T. Hurley while maintaining a degree of autonomy at Studebaker-Packard, or rallying his staff and work force to develop and produce the Lark, or helping engineer the placement of General Motors engines in Canadian-built Studebakers, Churchill consistently exhibited characteristics of leadership. From interviews of workers at all levels at Studebaker to statements by members of the Board of Directors, it is evident that "Church" was both deeply respected as an administrator and leader and liked as a person. It appears his motivational style was one of positive reinforcement of the efforts of his subordinates combined with a clear vision and specific focus on the task at hand.

The Lark, of course, was Churchill's greatest success. Yet one could argue it was also his greatest failure. It took both a vision of the emerging compact car market and courage to commit the limited resources of Studebaker to the production of the Lark. However, the initial success of the Lark could not be maintained, and competitive compacts of the Big Three and American Motors overwhelmed the Lark in the marketplace. Could an earlier commitment to a four-cylinder car — say for 1960 or 1961— have helped Studebaker? We will never know the answer to that question. Even if the four-cylinder car on a 100-inch wheelbase and its companion 108.5-inch wheelbase six and V8 models

Harold E. Churchill at his desk in the Studebaker administration building, holding a dealer promotional model of a 1956 Studebaker Golden Hawk. Churchill's vision of a compact car, the Lark, was the only vision for the Automotive Division of Studebaker-Packard Corporation that had even modest success in the 1954 to 1966 period (Richard Quinn).

had been produced and brought to market, there was no guarantee that the success of the 1959 Lark would have been repeated. In fact, one can argue that the designs of Randy Faurot for these cars, while being attractive, were not clearly distinguishable from earlier Larks. So we are left with the open question of whether these models could have saved Studebaker. In the auto industry, where large volumes and significant economies of scale determine the success or failure of firms, Studebaker and Churchill were faced with an enormous challenge they were not able to overcome.

When he became president of S-P, Churchill observed that it took an adjustment on his part to realize that now his responsibility was to the owners of the company, the stockholders, and not just to his fellow employees. Throughout the discussions within the Board of Directors meetings and even in the oral history interview of Churchill by R.T. King of Indiana University, one can detect the signs of an inner tension for Churchill between his passion for Studebaker the automobile producer and his responsibility for Studebaker the corporate entity. Perhaps the most telling moment in his career at Studebaker was when, at the November 28, 1960, Board meeting, he recommended against spending $24 million to tool the four-cylinder car line that he had so passionately been instrumental in developing. The "corporate" Harold Churchill had finally won out. That devotion to the corporation, in the very positive sense of the word, manifested itself in continued selfless efforts on his part to help in the transition of Studebaker to Canadian production and then assistance with the ongoing acquisition program of the company. When asked in the oral history interview about his views concerning diversification by Studebaker, Churchill responded: "I supported the program. Well, my heart and soul was automobiles. You have to be realistic about these things. After all, the people who had money invested in the Studebaker Corporation had a right to expect a return on their investment. And, this was a field in which I felt we could get a return on their investment."

In that oral interview, Churchill was asked if, by 1960, he felt the automotive part of Studebaker was going to continue to be viable. He responded, "I was concerned that they couldn't. I have to be honest about it." Asked if he thought others in management shared that concern, he said it wouldn't have surprised him if they did. But, as he did many times in describing his successes, he gave credit to those with whom he worked and noted that if that concern existed it didn't display itself in lack of zeal and response to the automotive programs of the corporation.

When asked in the oral history interview what he thought his major contribution at Studebaker was, he responded: "I think we did some things in the automobile business that preserved the Studebaker Corporation." He qualified his statement by observing his personal successes were primarily in engineering and manufacturing but not marketing.

It is unusual for a person who had been the chief executive officer of a corporation to continue on as a director and consultant to the firm after leaving the presidency. Yet in spite of the tumultuous conditions under which Churchill left the CEO position of Studebaker-Packard in September 1960, and then the staff position of president on February 1, 1961, he continued on as an active director and consultant to the firm. Those positions for him were more than honorary; he made very real contributions to the company through analysis of potential acquisitions and in assessing the engineering needs associated with the moving of all Studebaker automobile production to Canada in 1964. His loyalty and selfless approach to responsibilities were indicative of the character of the man who had devoted over 40 years of his life to Studebaker-Packard and had led the company as CEO for nearly five years. Harold E. Churchill died at age 77 on August 1, 1980, in South Bend.

Four Presidents, Four Visions for Studebaker-Packard Corporation

An examination of the history of Studebaker-Packard Corporation, and its successor after 1962, the Studebaker Corporation, from the time of the merger in 1954 to the ending of automobile production in 1966, encompasses the period of leadership of four persons as president of the company — James J. Nance, Harold E. Churchill, Sherwood H. Egbert, and Byers A. Burlingame. These four presidents represented four distinct leadership styles. They also represented four distinctly different visions for the firm's position in the automobile industry.

Before comparing the visions of Nance, Churchill, Egbert, and Burlingame, it is interesting to make some further comparisons based on their backgrounds. Nance and Egbert came to their leadership positions in the auto industry as outsiders: Nance came from the Hotpoint Division of appliance maker General Electric, and Egbert came from the industrial firm McCulloch, known for products ranging from chain saws to automobile superchargers. To lead the automaker, therefore, they had to undergo a very steep learning curve. Churchill and Burlingame, though, each had many years of experience in the auto industry before assuming the presidency of Studebaker. Churchill's experience, however, was quite different from that of Burlingame. Churchill's career path from 1926 to 1956, prior to becoming president of the corporation, had been as an engineer steeped in the automotive heritage of Studebaker. He fully understood the mechanics of the automobile and had an appreciation for what kind of vehicle the market was calling for when he assumed the presidency — i.e., a compact car that became the Lark. Burlingame, on the other hand, understood the finances of the automobile industry after a 40-year career at Packard and then Studebaker, but did not have a noticeable background in product and market development.

Each of the four men had a clear vision of where he wanted to take Studebaker-Packard. Nance, although lacking depth in the automobile industry, had the vision of making S-P the fourth full-line producer of automobiles in the United States after General Motors, Ford, and Chrysler. Whether he fully understood the economies of scale, marketing, and financial implications of his dream to make Studebaker-Packard a full-line producer of automobiles is problematic. In all fairness, Nance was constrained by the unexpected death of George Mason of Nash, who, together with Nance, had dreamt of combining Studebaker, Packard, Nash, and Hudson into that fourth full-line automobile company. But no one can claim that Nance did not give the full-line concept a noble attempt at Studebaker-Packard. The economic realities of the industry, however, doomed his vision before it ever got off the ground in the way he had hoped.

In a sense, Egbert also had grandiose visions for Studebaker's position in the automobile industry. He apparently could be described as a "car guy" who was interested in high-performance and stylish vehicles. He did recognize the need for Studebaker to have products that would draw customers into the showroom. However, the vision he had of the Avanti serving that purpose could be characterized as somewhat naïve from a marketing standpoint. Although the Avanti was developed in a remarkably short period of time, the production problems associated with the car erased any marketing and public relations benefit the company may have received from the car. Also, the Avanti was a niche vehicle geared to the personal sports car, high-performance market. Egbert's inexperience in the auto industry may have caused him not to understand fully what draws actual buyers (as opposed to curiosity seekers) into the showroom: i.e., a car they can relate to, afford, and feel good about owning. In that sense, Churchill of Studebaker-Packard, George Romney of American Motors, and then, by 1960, the Big Three automakers, recognized the compact car as a means of drawing large numbers of actual buyers into the showroom.

Byers Burlingame's vision for Studebaker was quite different from that of Churchill, Nance, and Egbert. He could be described as a pure finance person. The automobile appears to have been simply a means to an end — that end being profits to be distributed to the shareholders of the corporation. From what has been discovered thus far in Board of Director's minutes, letters, and public statements by Burlingame, he had no vision for the automobile as a concept, *per se*. There is no evidence he had any plan for the type of car Studebaker could or should build or the styling or engineering features it should encompass. Gordon Grundy, serving as president of the Studebaker Automotive Division under Burlingame, did have such a vision, but Burlingame's preoccupation with reducing costs and enhancing corporate profits constrained Grundy from carrying out his (Grundy's) vision for the Automotive Division.

While it is tempting to be critical of Burlingame for his lack of vision for Studebaker's Automotive Division, it is necessary to understand that the CEO of a corporation does have a responsibility to the shareholders. Churchill made that observation as well, in the oral history interview of him done by Indiana University, when he said his responsibility switched from being an employee to having to look out for the interests of the shareholders when he became president.

None of this is to imply that Nance and Egbert did not have the interests of shareholders in mind in their vision and decisions. However, it may be concluded that Burlingame and Churchill, with the resources and knowledge available to them at the moment they assumed the presidency of Studebaker-Packard, had a firmer grasp of what could and could not be done to enhance shareholder value.

It is significant that although the four presidents of Studebaker-Packard that have been discussed in this book each had a vision, and quite different visions at that, for the automotive operations of the company, none of those visions was successful in assuring the permanence of production of the Studebaker or Packard automobiles. As discussed in earlier chapters, the economics of the automobile industry as related to economies of scale and the costs of developing new products were severe constraints on the ability of independent automobile producers to survive. The survival of American Motors during this period (i.e., the 1950s and 1960s) can be attributed to the foresight of George Mason and his management team at Nash to develop the Rambler and the courage and foresight of George Romney as he assumed the leadership of American Motors to further develop and cultivate the market for the Rambler. As such, AMC had a strong head start in the compact car market, which enabled it to survive the onslaught of the Big Three in compact cars in 1960. Ultimately, though, even AMC succumbed to the pressures and realities of the automobile industry after the resignation of George Romney (to become governor of Michigan) in 1962. After merging with Kaiser Jeep Corporation in 1970, AMC was controlled through heavy investment by Renault of France in 1979, and then was absorbed into Chrysler Corporation in 1987.[48]

Thus, the scenario under which Studebaker could have survived as an automobile producer is not intuitively clear. All four presidents discussed here gave that survival a chance, although they approached the Automotive Division with quite differing strategies. That Studebaker was able to survive as a corporate entity through its diversification program, ultimately to be absorbed as a going concern into other corporate entities through a series of mergers after Byers Burlingame retired in the late 1960s, was of benefit to the shareholders but of little comfort to the thousands of workers in South Bend and Hamilton who lost their jobs when automobile production ended in those facilities. However, the argument also can be made that all employees of Studebaker, administrative, clerical, etc., in addition to the automotive production workers, might have lost their jobs if the company had gone into bankruptcy and was liquidated. So, while there were clear losers in the failure of automotive operations at Studebaker, there also were gainers — those persons whose jobs were saved and the investment of the shareholders.

The history of Studebaker-Packard Corporation during the period of the presidency of Harold Churchill from 1956 through early 1961, and then his role as a consultant into 1968, confirm that he was a successful president of the company. He was not successful in building a basis for the long-term survival of the Studebaker or Packard automobiles. However, as Churchill himself observed, he was successful in rescuing the company from what many thought was certain bankruptcy in both 1956 and 1958. As such, his vision for Studebaker-Packard to enter the compact car market with the Lark in 1959 laid the foundation for the carrying out of the diversification program of S-P and ultimate financial success in the Burlingame administration. From an historical perspective, Churchill's decision to build the Lark had its roots in his experience at Studebaker when he was involved in the development of the Champion in 1939. Therefore, it can be argued that Churchill's vision to "Champion" the development of the Lark, which ultimately made possible the preserving of Studebaker as a corporate entity, reflected not only his understanding of the automotive market in 1959, but also was a reflection of his long years of experience in the industry and at Studebaker. It is interesting to note, as well, that his term as president of the automotive company lasted the longest of the four presidents discussed here. Perhaps in a broader and more philosophical sense, Harold E. Churchill was successful, not only as a corporate leader, but as a determined, positive, visionary, understanding, and decent human being.

Appendix A: Studebaker Sedan Styling Evolution, 1953–1966

One of the challenges confronted by Harold Churchill, and the entire Studebaker-Packard Corporation, throughout the 1953 to 1966 period, and certainly during the presidency of Churchill between 1956 and 1961, was how to keep the body styling looking up-to-date without incurring very expensive model changeover and tooling costs. As Churchill acknowledged, the engineering of the cars was excellent, but the financial condition of the company precluded extensive and frequent styling changes. The result was that the body shell introduced in 1953 for the Studebaker sedans served as the basis for all the sedans Studebaker built from 1953 to 1966, including the 1957 and 1958 Packards. This Appendix uses illustrations and photographs from Studebaker and Studebaker-Packard showroom literature to trace the evolution of the styling of the cars under the conditions of severe budgetary constraints.

Top: The 1953 and 1954 Champion and Commander sedans were virtually identical except for minor trim changes. The basic body shell was introduced in 1953. Shown here is a 1954 Champion sedan on the 116.5-inch wheelbase. This basic body shell, with modifications, served Studebaker through the 1966 model year. *Middle:* The Land Cruiser on the 120.5-inch wheelbase was the top-of-the-line sedan in 1953 and 1954. Long wheelbase sedans through the end of Studebaker production in 1966 were based on the Land Cruiser body shell introduced in 1953. *Bottom:* The 1956 sedans departed from the sleeker style of the 1953 through 1955s because President James Nance wanted them to have a more conventional appearance. Pictured here is a 1956 Commander V8 sedan on the 116.5-inch wheelbase. Note that although the front clip and rear sheet metal are significantly changed from the 1953–1955 models, the basic body shell remained the same.

Appendix A: Studebaker Sedan Styling Evolution, 1953–1966

Top: The 1956 President Classic on the 120.5-inch wheelbase continued the luxury heritage of the Land Cruisers and the 1955 President State sedans. *Middle:* When Studebaker-Packard made the decision to consolidate Packard production in South Bend, the 1957 Packard Clippers were built on the 120.5-inch Studebaker President Classic body shell and chassis, which had its origins with the 1953 Studebaker Land Cruiser, but with a supercharger to enhance performance. *Bottom:* A subtle change to the old 1953 body shell was incorporated into the 1958 Studebaker and Packard sedans. That change was a slight lowering of the roof line, but the basic body still continued the original design. Pictured here is a sedan on the 116.5-inch wheelbase available in the Commander and Champion series.

Appendix A: Studebaker Sedan Styling Evolution, 1953–1966

Top: The 1958 Packard 4-door sedan on the 120.5-inch wheelbase was the most luxurious evolution of the 1953 body shell, but was the last of the Packard line, which was discontinued after the 1958 model year. *Bottom:* The 1959 Lark was a clever and ingenious adaptation of the 1953 body shell to a shorter 108.5-inch wheelbase. Interior space was essentially the same as the 116.5-inch wheelbase models of earlier years with a refreshing new look for the compact cars. Note, however, that the basic body shell maintained the original styling.

Top: The 1961 Larks on the 108.5-inch wheelbase featured a significant change in the basic body shell. Note that the "C" pillar (rear pillar) had a subtle change in its configuration to give the sedans a somewhat more modern look. *Bottom:* The last year for Studebaker production, and, therefore, the final evolution of the basic 1953 body shell, was in 1966. The 1966 Studebakers had only minor trim changes from the 1964 and 1965 models. By 1966, the basic 1953 body shell was somewhat disguised as a result of modified B (center) and C (rear) pillars. Four-door sedans continued on the 113-inch wheelbase and 2-door models were on the 108.5-inch wheelbase.

Appendix B: Studebaker Sport Coupe Styling Evolution, 1953–1964

As Churchill struggled with the issue of how to keep the Studebaker model lineup reasonably modern and attractive to the car-buying public, the question of what to do about the sporty coupes originally introduced in 1953, often called "Loewy coupes" but actually the styling work principally of Bob Bourke, confronted the company. The Hawk line introduced in 1956 was a major styling and performance victory for Studebaker-Packard. Likewise, the supercharged 1957 Golden Hawk and the companion Silver Hawks continued both the styling and performance heritage of the sport coupes. However, by 1959, as discussed in the text of the book, sales of Hawks had dropped off and Churchill almost eliminated them from the Studebaker product line. Dealer pressure convinced him to continue producing the Hawk, but on a more limited basis. Under Egbert, the Hawks underwent a major change with the introduction of the Gran Turismo Hawks. However, the body shell introduced in 1953 for the Studebaker coupes served as the basis for all the coupes and Hawks Studebaker-Packard built from 1953 to 1964, including the 1958 Packard Hawk. All Studebaker sport coupes were built on the 120.5-inch wheelbase. This Appendix uses illustrations and photographs from Studebaker and Studebaker-Packard showroom literature to trace the evolution of the styling of the coupes under the conditions of severe budgetary constraints.

Top: Bob Bourke's design for the 1953 Studebaker Starliner was one of the most beautiful automotive designs of the 20th century. Unfortunately, manufacturing problems prevented the cars from reaching their full market potential. Pictured here is a pillarless hardtop 1953 Commander Starliner. This design was the basis of all Studebaker sport coupes and Hawks built between 1953 and 1964. Except for minor trim changes, 1953 and 1954 Starliners were virtually identical. *Middle:* The sleek Starliner design also was applied to a pillared coupe. Pictured is a 1953 Starlight coupe available in the Commander and Champion series. The 1954 Starlight coupes had the same basic styling as the 1953s except for minor trim changes. *Bottom:* In 1956, Studebaker introduced its Hawk line of sports coupes. Top of the line was the Golden Hawk pillarless sport coupe hardtop, pictured here, which was based on the basic body shell of the 1953 Starliners. It was the only Hawk in 1956 to have the small fins on the rear fender.

Top: The 1956 Studebaker Hawk line had four models: the Golden Hawk, Silver Hawk, Power Hawk, and Flight Hawk. The Power Hawk and Flight Hawk, shown here, had identical styling based on the 1953 Starlight pillared sport coupe design. Power Hawks had the Studebaker 259-cubic-inch V8 engine and the Flight Hawks had the 185-cubic-inch six-cylinder engine. *Middle:* Top of the Studebaker Hawk line in 1957 and 1958 were the supercharged Golden Hawks based on the Starliner hardtop design. Styling differences between 1957 and 1958 models were confined to minor trim changes. *Bottom:* The Hawk line was simplified for 1957 and 1958. The Silver Hawk had the same fin design as the Golden Hawk with slightly different trim. The basic body for the Silver Hawk no longer was the Starliner (as had been the case in 1956), but rather the pillared Starlight coupe design. The 1957 and 1958 Silver Hawks were available with the 289-cubic-inch V8, 259-cubic-inch V8, or 185-cubic-inch six-cylinder engines. The pillared Silver Hawk design was kept in production with only minor trim and interior changes through 1961.

Appendix B: Studebaker Sport Coupe Styling Evolution, 1953–1964 165

Top: The major news in the Hawk series for 1958 was the addition of a Packard Hawk to the line. The Packard Hawk was based on 1958 Golden Hawk running gear, including the supercharged 289-cubic-inch engine. The front-end styling of the Packard Hawk featured a sloping fiberglass hood. The car had a leather interior and was the highest-priced Studebaker-Packard automobile in 1958. Like the Golden Hawk, its basic body design was based on the 1953 Starliner hardtop. *Bottom:* Brooks Stevens restyled the Hawk for 1962, with the result that the basic 1953 Starliner pillarless body shell was given a whole new look of sporty elegance. Pictured here is the 1962 Gran Turismo Hawk. The Gran Turismo design was maintained with minor changes through the end of Hawk production in the 1964 model year.

Appendix C: Studebaker-Packard Vehicle Specifications, 1953–1966

Harold E. Churchill was president of the Studebaker-Packard Corporation from July 1956 to February 1, 1961. This Appendix, however, covers Studebaker products from 1953 to 1966 to give some comparison of the cars and trucks built in the Churchill years to what came immediately before and after Churchill's time as president. Justification for including the 1953 through 1956 and 1962 through 1966 Studebakers in this list of specifications is that all the cars produced by Studebaker-Packard during the Churchill years, and afterward in the Egbert and Burlingame years, were based on the 1953 basic Studebaker sedan and sport coupe body shells (except the Avanti) and running gear (including the Avanti). Also, as a means of comparison with the 1957 and 1958 Packards, specifications for the 1955 and 1956 Packards and Clippers are given. While every effort has been made to be as complete as possible, the list of models and specifications shown here is claimed to be only a representative summary of the cars and trucks built by Studebaker-Packard that Churchill had any real influence over as president of the company. S-P built many variations of its models, all of which had many options available. Particularly in the truck line, there were many engine, transmission, wheelbase, Gross Vehicle Weight, and other options available, making the number of possible combinations to configure a truck almost infinite. Therefore, a 100 percent comprehensive listing is very difficult to achieve. The source of the information contained in these charts is printed literature produced by Studebaker-Packard, primarily for showroom distribution, during the 1953 through 1966 model years.

To aid the reading and understanding of the charts, the following guide is provided:

- Wheelbase, length, and bore and stroke dimensions are in inches.
- The 1953 and 1954 V8 engines built by Studebaker were the 232-cubic-inch version with a 3⅜-inch bore and 3¼-inch stroke.
- The V8 engine available in 1955 was the 259-cubic-inch version.
- During the 1956–1964 period, the V8 engines produced by Studebaker-Packard were the 259- and 289-cubic-inch models. In the chart they are simply referred

to as "259" or "289." One exception is the Avanti, which had both a 289-cubic-inch engine available and a 304-cubic-inch engine option.
- In 1963 and 1964, Studebaker four- and two-door sedans, and Hawks, were available with the 289 V8 "Thunderbolt" engine, or with the high-performance 289 V8 Avanti "Jet Thrust" engine, or the Avanti 289 V8 supercharged V8 "Jet Thrust" engine.
- The Packard-built V8 engines in 1955 were as follows:
  - 352-cubic-inch with a 4-inch bore and 3½-inch stroke was standard on the Packards and Clipper Customs.
  - 320-cubic-inch with a 3.8125-inch bore and 3½-inch stroke was standard on the Clipper Super and Deluxe models.
- The Packard-built V8 engines in 1956 were as follows:
  - 374 cubic inches with a 4⅛-inch bore and 3½-inch stroke was standard on the Packard Patrician, Caribbean, and "400" Hardtop.
  - 352 cubic inches with a 4-inch bore and 3½-inch stroke was used on all Clippers and the mid-year introduced Packard Executive models and the Studebaker Golden Hawk.
- Supercharged models are designated by "SC."
- Bore and stroke of the 289 engine were: 3.56-inch bore, 3.62-inch stroke.
- Bore and stroke of the 259 engine were: 3.56-inch bore, 3.25-inch stroke.
- The Avanti 304 engine option had a bore of 3.65 inches and a stroke of 3.62 inches.
- Note: The 289 engine with a two-barrel carburetor produced 210 horsepower. With a four-barrel carburetor, available as an option on some models, it produced 225 horsepower. Supercharged versions of the 289 engine in 1957 and 1958 produced 275 horsepower.
- Note: The 259 engine with a two-barrel carburetor produced 180 horsepower. With a four-barrel carburetor available as an option on some models, it produced 195 horsepower.
- During the 1957–1961 period, at various times, Studebaker-Packard produced 185- and 169-cubic-inch L-head six-cylinder engines for passenger cars and trucks. A 245-cubic-inch engine was made as an option for some trucks. These various engines are referred to as "245," or "185," or "169." OHV (overhead valve) 169-cubic-inch six-cylinder engines were introduced in 1961.
- Bore and stroke of the 185 engine were: 3-inch bore, 4⅜-inch stroke.
- Bore and stroke of the 169 engine were: 3-inch bore, 4-inch stroke.
- Bore and stroke of the 245 engine were: 3 5/16-inch bore, 4¾-inch stroke
- Note: The 185 engine produced 101 horsepower in passenger cars and 92 horsepower in trucks.
- In 1955, Studebaker introduced a 224-cubic-inch V8 engine on its ½-ton light duty trucks. The engine had an 3.5625-inch bore and 2.812-inch stroke.
- Note: the 169 L-head engine produced 90 horsepower; the 169 OHV engine produced 112 horsepower.

- Note: the 245 L-head engine produced 106 horsepower.
- In 1965 and 1966, Studebaker used engines built by General Motors in Canada.
  - In 1965 and 1966 a 194-cubic-inch 6-cylinder engine with 3.563-inch bore and 3.25-inch stroke was available.
  - In 1966 only, a 230-cubic-inch 6-cylinder engine with 3.875-inch bore and 3.25-inch stroke was an option.
  - In both 1965 and 1966, a 283-cubic-inch V8 engine with 3.875-inch bore and 3.00-inch stroke was available.
- Beginning in 1962, Studebaker Lark model designations changed.
  - In 1962, hardtops and convertibles were available in either "Regal" or "Daytona" trim, with the Daytona being the more upscale of the two. However, dimensions and engine options were the same for both trim levels.
  - In 1963, two- and four-door Lark sedans were available as Standard, Regal, or Custom models (Custom being the highest trim level). The Cruiser no longer was referred to as a Lark and was the top of the line of the sedans, as in previous years. Hardtops and convertibles were designated only as Daytonas. The new Wagonaire station wagon with a sliding roof was available in either Regal or Daytona trim levels.
  - In 1964, the Lark name was used sparingly in advertising and model designation. The Commander name returned to the Studebaker line for its midline two- and four-door sedans for either 6-cylinder or 8-cylinder models. In showroom literature, only the Commander and Challenger two- and four-door sedans were referred to as Larks. The lowest trim level for the 6- and 8-cylinder sedans was the Challenger. Hardtops and convertibles continued to be called Daytonas. Wagonaires and 4-door sedans were available as Challengers, Commanders, or Daytonas.
  - In 1965 and 1966, basic two- and four-door sedans were designated Commanders. A sport two-door sedan (no longer a hardtop, but a two-door pillared sedan with sport trim and interior) was designated the Daytona. Top of the line was the four-door Cruiser.
- On the charts, if an "x" appears in a box, it indicates that feature was available, sometimes as an option, in that model. "Automatic" indicates automatic transmission available in that model.
- GVW in truck specifications is Gross Vehicle Weight.
- Specification data presented here were taken primarily from Studebaker-Packard factory literature.

Studebaker-Packard Models and Specifications, 1953–1966

Note: Harold Churchill was President of Studebaker-Packard Corporation during the 1957–1961 model years.

Representative Examples of Passenger Cars

Year	Make	Model	Wheelbase	Length	Engines	Automatic
1953	Studebaker	Land Cruiser V8	120.5	202.6	232	X
1953	Studebaker	Commander V8 Sedan	116.5	198.6	232	X
1953	Studebaker	Commander V8 Coupe	120.5	202	232	X
1953	Studebaker	Champion 6 Sedan	116.5	198.6	169	X
1953	Studebaker	Champion 6 Coupe	120.5	202	169	X
1954	Studebaker	Land Cruiser V8	120.5	202.6	232	X
1954	Studebaker	Commander V8 Sedan	116.5	198.6	232	X
1954	Studebaker	Commander V8 Coupe	120.5	202	232	X
1954	Studebaker	Champion 6 Sedan	116.5	198.6	169	X
1954	Studebaker	Champion 6 Coupe	120.5	202	169	X
1955	Studebaker	President V8	120.5	206.25	259	X
1955	Studebaker	Commander V8 Sedan	116.5	202.25	259	X
1955	Studebaker	Commander V8 Coupe	120.5	204.4	259	X
1955	Studebaker	Champion 6 Coupe	120.5	204.4	185	X
1955	Packard	Patrician, Caribbean, "400"	127	218.5	352	X
1955	Packard	Clipper Custom	122	214.8	352	X
1955	Packard	Clipper Super & Deluxe	122	214.8	320	X
1956	Studebaker	Golden Hawk V8	120.5	203.9	352	X
1956	Studebaker	President Classic V8	120.5	204.75	289	X
1956	Studebaker	President V8	116.5	200.75	289	X
1956	Studebaker	Sky Hawk V8	120.5	204	289	X
1956	Studebaker	Power Hawk V8	120.5	204	259	X
1956	Studebaker	Commander Sedan V8	116.5	200.75	259	X
1956	Studebaker	Flight Hawk 6	120.5	204	185	X
1956	Studebaker	Champion 6 Sedan	116.5	200.75	185	X
1956	Packard	Patrician, Caribbean, "400"	127	218.5	374	X
1956	Packard	Clipper	122	214.8	352	X
1957	Packard	Clipper V8 Town Sedan	120.5	211.8	289-SC	X
1957	Packard	Clipper V8 Country Sedan	116.5	204.8	289-SC	X
1957	Studebaker	Golden Hawk V8	120.5	204	289 SC	X
1957	Studebaker	Silver Hawk V8	120.5	204	289	X
1957	Studebaker	Silver Hawk 6	120.5	204	185	X
1957	Studebaker	President Classic V8	120.5	206.4	289	X
1957	Studebaker	President V8	116.5	202.4	289	X
1957	Studebaker	Broadmoor Wagon V8	116.5	202.4	289	X
1957	Studebaker	Commander V8 Sedans	116.5	202.4	259	X
1957	Studebaker	Provincial V8 Wagon	116.5	202.4	259	X
1957	Studebaker	Parkview V8 Wagon	116.5	202.4	259	X
1957	Studebaker	Champion 6 Sedans	116.5	202.4	185	X
1957	Studebaker	Pelham 6 Wagon	116.5	202.4	185	X
1957	Studebaker	Scotsman 6 Sedan	116.5	202.4	185	
1958	Packard	Hawk V8	120.5	205.1	289-SC	X
1958	Packard	Sedan V8	120.5	213.2	289	X
1958	Packard	Hardtop V8	116.5	209.2	289	X
1958	Packard	Wagon V8	116.5	206.2	289	X
1958	Studebaker	Golden Hawk V8	120.5	204	289-SC	X

Appendix C: Studebaker-Packard Vehicle Specifications, 1953–1966

Year	Make	Model	Wheelbase	Length	Engines	Automatic
1958	Studebaker	Silver Hawk V8	120.5	204	259 & 289	X
1958	Studebaker	Silver Hawk 6	120.5	204	185	X
1958	Studebaker	President 4-Door	120.5	206.4	289	X
1958	Studebaker	President V8 Hardtop	116.5	202.4	289	X
1958	Studebaker	Provincial V8 Wagon	116.5	202.4	259	X
1958	Studebaker	Commander V8 Sedan	116.5	202.4	259	X
1958	Studebaker	Champion 6 Sedan	116.5	202.4	185	X
1958	Studebaker	Scotsman 6 Sedan	116.5	202.4	185	
1959	Studebaker	Lark V8 Sedan	108.5	175	259	X
1959	Studebaker	Lark 6 Sedan	108.5	175	169	X
1959	Studebaker	Lark V8 Hardtop	108.5	175	259	X
1959	Studebaker	Lark 6 Hardtop	108.5	175	169	X
1959	Studebaker	Lark V8 Wagon	113	184.5	259	X
1959	Studebaker	Lark 6 Wagon	113	184.5	169	X
1959	Studebaker	Econ-O-Miler V8 Taxi	113	179	259	X
1959	Studebaker	Econ-O-Miler 6 Taxi	113	179	169	X
1959	Studebaker	Silver Hawk V8	120.5	204	259	X
1959	Studebaker	Silver Hawk 6	120.5	204	169	X
1960	Studebaker	Lark V8 Sedan	108.5	175	259	X
1960	Studebaker	Lark 6 Sedan	108.5	175	169	X
1960	Studebaker	Lark V8 Hardtop	108.5	175	259	X
1960	Studebaker	Lark 6 Hardtop	108.5	175	169	X
1960	Studebaker	Lark V8 Wagon	113	184.5	259	X
1960	Studebaker	Lark 6 Wagon	113	184.5	169	X
1960	Studebaker	Econ-O-Miler V8 Taxi	113	179	259	X
1960	Studebaker	Econ-O-Miler 6 Taxi	113	179	169	X
1960	Studebaker	Silver Hawk V8	120.5	204	289	X
1961	Studebaker	Lark V8 Sedan	108.5	175	259	X
1961	Studebaker	Lark OHV 6 Sedan	108.5	175	169	X
1961	Studebaker	Lark V8 Hardtop	108.5	175	259	X
1961	Studebaker	Lark OHV 6 Hardtop	108.5	175	169	X
1961	Studebaker	Lark V8 Wagon	113	184.5	259	X
1961	Studebaker	Lark OHV 6 Wagon	113	184.5	169	X
1961	Studebaker	Econ-O-Miler V8 Taxi	113	179	259	X
1961	Studebaker	Econ-O-Miler OHV 6 Taxi	113	179	169	X
1961	Studebaker	Lark V8 Cruiser	113	179	259 or 289	X
1961	Studebaker	Silver Hawk V8	120.5	204	289	X
1962	Studebaker	Lark Cruiser V8	113	188	259 or 289	X
1962	Studebaker	Lark Cruiser OHV 6	113	188	169	X
1962	Studebaker	Lark 4-door Sedan V8	113	188	259 or 289	X
1962	Studebaker	Lark 4-door Sedan OHV 6	113	188	169	X
1962	Studebaker	Lark all 2-door V8 models	109	184	259 or 289	X
1962	Studebaker	Lark all 2-door model OHV 6	109	184	169	X
1962	Studebaker	Lark 4-door Wagon V8	113	187	259 or 289	X
1962	Studebaker	Lark 4-door Wagon OHV 6	113	187	169	X
1962	Studebaker	Gran Turismo Hawk	120.5	204	289	X
1963	Studebaker	Cruiser V8	113	188	289*	X
1963	Studebaker	All 4-door Sedans V8	113	188	259 or 289*	X
1963	Studebaker	All 4-door Sedans OHV 6	113	188	169	X
1963	Studebaker	All 2-door V8 models	109	184	259 or 289*	X
1963	Studebaker	All 2-door models OHV 6	108.5	184	169	X

Appendix C: Studebaker-Packard Vehicle Specifications, 1953–1966

Year	Make	Model	Wheelbase	Length	Engines	Automatic
1963	Studebaker	4-door Wagonaire V8	113	187	259 or 289*	X
1963	Studebaker	4-door Wagonaire OHV 6	113	187	169	X
1963	Studebaker	Gran Turismo Hawk	120.5	204	289*	X
1963	Studebaker	Avanti	109	192.5	289*	X
1964	Studebaker	Cruiser V8	113	194	289*	X
1964	Studebaker	All 4-door Sedan V8	113	194	259 or 289*	X
1964	Studebaker	All 4-door Sedan OHV 6	113	194	169	X
1964	Studebaker	All 2-door V8 models	108.5	190	259 or 289*	X
1964	Studebaker	All 2-door model OHV 6	108.5	190	169	X
1964	Studebaker	Wagonaire V8	113	193	259 or 289*	X
1964	Studebaker	Wagonaire OHV 6	113	193	169	X
1964	Studebaker	Gran Turismo Hawk	120.5	204	289*	X
1964	Studebaker	Avanti	109	192.5	289*	X
1965	Studebaker	Cruiser OHV 6	113	194	194	X
1965	Studebaker	Cruiser V8	113	194	283	X
1965	Studebaker	Commander 2-door OHV 6	109	190	194	X
1965	Studebaker	Commander 2-door V8	109	190	283	X
1965	Studebaker	Commander 4-door OHV 6	113	194	194	X
1965	Studebaker	Commander 4-door V8	113	194	283	X
1965	Studebaker	Daytona 2-door OHV 6	109	190	194	X
1965	Studebaker	Daytona 2-door V8	109	190	283	X
1965	Studebaker	Wagonaire OHV 6	113	193	194	X
1965	Studebaker	Wagonaire V8	113	193	283	X
1966	Studebaker	Cruiser OHV 6	113	194	194 or 230	X
1966	Studebaker	Cruiser V8	113	194	283	X
1966	Studebaker	Commander 2-door OHV 6	109	190	194 or 230	X
1966	Studebaker	Commander 2-door V8	109	190	283	X
1966	Studebaker	Commander 4-door OHV 6	113	194	194 or 230	X
1966	Studebaker	Commander 4-door V8	113	194	283	X
1966	Studebaker	Daytona 2-door OHV 6	109	190	194 or 230	X
1966	Studebaker	Daytona 2-door V8	109	190	283	X
1966	Studebaker	Wagonaire OHV 6 cyl	113	193	194 or 230	X
1966	Studebaker	Wagonaire V8	113	193	283	X

* Available in either normal or supercharged form.

Studebaker Trucks: Representative Examples of Studebaker Trucks Available: 1954–1964 Models

Note: Many combinations of truck specifications were available in Studebaker trucks; not all could be shown here.

Year	Make	Model	Wheelbases	Engines					
				169-6	185-6	245-6	259-V8	289-V8	224-V8	232-V8
1954	Studebaker	Pickup ½-ton	112	X	X					
1954	Studebaker	Pickup ¾-ton	122	X	X					
1954	Studebaker	1-ton	131			X				
1954	Studebaker	1½-ton	155			X				
1954	Studebaker	1½-ton	171			X				X

Appendix C: Studebaker-Packard Vehicle Specifications, 1953–1966

Year	Make	Model	Wheelbases	169-6	185-6	245-6	259-V8	289-V8	224-V8	232-V8
1954	Studebaker	2-ton	171			X				X
1955	Studebaker	Pickup ½-ton	112		X				X	
1955	Studebaker	¾-ton	122						X	
1955	Studebaker	1-ton	122						X	
1955	Studebaker	1½-ton	131				X			
1955	Studebaker	2-ton	212				X			
1956	Studebaker	Pickup ½-ton	112		X				X	
1956	Studebaker	Pickup ½-ton	122		X				X	
1956	Studebaker	¾-ton	122				X			
1956	Studebaker	1-ton	131				X			
1957–1958	Studebaker	Pickup & Stake ½-ton	112, 122		X		X			
1957–1958	Studebaker	Pickup & Stake ¾-ton	122			X	X			
1957–1958	Studebaker	Pickup & Stake 1-ton	131			X	X			
1957–1958	Studebaker	Dump 2-ton HD	155					X		
1957–1958	Studebaker	Tractor	131, 155, 171, 195			X				
1958	Studebaker	Scotsman Pickup	112		X					
1959	Studebaker	Pickup-Stake ½-ton	112, 122			X	X	X		
1959	Studebaker	Pickup-Stake ¾-ton	122			X		X		
1959	Studebaker	Med. Duty Tractor	155					X		
1959	Studebaker	Pickup-Stake/ 4 × 4	112, 122, 131			X		X		
1959	Studebaker	Scotsman Pickup	112, 122	X	X	X	X			
1960–1961	Studebaker	Stakes, Flatbeds, Dumps, 1-ton 4 × 4 also available	131			X	X			
1960–1961	Studebaker	Dumps, etc. 1½ & 2-ton	131, 155, 171			X	X			
1960–1961	Studebaker	Tractors, etc. @ ton Heavy Duty	131, 155, 171, 195					X		
1960	Studebaker	Champ Pickup-Stake-Platform ½-ton	112, 122	X		X	X			
1960	Studebaker	Champ Pickup-Stake-Platform ¾-ton	122	X		X	X			
1961	Studebaker	Champ Pickup-Stake-Platform ½-ton	112, 122	X (OHV)			X			
1961	Studebaker	Champ-Stake-Platform ¾-ton	122	X (OHV)			X			

Appendix C: Studebaker-Packard Vehicle Specifications, 1953–1966

Year	Make	Model	Wheelbases	169-6	185-6	245-6	259-V8	289-V8	224-V8	232-V8
1961–1964	Studebaker	Diesels; Tractors, Dumps, etc. HD	131, 155, 171, 195	Engine was General Motors 4-cyl. Diesel, 212 c.i.d. which produced 130 horsepower						
1962	Studebaker	Champ ½-ton	112. 122	X (OHV)			X			
1962	Studebaker	Champ ¾-ton	122	X (OHV)			X			
1962	Studebaker	1-ton	131					X	X	
1962	Studebaker	1½-ton	155					X	X	
1962	Studebaker	2-ton	195						X	
1962	Studebaker	1-ton 4 × 4	131					X	X	
1963–1964	Studebaker	Champ ½-ton	112/122	X (OHV)			X			
1963–1964	Studebaker	Champ ¾-ton	122	X (OHV)			X			
1963–1964	Studebaker	1-ton	143					X	X	
1963–1964	Studebaker	1½-ton	155					X	X	
1963–1964	Studebaker	2-ton							X	

Chapter Notes

Introduction

1. S. Longstreet, *A Century on Wheels* (New York: Henry Holt, 1952), pp. 1–36.
2. B.R. Kimes, *Packard: A History of the Motor Car and the Company* (Princeton, NJ: Princeton Publishing, 1978), pp. 28–37.
3. J.A. Ward, *The Fall of the Packard Motor Car Company* (Stanford, CA: Stanford University Press, 1995), pp. 1–24.
4. T. Bonsall, T., *More Than They Promised: The Studebaker Story* (Stanford, CA: Stanford University Press, 2000), pp. 47–82.
5. R.R. Ebert and A.D. Wyant, "From Garfords to Fords: Prosperity and Crisis in the Lorain County Auto Industry," *Automotive History Review*, no. 53 (Autumn 2011): pp. 5–7.
6. Kimes, pp. 806–807.
7. Bonsall, Chapters 2, 3, and 4.
8. Sales and profit and loss data were obtained from the Studebaker Corporation *Annual Reports*, a Packard Motor Car Company Proxy Statement dated July 9, 1954, and selected issues of *Ward's Automotive Reports* and *Automotive News*.
9. Ward, pp. 53–81.
10. Ward, pp. 107–160; W.B. Harris, "The Breakdown of Studebaker-Packard," *Fortune* (October 1956): pp. 139–141, 222–232.
11. Ward, pp. 3–4.
12. D.T. Critchlow, *Studebaker: The Life and Death of an American Corporation* (Bloomington: Indiana University Press, 1996), p. 114.
13. Studebaker-Packard Corporation. *Annual Reports, 1955–1961*, and selected issues of *Ward's Automotive Reports*.
14. Kimes, pp. 624–640.
15. Council of Economic Advisors, *Economic Report of the President* (Washington, DC: United States Government Printing Office, January 1967), Tables B-2 and B-22.
16. "100 Year Almanac and Market Data Book," *Automotive News*, April 24, 1996.

Chapter 1

1. H.E. Churchill, interview by R.T. King, February 28–29, 1980. Economic History of Indiana in the Twentieth Century, 1976–1980 Project. Indiana University, Bloomington, IN. Call Number 80-013.
2. Churchill interview.
3. Ibid.
4. Ibid.
5. Ibid.
6. "Churchill Becomes Auto Firm President," *South Bend Tribune*, August 5, 1956, p. 1.
7. Critchlow, pp. 66–103.
8. M.D. Hendry, "One Can Do a Lot of Remembering in South Bend," *Automotive Quarterly* 10, no. 3 (Third Quarter 1972): p. 228–257.

9. Churchill interview.
10. Hendry, pp. 237–240.
11. Churchill interview.
12. Critchlow, pp. 66–103.
13. Churchill interview.
14. Ibid.
15. Bonsall, pp. 154–156.
16. Hendry, p. 247.
17. Churchill interview.
18. "Studebaker Chief Faces Big Job," *New York Times*, August 8, 1956, p. 46.

Chapter 2

1. Hendry, p. 237.
2. Bonsall, pp. 135–137.
3. Hendry, p. 240.
4. "Studebaker Chief Faces Big Job," p. 46.
5. Bonsall, pp. 157–159.
6. Hendry, p. 244.
7. Bonsall, pp. 182–209.
8. Hendry, p. 247.
9. Churchill interview.
10. Critchlow, p. 114.
11. S. Longstreet, *A Century on Wheels* (New York: Henry Holt, 1952), p. 109.
12. Churchill interview.
13. "Studebaker Chief Faces Big Job," p. 46.
14. Bonsall, pp. 218–219.
15. W.B. Harris, "The Breakdown of Studebaker-Packard" *Fortune* (October 1956), p. 222.
16. Harris, pp. 139–141; 222.
17. Studebaker-Packard Corporation, *Annual Reports*, 1955 and 1956. South Bend, IN.
18. J.S. Bain, *Barriers to New Competition* (Cambridge, MA: Harvard University Press, 1956).
19. C.E. Edwards, *Dynamics of the United States Automobile Industry* (Columbia, SC: University of South Carolina Press, 1965).

Chapter 3

1. Churchill interview.
2. "Soaring on Wings of the Lark," *Business Week*, June 20, 1959.
3. Complete bibliographic information of minutes of the Board of Directors and Board Executive Committee of Studebaker-Packard Corporation and the Studebaker Corporation referenced in this chapter may be found in the Bibliography.
4. D. Fettig, *The Region*, publication of the Federal Reserve Bank of Minneapolis, June 2008, pp. 33–34. http://www.minneapolisfed.org/publications_papers/pub_display.cfm?id=3485 (accessed December 21, 2008).
5. "Churchill Becomes Auto Firm President," *South Bend Tribune*, August 5, 1956, p. 1.
6. Churchill interview.
7. Churchill, Harold E., President, Studebaker-Packard Corporation. "Studebaker-Packard's Comeback Program for 1957." Remarks to Automotive and Financial Editors Press Conference, New York City, September 5, 1956. Harold E. Churchill Papers, Studebaker National Museum, Series I, Box 14, Index Code 2B-13-14.
8. Churchill Press Conference, September 5, 1956.
9. "Management Seeks Studebaker Votes," *New York Times*, September 27, 1956, p. 55.
10. "Studebaker Sees Victory in Vote," *New York Times*, November 1, 1956, p. 57.
11. R.R. Ebert and N.M. Pamphilis, "Packards From South Bend: Economic Perspectives on 'The Last Packards Decision,'" Parts 1 and 2, *Automotive History Review*, no. 46 (Fall 2006) and 47 (Spring 2007).
12. W.M. Schmidt, interview by David Crippen, August 1, 1984. Design Oral History Project of The Henry Ford, Benson Ford Research Center, Dearborn, Michigan, vol. II.

13. R.A. Teague, interview by David Crippen, July 2, 1985. Design Oral History Project of The Henry Ford, Benson Ford Research Center, Dearborn, Michigan, vol. II.
14. G.H. Brodie, to J.J. Nance, June 11, 1956. In Nance Papers, ser. 2, box 12, Studebaker National Museum Archives.
15. Packard Division, Studebaker-Packard Corporation, National Dealer Council Meeting Minutes, August 28, 1956.
16. Ibid.
17. Ibid.
18. Ibid.
19. Bain.
20. Edwards; L.J. White, *The Automobile Industry Since 1945* (Cambridge, MA: Harvard University Press, 1971).
21. Bonsall, p. 319.
22. Robert Heller and Associates, "Record of Efforts Directed at Preserving the Corporation, January–June 1956," July 31, 1956. Attached to Board of Directors Minutes, Studebaker-Packard Corporation, August 6, 1956.
23. Studebaker-Packard Corporation, *Annual Report for 1954*. South Bend, IN.
24. R.I. Heikkinen, "Consolidation of Studebaker-Packard Dealer Organization," November 20, 1956. Attached as Item 10 of the Agenda, Studebaker-Packard Corporation Board of Directors Minutes, November 28, 1956.
25. Churchill interview.
26. Ibid.
27. Ibid.
28. Churchill, Press Conference, September 5, 1956.
29. Ward, p. 249.
30. C.K. Hyde, *Storied Independent Automakers* (Detroit: Wayne State University Press, 2009), p. 185.
31. "Economy Car Makes Debut," *South Bend Tribune*, May 27, 1957, p. 1.
32. Studebaker-Packard Corporation, *Annual Report for 1956*, South Bend, IN.

Chapter 4

1. Churchill interview.
2. Ibid.
3. Ibid.
4. Bonsall, pp. 269–271.
5. Board of Directors Meeting Minutes Book III (March 14, 1958). Studebaker-Packard Corporation, Archives of the Studebaker National Museum.
6. "Soaring on Wings of the Lark."
7. H.E. Churchill. To the Shareholders (September 4, 1958). Studebaker-Packard Corporation letter to accompany Proxy Statement.
8. "Stockholders Approve Studebaker Refinancing: Churchill Announces Aggressive Merchandising of New 'Lark,'" October 15, 1958. Public Relations Department. Studebaker-Packard Corporation, South Bend, Indiana.
9. F.K. Fox, "Studebaker's 1959–61 Larks: A Story About Great Cars," *Turning Wheels* (September 2009): pp. 6–15.
10. Critchlow, pp. 66–103.
11. M. Beatty, P. Furlong, and L. Pennington, *Studebaker: Less Than They Promised* (South Bend, IN: And Books, 1984).
12. Beatty et al., p. 25.
13. Critchlow, pp. 135–137.
14. Ibid., pp. 149–151.
15. Churchill interview.
16. "Studebaker Strike Ends After 4 Days," *New York Times*, November 26, 1958, p. 19.
17. "Auto Pact Ratified," *New York Times*, December 1, 1958, p. 32.
18. Churchill interview.
19. F.K. Fox.
20. "Celebration Marks Delivery of 100,000th Lark," *Studebaker News* 1, no. 3 (1959): p. 3.
21. L.A. Fleener to H.E. Churchill and Royall Victor, October 14, 1960, with attached memo;

L.A. Fleener to A. Wychodil, Auto Union–DKW, October 11, 1960. Harold Churchill Papers, Studebaker National Museum, Series I, Box 23, Index Code 2B-12-5.

Chapter 5

1. J.J. Nance H.J. and Ferry. To Packard Shareholders, July 9, 1954. Letter and Proxy Statement.
2. J. Weed, "Truckin,'" *Automotive News* December 5, 1955.
3. A.J. Porta, "Studebaker-Packard Sales, Passenger Cars and Trucks," December 20, 1957. Report to Studebaker-Packard Corporation Board of Directors.
4. O. Romine, "Conversations with Otis, Part IV," interview by L. Pennington, May 18, 1972, *Turning Wheels* (June 2010): pp. 6–8.
5. Dealer Council Meeting Minutes, Summer 1959. Studebaker-Packard Corporation, South Bend, IN. Harold E. Churchill Papers, Studebaker National Museum, Series I, Box 22, Index Code 2b-12-4.
6. Ibid.
7. H.E. Churchill, "The Case for Competition," Remarks to the National Press Club, November 6, 1959. Washington, DC. Harold E. Churchill Papers, Studebaker National Museum, Series I, Box 27, Index Code 2B-12-9.
8. Bonsall, p. 342.
9. H. Johnson, "The Studebaker Flat Four Engine," *Turning Wheels* (September 2005): pp. 6–15.
10. R. Quinn, "The Car That Never Was," *Turning Wheels* (September 2005): p. 10.
11. Ibid.
12. Ibid.
13. A.R Hammer, "Car Changeovers Include Officers," *New York Times*, September 11, 1960, p. F5.

Chapter 6

1. A.R. Zipser, "Francis Out to Replace Himself," *New York Times*, November 6, 1960, p. F1.
2. Board of Directors, Studebaker-Packard Corporation, Handwritten Meeting Minutes, December 28, 1960. Board Minutes Book V. Archives of the Studebaker National Museum, South Bend, IN.
3. Ibid.
4. A.R. Hammer, "Sonnabend Discloses the Sale of All His Stock in Studebaker," *New York Times*, December 30, 1960, p. 26.
5. Churchill interview.
6. R.R. Ebert, "On Wings of Larks and Hawks: The Last Flight of Studebaker, 1956–1966, Part Three," *The Bulb Horn* 53, no. 1 (January–March 1992): pp. 35–42.

Chapter 7

1. Churchill, Press Conference, September 5, 1956.
2. D'Arcy Advertising Company, "A Report to Studebaker on a Study of Lark Owners," no date. Unpublished. Harold E. Churchill Papers, Studebaker National Museum. Series I, Box 25, Index code 2B-12-7.
3. Details of the six major findings of the D'Arcy study are contained in its Report to Studebaker (see footnote 2).
4. D'Arcy, "Report to Studebaker."
5. Dealer Council Meeting Minutes, Summer 1959.

Chapter 8

1. M.E. Lynch, "Our Own Hall of Fame, James J. Nance," *Dayton Daily News*, February 17, 1961. www.daytonhistorybooks.com/halloffamenance.html (accessed June 5, 2012).
2. R.E. Bedingfield, "Along the Highways and Byways of Finance," *New York Times*, October 10, 1954, p. F3.

3. Lynch.
4. Ward, pp. 25–50.
5. "Packard's Road Back," *Fortune* (November 1952): p. 116.
6. Ibid.
7. Kimes, p. 546.
8. "Packard's Road Back," p. 116.
9. Ibid.
10. Ibid.
11. Ibid.
12. "Packard to Take a Year to Adjust," *New York Times*, April 20, 1954, p. 43.
13. "Studebaker Merger with Packard Voted," *New York Times*, August 18, 1954, p. 1.
14. W.B. Harris, "The Breakdown of Studebaker-Packard," *Fortune* (October 1956): p. 228.
15. Harris, p. 224.
16. Ward, p. 223.
17. Harris, p. 232.
18. Lynch.
19. Ohio Wesleyan University, June 21, 1980. Distinguished Achievement Citation–James J. Nance. http://alumni.owu.edu/pdfs/awards/Nance.pdf (accessed June 5, 2012).
20. D. Peterson, "Sherwood Harry Egbert," November 6, 2010. *Find a Grave*. http://www.findagrave.com (accessed June 5, 2012).
21. R. Hammer, "Welcome Sherwood Egbert," *Fortune* (December 1961): pp. 94–97 and 152–163.
22. Peterson.
23. Hammer.
24. Ibid.
25. Ibid.
26. Ibid.
27. "Studebaker Is Hit By Strike: Quick Peace Doubted," *Wall Street Journal*, January 3, 1962, p. 2.
28. R. Gregg, "Egbert Joins Scuffle; Picket Arrested," *South Bend Tribune*, January 17, 1962, p. 1.
29. R. Gregg and W. Fidati, "S-P President, Picket Face Charges," *South Bend Tribune*, January 18, 1962, p. 1.
30. "Disorderly Conduct Charge Against Egbert Dropped," *Wall Street Journal*, February 27, 1962.
31. J. Colwell, "S-P Plans Full Production Tuesday," *South Bend Tribune*, February 11, 1962, p. 1.
32. Bonsall, pp. 358–361.
33. Ibid., pp. 361–366.
34. Studebaker Corporation, *Annual Report for 1962*, South Bend, IN.
35. J. Hull, *Avanti: The Complete Story* (Hudson, WI: Iconografix, 2008), pp. 14–17.
36. Bonsall, pp. 371–372.
37. B. Thomas, "Ex-South Bend Signal Caller Won't 2nd Guess," *Los Angeles Times*, December 15, 1963, p. 7.
38. Peterson.
39. "Burlingame Is Appointed to Run Auto Company," *South Bend Tribune*, November 11, 1963, p. 1; R.H. Guthrie, Official Factory Bulletin, November 25, 1963. Studebaker Corporation.
40. S. Chapman, "The Survivor Responds," *Turning Wheels* (June 2008): pp. 16–18.
41. Ibid.
42. R. Quinn, "Historic Document Sheds Light on Canadian Operation," *Turning Wheels* (April 2008): pp. 26–30. Reprint of August 24, 1965, letter from B.A. Burlingame to Gordon E. Grundy.
43. Beatty et al., pp. 48–50; S. Chapman, *My Father the Car* (Evansville, IN: M.T. Publishing, 2009), pp. 96–99.
44. Quinn, "Historic Document."
45. E. Reynolds, "1967 + Design – The Final Proposals," *Turning Wheels* (June 1990): pp. 30–32.
46. Beatty et al., p. 50.
47. B. Palma, "The Deck Lid Die Broke," *Turning Wheels* (April 2012): p. 20.
48. Hyde.

Bibliography

Primary Sources

Altman, N.D., President, Avanti Motor Corporation, interview with by Robert R. Ebert, December 18, 1974. South Bend, IN.
"Announcement of Resignation of Sherwood H. Egbert as President and Member of the Board: Burlingame Elected as President." Studebaker Corporation Official Factory Bulletin, November 25, 1963. South Bend, IN.
"Announcement of Shifting Automotive Operations to Canada." Studebaker Corporation Public Relations Department, December 9, 1963. South Bend, IN.
Board of Directors, Studebaker-Packard Corporation. *Minutes*. The following lists the dates of meetings cited within this work and retrieved at the Archives of the Studebaker National Museum, South Bend, Indiana:
    Book I: 1954: December 17.
        1955: January 21, March 18, April 18, August 19, September 15.
        1956: January 20, February 27, March 23, April 16, May 2, May 9, May 29, June 2, June 4, June 7, June 27, July 25.
    Book II: 1956: July 26, August 6.
        1957: January 29, February 28, March 20, April 5, April 25, June 20, July 25, September 16.
    Book III: 1957: October 31, November 15, December 20.
        1958: January 30, February 24, February 24 (Supplementary Materials), March 14, March 27, April 24, May 8, May 8 (Supplementary Materials), June 18, July 24, August 26, September 25.
    Book IV: 1958: October 21, November 17, December 15.
        1959: January 25, February 16.
    Book V: 1959: April 27, April 27 (Supplementary Materials), May 4, June 15, July 7.
        1960: September 2 (Special Meeting, pencil draft), September 2 (Special Meeting, typed version), November 28 (Special Meeting, pencil draft), November 28 (Special Meeting, typed version), December 19 (pencil draft), December 19 (typed version), December 28 (pencil draft), December 28 (typed version).
        1961: February 6 (pencil draft), February 6 (typed version), February 28 (Pencil draft).
Board of Directors, Studebaker Corporation. *Minutes*. The following lists the dates of meetings cited here and retrieved at the archives of the Studebaker National Museum, South Bend, Indiana:
        1963: January 10–11, February 7, February 18 (Special Meeting), March 1, August 8 (Special Meeting), November 9, November 22 (Special Meeting), December 1 (Special Meeting), December 12 (Special Meeting), December 19 (Special Meeting).
        1964: January 3, January 17, February 7.
Board of Directors, Executive Committee, Studebaker-Packard Corporation. *Minutes*. The following lists the dates of meetings cited here and retrieved at the archives of the Studebaker National Museum, South Bend, Indiana. These Minutes are in the same books as Board of Directors Minutes.
    Book IV: 1958: November 14, December 1.
        1959: January 6.

Board of Directors, Executive Committee, Studebaker Corporation. *Minutes.* The following lists the dates of meetings cited here and retrieved at the archives of The Studebaker National Museum, South Bend, Indiana. These Minutes are in the same books as Board of Directors Minutes.
>Book V: 1960: June 3 (pencil draft), June 3 (typed version), July 6, August 30, December 5. 1963: September 2.

Brodie, G.H. to J.J. Nance, June 11, 1956. In Nance Papers, ser. 2, box 12, Studebaker National Museum archives.

Burlingame, B. Letter to Gordon E. Grundy, August 25, 1965.

_____. Letter to Studebaker Employees, December 3, 1963. Studebaker Corporation.

_____. Public relations release, December 9, 1963. Studebaker Corporation.

_____. Telegram to all Studebaker Dealers, December 9, 1963.

Churchill, H.E. Letter to All Studebaker-Packard Dealers, August 8, 1956. Harold E. Churchill Papers, Studebaker National Museum, Series I, Box 13, Code 2B-13-13.

_____. "Studebaker-Packard's Comeback Program for 1957." Remarks to Automotive and Financial Editors Press Conference, New York City, September 5, 1956. Harold E. Churchill Papers, Studebaker National Museum, Series I, Box 14, Index code 2B-13-14.

_____. "Remarks for National Press Demonstration Day," South Bend, Indiana, September 12, 1956. Harold E. Churchill Papers, Studebaker National Museum, Series I, Box 14, Index code 2B-13-14.

_____. "Remarks to the Studebaker-Packard Corporation Annual Meeting of Shareholders," April 24, 1958. South Bend, Indiana. Harold E. Churchill Papers, Studebaker National Museum, Series I, Box 21, Index Code 2B-12-3.

_____. To the Shareholders, September 4, 1958. Studebaker-Packard Corporation. Letter to accompany Proxy Statement.

_____. "Remarks to the Studebaker-Packard Corporation Annual Meeting of Shareholders," April 23, 1959. South Bend, Indiana. Harold E. Churchill Papers, Studebaker National Museum, Series I, Box 24, Index Code 2B-12-6.

_____. "The Case for Competition: Remarks to the National Press Club." November 6, 1959. Washington, D.C. Harold E. Churchill Papers, Studebaker National Museum, Series I, Box 27, Index Code 2B-12-9.

_____. To Lewis G. Vander Veide, Director, Michigan Historical Collections, University of Michigan, January 20, 1960. Harold E. Churchill Papers, Studebaker National Museum, South Bend, IN. Series I, Box 25.

_____. Letter to Raymond Loewy. March 18, 1960. Harold E. Churchill Papers, Studebaker National Museum, Series I, Box 27, Index Code 2B-12-9.

_____. Memo to A.J. Porta and E.J. Hardig. March 18, 1960. Harold E. Churchill Papers, Studebaker National Museum, Series I, Box 27, Index Code 2B-12-9.

_____. "Dear Studebaker-Packard Dealer": Letter to Studebaker-Packard dealers, January 24, 1961.

_____. Interview by R.T. King, February 28–29, 1980. *Economic History of Indiana in the Twentieth Century, 1976–1980 Project.* Indiana University, Bloomington, IN. Call Number 80–013.

Council of Economic Advisors. *Economic Report of the President.* Washington, DC: United States Government Printing Office, January 1967.

D'Arcy Advertising Company. "A Report to Studebaker on a Study of Lark Owners" (no date). Unpublished. Harold E. Churchill Papers, Studebaker National Museum. Series I, Box 25, Index Code 2B-12-7.

Dealer Council Meeting Minutes, Summer 1959. Studebaker-Packard Corporation, South Bend, Indiana. Harold E. Churchill Papers, Studebaker National Museum, Series I, Box 22, Index Code 2B-12-4.

DeBlumenthal, M.P. to H.E. Churchill, August 7, 1957. Gogomobil Evaluation, Report No. 1. Harold E. Churchill Papers, Studebaker National Museum, Series I, Box 16, Index Code 2B-13-16.

Fleener, L.A., to H.E. Churchill and Royall Victor, October 14, 1960, with attached memo; L.A. Fleener to A. Wychodil, Auto Union–DKW, October 11, 1960. Harold Churchill Papers, Studebaker National Museum, Series I, Box 23, Index Code 2B-12-5.

Fox, L. Interview by R.L. Zeff, July 1 and July 3, 1985. Indiana University Oral History Project. Studebaker Employees, Project No. 097. Bloomington, IN. Call no. 85–045.

Guthrie, R.H. Official Factory Bulletin, November 25, 1963. Studebaker Corporation.

Hardig, E.J., to H.E. Churchill and J.P. Mullaney, January 24, 1957. "Cost Reductions in Champion Custom 2 & 4 Door Sedans." Harold E. Churchill Papers, Studebaker National Museum, Series I, Box 16, Index code 2B-13-16.

"It Is with Deep Regret That a Decision Has Been Reached to Move Automotive Assembly to Our Canadian Plant." Studebaker Corporation Official Factory Bulletin, December 10, 1963. South Bend, IN.

Klausmeyer, O. Interview by J. Bodnar, May 11, 1984. Indiana University Oral History Project. Studebaker Employees, Project No. 097. Bloomington, IN. Call no. 84–027.
MacMillan, C. Interview by J. Bodnar, May 11, 1984. Indiana University Oral History Project. Studebaker Employees, Project No. 097. Bloomington, IN. Call no. 84–013.
Nance, J.J., and H.J. Ferry. To Packard Shareholders, July 9, 1954. Letter and proxy statement.
"Packard Division, Studebaker-Packard Corporation." National Dealer Council Meeting, Minutes, August 28, 1956.
Packard Motor Car Company. *Annual Report for 1952*. March 2, 1953. Detroit, MI.
Packard Motor Car Company. *Annual Report for 1953*. March 1, 1954. Detroit, MI.
Peterson, D. "Sherwood Harry Egbert," November 6, 2010. *Find A Grave*. findagrave.com (accessed June 5, 2012).
Piechowiak, J.M. Interview by J.B. Wolford, October 8, 1984. Indiana University Oral History Project. Studebaker Employees, Project No. 097. Bloomington, IN. Call no. 84–015.
Porta, A.J. "Studebaker-Packard Sales, Passenger Cars and Trucks." Report to Studebaker-Packard Corporation Board of Directors, December 20, 1957.
Public Relations Department Studebaker-Packard Corporation, October 12, 1960. To: All Officers and Department Heads — Confidential, as reprinted in *Turning Wheels* (September 2005): p. 7.
Rosenbaum, F. Interview by J.B. Wolford, August 8, 1984. Indiana University Oral History Project. Studebaker Employees, Project No. 097. Bloomington, IN. Call No. 84–010.
Schmidt, W.M. Interview by David Crippen, August 1, 1984. "Design Oral History Project," The Henry Ford, Benson Ford Research Center, Dearborn, Michigan.
Sitarz, F. Interview by J.B. Wolford, March 30, 1985. Indiana University Oral History Project. Studebaker Employees, Project No. 097. Bloomington, IN. Call No. 85–040.
Snaith, W.T., Partner, Raymond Loewy Associates. *Environment Study of the Automobile for Studebaker-Packard*. February 26, 1960. Harold E. Churchill Papers, Studebaker National Museum, Series I, Box 27, Index code 2B-12-9.
"Stockholders Approve Studebaker Refinancing: Churchill Announces Aggressive Merchandising of New 'Lark.'" October 15, 1958. Public Relations Department. Studebaker-Packard Corporation, South Bend, Indiana.
Studebaker Corporation. *Annual Reports* for the years 1941, 1944, 1945, 1952, 1953, 1962, 1963, 1964, 1965, 1966, and 1967, South Bend, Indiana.
Studebaker-Packard Corporation. *Annual Reports* for the years 1954, 1955, 1956, 1957, 1958, 1959, 1960, 1961. South Bend, IN.
Studebaker-Packard Corporation. National Dealer Council Meeting, June 26, 1957, South Bend, IN; transcript of Studebaker National Museum Archives, Harold E. Churchill Papers, Series I, Box 19, Index 2B-12-1.
Studebaker-Packard Corporation. Proxy Statement and Notice of Special Meeting of Shareholders to be held October 15, 1958. September 4, 1958.
Studebaker-Packard Corporation, Packard Division. National Dealer Council Meeting, August 28, 1956. South Bend, IN; transcript of Studebaker National Museum Archives, Harold E. Churchill Papers, Series I, Box 7, Index 2B-13-7.
Teague, R.A. Interview by David Crippen, July 2, 1985. "Design Oral History Project" of the Henry Ford, Benson Ford Research Center, Dearborn, MI, vol. II.
Thompson, C. Interview by J.B. Wolford, July 9, 1984. Indiana University Oral History Project. Studebaker Employees Project No. 097. Bloomington, IN. Call No. 84–016.
Warren, M. Interview by J.B. Wolford, August 28, 1984. Indiana University Oral History Project. Studebaker Employees Project No. 097. Bloomington, IN. Call No. 84–021.
Zenzinger, Theodore. Interview by J.B. Wolford, July 1984. Indiana University Oral History Project. Studebaker Employees Project No. 097. Bloomington, IN. Call No. 84–003.

Secondary Sources

"All's Right in South Bend." *Time*, March 2, 1959. Studebaker-Packard Corporate Reprint.
"Auto Maker Explains." *New York Times*, December 11, 1969, p. 69.
"Auto Pact Ratified." *New York Times*, December 1, 1958, p. 32.
Bain, J.S. *Barriers to New Competition*. Cambridge, MA: Harvard University Press, 1956.
Beatty, M., P. Furlong, and L. Pennington. *Studebaker: Less Than They Promised*. South Bend, IN: And Books, 1984.
Bedingfield, R.E. "Along the Highways and Byways of Finance." *New York Times*, October 10, 1954, p. F3.

Berger, A. "Miracle in South Bend." *Speed Age* 12, no. 3 (December 1958): p. 10.
_____. "Studebaker Lark–Biggest Little Car in the World." *Speed Age* 12, no. 3 (December 1958): p. 12.
"Best Overall Buy." *Cars* magazine (June 1960).
Bodnar, J. "Power and Memory in Oral History: Workers and Managers at Studebaker." *Journal of American History* 75, no. 4 (March 1989): 1201–1221.
Bonsall, T. *More Than They Promised: The Studebaker Story*. Stanford, CA: Stanford University Press, 2000.
Brock, R. "Packard Hawk Performance Test." *Hot Rod* 11, no. 5 (May 1958): p. 18.
_____. "Lark–The People's Car." *Hot Rod* 12, no. 1 (January 1959): p. 18.
"Burlingame Is Appointed to Run Auto Company." *South Bend Tribune*, November 11, 1963, p. 1.
Callahan, B. "Valiant, Corvair, Falcon, Rambler, Lark, How They Compare." *Motor Trend* 11, no. 12 (December 1959): p. 20.
"Car Changeovers Include Officers." *New York Times*, September 11, 1960, p. F5.
"Celebration Marks Delivery of 100,000th Lark." *Studebaker News* 1, no. 3 (1959): p. 3.
Chapman, S. "The Survivor Responds." *Turning Wheels* (June 2008): pp. 16–18.
_____. *My Father the Car*. Evansville, IN: M.T. Publishing, 2009.
"Churchill Becomes Auto Firm President." *South Bend Tribune*, August 5, 1956, p. 1.
Colwell, J. "S-P Plans Full Production Tuesday." *South Bend Tribune*, February 11, 1962, p. 1.
"Compact Wagons." *Motor Trend* 13, no. 6 (June 1961): pp. 58–63.
"Comparative Check Lists — Studebaker." *Car Life* 5, no. 7 (July 1958): pp. 12–23.
Critchlow, D.T. *Studebaker: The Life and Death of an American Corporation*. Bloomington: Indiana University Press, 1996.
"Disorderly Conduct Charge Against Egbert Dropped." *Wall Street Journal*, February 27, 1962.
Ebert, R.R. "On Wings of Larks and Hawks: The Last Flight of Studebaker 1956–66, Part One." *The Bulb Horn* 52, no. 3 (July–September 1991): pp. 13–19.
_____. "On Wings of Larks and Hawks: The Last Flight of Studebaker 1956–66, Part Two." *The Bulb Horn* 52, no. 4 (October–December, 1991): pp. 9–15.
_____. "On Wings of Larks and Hawks: The Last Flight of Studebaker 1956–66, Part Three." *The Bulb Horn* 53, no. 1 (January–March, 1992): pp. 35–42.
_____, and A.D. Wyant. "From Garfords to Fords: Prosperity and Crisis in the Lorain County Auto Industry." *Automotive History Review*, no. 53 (Fall 2011): pp. 4–18.
Ebert, R.R., and N.M. Pamphilis. "Packards From South Bend: Economic Perspective on 'The Last Packards Decision,'" Parts 1 and 2. *Automotive History Review*, no. 46 (Fall 2006) and 47 (Spring 2007).
"Economy Car Makes Debut." *South Bend Tribune*, May 27, 1957, p. 1.
Edwards, C.E. *Dynamics of the United States Automobile Industry*. Columbia: University of South Carolina Press, 1965.
Egbert, S.H. "To All Studebaker-Packard Shareholders." Letter, February 23, 1961.
Fendell, B. "The Perfect Family Car." *Car Life* 5, no. 3 (March 1958): p. 22.
Fettig, D. *The Region*, publication of the Federal Reserve Bank of Minneapolis, June 2008, pp. 33–34. http://www.minneapolisfed.org/publications_papers/pub_display.cfm?id=3485 (accessed December 21, 2008).
"'58 Studebaker-Packard." *Motor Trend* 9, no. 11 (November 1957): p. 28.
"First Look at the Lark." *Motor Life* 8, no. 5 (December 1958): p. 20.
Fox, F.K. "Studebaker's 1959–61 Larks: A Story About Great Cars." *Turning Wheels* (September 2009): pp. 6–15.
"Francis, Now in Charge, Is Known as a Fireball." *New York Times*, September 3, 1960, p. 21.
Gregg, R. "Californian, 40, New S-P President." *South Bend Tribune*, December 29, 1960, p. 1.
_____. "Egbert Joins Scuffle; Picket Arrested." *South Bend Tribune*, January 17, 1962, p. 1.
_____, and W. Fidati. "S-P President, Picket Face Charges." *South Bend Tribune*, January 18, 1962, p. 1.
Hammer, A.R. "Car Changeovers Include Officers." *New York Times*, September 11, 1960, p. F5.
_____. "Sonnabend Discloses the Sale of All His Stock in Studebaker." *New York Times*, December 30, 1960, p. 26.
_____. "Welcome, Sherwood Egbert." *Fortune* (December 1961): pp. 94–97, 152–163.
Harris, W.B. "The Breakdown of Studebaker-Packard." *Fortune* (October 1956): pp. 139–141, 222–232.
Hassfurther, G. "Toughest Use-Test of All (Fleet Usage)." *Cars* 2, no. 1 (August 1960)" p. 50.
"The Hawk for 1959." *Motor Life* 8, no. 5 (December 1958): p. 25.
Heikkinen, R.I. "Consolidation of Studebaker-Packard Dealer Organization," November 20, 1956. Attached as Item 10 of the Agenda, Studebaker-Packard Corporation Board of Directors Minutes, November 28, 1956.

Heller, Robert, and Associates. "Record of Efforts Directed at Preserving the Corporation, January–June 1956," July 31, 1956. Attached to Board of Directors Minutes, Studebaker-Packard Corporation, August 6, 1956.
Hendry, M.D. "One Can Do a Lot of Remembering in South Bend." *Automobile Quarterly* 10, no. 3 (Third Quarter 1972): pp. 228–257.
"High McCulloch Official Named Studebaker-Packard President." *New York Times*, December 29, 1960, p. 33.
"How the Lark Compares." *Motor Life* 8, no. 5 (December 1958): p. 26.
"How the Lark Was Hatched." *Sports Car Wheel* 1, no. 1 (January 1960): p. 8.
Hull, J. *Avanti: The Complete Story*. Hudson, WI: Iconografix, 2008.
"Hurley is Leading Production Expert." *South Bend Tribune*, August 5, 1956, p. 6.
Hyde, C.K. *Storied Independent Automakers*. Detroit: Wayne State University Press, 2009.
Johnson, H. "The Studebaker Flat Four Engine." *Turning Wheels* (September 2005): pp. 6–15.
Kimes, B.R., ed. *Packard: A History of the Motor Car and the Company*. Princeton, NJ: Princeton Publishing, 1978.
Lackie, S. "A Brief History of Studebaker Trucks: An Analysis of Production Records." www.studebakerdriversclub.com/StudebakerTruckHistory.asp (accessed January 28, 2012).
"Lark Cruiser — luxurious compact." *Car Life* 8, no. 2 (March 1961): p. 43.
"Lark Hopped Up V-8." *Motor Life* 9, no. 10 (May 1960): p. 30.
"Lark Six (for 1960)." *Motor Life* 9, no. 7 (February 1960): p. 34.
"Lark VI Road Test (1961)." *Motor Trend* 13, no. 5 (May 1961): p. 51.
"Lark V-8." *Motor Life* 9, no. 9 (April 1960): p. 44.
"The Lark V8s." *Motor Trend* 13, no. 2 (February 1961): p. 40.
"Lark Wagon." *Motor Life* 9, no. 12 (July 1960): p. 33.
Lawrence, H. "Last Stand for Packard?" *Speed Age* 11, no. 4 (January 1958): p. 10.
Lodge, J. "'56 Studebaker Golden Hawk." *Motor Trend* 8, no. 2 (February 1956): p. 20.
Longstreet, S. *A Century on Wheels*. New York: Henry Holt, 1952.
Lynch, M.E. "Our Own Hall of Fame, James J. Nance." *Dayton Daily News*, February 17, 1961. www.daytonhistorybooks.com/halloffamenance.html (accessed June 5, 2012).
MacDonald, D. "'56 Studebaker President." *Motor Trend* 8, no. 2 (February 1956): p. 24.
"Management Seeks Studebaker Votes." *New York Times*, September 27, 1956, p. 55.
Maxwell, D. "The '61 Hawk Sporty, Stick-Shift Speedster." *Cars* 2, no. 6 (March 1961): p. 18.
"Meeting Ratifies Studebaker Deal." *New York Times*, November 3, 1956, p. 33.
"MT Tests the Compact Wagons." *Motor Trend* 13, no. 6 (June 1961): p. 58.
Nerpel, C. "1960 Lark Convertible." *Motor Trend* 12, no. 6 (June 1960): p. 32.
_____. "Studebaker Hawk Road Test." *Motor Life* 10, no. 11 (June 1961): p. 18.
_____, and B. Callahan. "Lark vs. the American." *Motor Trend* 10, no. 12 (December 1958): p. 16.
"New Engine for the Lark." *Motor Trend* 12, no. 10 (October 1960): p. 60.
"New Spark for the '61 Lark." *Motor Life* 10, no. 3 (October 1960): p. 26.
"The 1957 Car Market." *Consumer Reports* 22, no. 4 (April 1957): pp. 148–205.
"The 1957 Engines." *Motor Life* 6, no. 9 (April 1957): p. 36.
"The 1957 Packard." *Motor Life* 6, no. 7 (February 1957): p. 64.
"1956–1958 Studebaker Hawk." www.studebakergarage.com (accessed February 20, 2012).
"The 1960 Road Test Review." *Motor Life* 9, no. 10 (May 1960): p. 56.
"1960 Studebaker." *Motor Life* 9, no. 5 (December 1959): p. 60.
Ohio Wesleyan University. Distinguished Achievement Citation — James J. Nance. June 21, 1980. http://alumni.owu.edu/pdfs/awards/Nance.pdf (accessed June 5, 2012).
"100 Year Almanac and Market Data Book." *Automotive News*, April 24, 1996.
"Packard." *Motor Life* 6, no. 10 (May 1957): p. 54.
"Packard Hawk Road Test." *Motor Life* 7, no. 11 (June 1958): p. 66.
"Packard to Take a Year to Adjust." *New York Times*, April 20, 1954, p. 43.
"Packard's Road Back." *Fortune* 46 (November 1952): p. 116.
Palma, B. "The Deck Lid Die Broke." *Turning Wheels* (April 2012): p. 20.
Quinn, R. "The Car That Never Was." *Turning Wheels* (September 2005): p. 10.
_____. "Otto Klausmeyer, 1899–1985." *Turning Wheels* (September 2005): p. 14.
_____. "Postwar Engine Development." *Turning Wheels* (September 2005): p. 15.
_____. "Heretofore Unpublished Letter from Raymond Loewy Offers Insight into His Work for Studebaker." *Turning Wheels* (September 2008): pp. 30–34.
_____. "Historic Document Sheds Light on Canadian Operation" (reprint of August 24, 1965, letter from B.A. Burlingame to Gordon E. Grundy). *Turning Wheels* (April 2008): pp. 26–30.

Railton, A. "The Studebaker Scotsman and the Rambler American." *Popular Mechanics* 110, no. 2 (August 1958): p. 78.
Reynolds, E. "1967 + Design — The Final Proposals." *Turning Wheels* (June 1990): pp. 30–31.
Romine, O. "Conversations with Otis, Part IV." Interview by L. Pennington, May 18, 1972. *Turning Wheels* (June 2010): pp. 6–8.
Russo, B. "'61 Lark V8 Cruiser Road Test." *Motor Life* (December 1960): pp. 58–61.
"'64 A Vital Year for Studebaker." *New York Times*, September 16, 1963, p. 55.
"'61 Lark V8 Cruiser." *Motor Life* 10, no. 5 (December 1960): p. 58.
"The Small Sixes." *Motor Life* 9, no. 9 (April 1960): p. 30.
"Soaring on Wings of the Lark." *Business Week*, June 20, 1959.
"Sonnabend Discloses the Sale of All His Stock in Studebaker." *New York Times*, December 30, 1960, p. 26.
"S-P Votes Francis Chairman." *South Bend Tribune*, September 2, 1960, p. 17.
"Station Wagons." *Consumer Reports* 23, no. 6 (June 1958): pp. 318–330.
"Studebaker Aims at Profit for '57." *New York Times*, September 6, 1957, p. 35.
"Studebaker Chief Faces Big Job." *New York Times*, August 8, 1956, p. 46.
"Studebaker Corporation Names New Chairman." *New York Times*, June 8, 1963, p. 32.
"Studebaker Hawk." *Motor Life* 6, no. 10 (May 1957): p. 44.
"Studebaker Hawk." *Motor Trend* 11, no. 1 (January 1959): p. 29.
"Studebaker Hawk Road Test." *Motor Trend* 13, no. 6 (June 1961): p. 54.
"Studebaker Is Hit by Strike: Quick Peace Doubted." *Wall Street Journal*, January 3, 1962, p. 2.
"Studebaker Lark." *Motor Trend* 11, no. 1 (January 1959): p. 49.
"Studebaker Merger with Packard Voted." *New York Times*, August 18, 1954, p. 1.
"Studebaker Ratings." *Car Life* 5, no. 7 (July 1958): p. 23.
"Studebaker Road Test." *Car Life* 5, no. 6 (June 1958): pp. 36–39.
"Studebaker Road Test." *Motor Life* 7, no. 12 (July 1958): p. 74.
"Studebaker Sees Gains." *New York Times*, December 31, 1963, p. 31.
"Studebaker Sees Victory in Vote." *New York Times*, November 1, 1956, p. 57.
"Studebaker Strike Ends After 4 Days." *New York Times*, November 28, 1958, p. 19.
"Studebaker's Lark." *Consumer Reports* 24, no. 2 (February 1959): p. 83.
"Studebaker's Lark." *Motor Life* 8, no. 5 (December 1958): p. 18.
Thomas, B. "Ex–South Bend Signal Caller Won't 2nd Guess." *Los Angeles Times*, December 15, 1963, p. 7.
"U.S. Antitrust Action Filed on Studebaker Oil Additive." *New York Times*, November 1, 1963, p. 68.
"U.S. Autos 1960." *Consumer Reports* 25, no. 4 (April 1960): pp. 168–205.
Vieth, B. "The Corvette, T-Bird, and Hawk." *Speed Age* 10, no. 8 (May 1957): p. 16.
Ward, J.A. *The Fall of the Packard Motor Car Company*. Stanford, CA: Stanford University Press, 1995.
Warren, A. "S-P's Super Economy Car?" *Car Life* 5, no. 2 (February 1958): p. 12.
Warren, D.A. "1958 Packard Hawk." *Speed Age* 11, no. 8 (May 1958): p. 22.
Weed, J. "Truckin'." *Automotive News*, December 5, 1955.
Wherry, J.H. Packard Clipper Drivescription." *Motor Trend* 9, no. 3 (March 1957): p. 27.
_____. "'58 Studebaker and Packard." *Motor Trend* (November 1957): pp. 28–33.
_____. "Packard First Feel Behind the Wheel." *Motor Trend* 10, no. 1 (January 1958): p. 22.
_____. "Driving the 1959 Silver Hawk." *Science and Mechanics* 29, no. 6 (December 1958): p. 84.
_____. "Driving the Small New Studebaker Larks." *Science and Mechanics* 29, no. 6 (December 1958): p. 81.
_____. "The Studebaker Champ — Pickup with Punch." *Cars* 2, no. 1 (August 1960): p. 25.
Whipple, J. "Studebaker Consumer Analysis." *Car Life* 5, no. 6 (June 1958).
_____. "Studebaker Lark." *Car Life* 5, no. 12 (December 1958): p. 28.
_____. "Lark & Rambler: The Old Pros." *Car Life* 7, no. 2 (February 1960): p. 13.
_____. "The Lively Lark of Studebaker." *Car Life* 7, no. 2 (February 1960): p. 16.
White, L.J. *The Automobile Industry Since 1945*. Cambridge, MA: Harvard University Press, 1971.
Wright, Robert A. "Studebaker President Resigns; Burlingame to Succeed Egbert." *New York Times*, November 26, 1963, p. 57.
Zipser, A.R. "Francis Out to Replace Himself." *New York Times*, November 6, 1960, p. F1.

Index

advertising *see* Studebaker-Packard advertising
American Motors 6–7, 22, 46, 153–154; *see also* Rambler
Andrews, Robert 141
Auto Union–DKW 68–70
Avanti *see* Studebaker Avanti
Avanti Motors Corporation 143

Bain, Joe S. 24, 25, 42
Bickelhaupt, R.E. 40
Big Four Division 96
Big Three competition 80
body rust *see* Studebaker body rust
Borden, D. C. 31
Bourke, Bob 162, 163
Brock, Ray 106–107
Brodie, George 39
Burke, Dowling, and Adams *64*

Callahan, Bill 120
Car Life 109, 110, 115, 120, 128
Cars 122–123, 126
Champ Trucks *see* Studebaker Trucks
Champion *see* Studebaker Champion
Chapman, Stuart 146–147
Chemical Compounds Division 96
Chevrolet 17
Chevrolet Corvair 24, 80, 120–122
Chevrolet Corvette 102
Christopher, George 5–6, 132
Chrysler Corporation 154
Churchill, Harold E. 3, 7–9, *10*, 11–21, 24–27, 28–54, 88–90, 91–99, 124, 130–131, 150, *151*, 152–155, 157, 162, 166; and Hawks 76–79; and the Lark 55–58, 60, 64–69, *70*, *71*, 72, 79, *81*, 83, 85–90; and trucks 73, 75, 76
Churchill, Josephine Thompson 10
Clarke Floor Machinery 96

Cole, Roy 12, 16
Commander *see* Studebaker Commander
compact car specifications 120
Consumer Reports 101, 103, 104, 107, 110, 111, 116, 117, 120, 121, 122
Critchlow, Donald 6
Curtiss-Wright 7–8, 29, 31–37, 39, 42, 46, 53, 59
Cyclone aircraft engines 18, *19*

Daimler-Benz 33, 68
Dann, Sol A. 37
D'Arcy Advertising 64, *65*, 118–119
dealers *see* Studebaker-Packard dealers
Dodge Brothers Manufacturing Co. 10
Dodge trucks 76

Ebstein, John 141
Edwards, Charles E. 24, 25, 42
Egbert, Sherwood H. 8, 88, 91–98, 131, 138–141, *142*, 143–144, 152–154, 162, 166
E-M-F *see* Everett-Metzger-Flanders
Erskine, Albert R. 5, 11, 14
Erskine automobile 5, 14, *15*
Everett-Metzger-Flanders 4

Faurot, Randy 85
Federal Reserve 33, 34
Fendell, Bob 110–112
Ferry, Hugh 6
Fish, Frederick 5
Fitzpatrick, Allen E. *49*
Ford Falcon 24, 80, 120–122
Ford Motor Company 17–18
Ford Thunderbird 102
Forgan, J. Russell 28, 32, 33, 64, 93
four cylinder Lark *see* Studebaker Lark four cylinder engine
Francis, Clarence 60, 88–89, 91–93, 125

Garford automobile 4
General Electric 22, 131–133
General Motors 18; engines 96, 98
Gerke, C.E. 85
Gilman, Max 132
Glas, Hans 53–54
Goggomobil 53–54
Granatelli, Andy 141
Gravely tractors 91, 93
Graves, William H. 132
Grundy, Gorden E. 146–150
Guthrie, Randolph 96, 143, *145*, 146

Hall, D. Ray 91–93
Hardig, Eugene 46, 61, 85
Hawk *see* Studebaker Hawk
Heaslet, James G. 11
Heller, Robert 31
Herzog, Mr. and Mrs. Frank 67
Hoffman, Paul 5–6, 12, 16, 34, 61
Hot Rod 106, 115
Hotpoint 22, 131–132
Hudson 6
Hurley, Roy T. 32, 33, 35, 39, 48

integrated automobile production 24

James, W.S. 12

Kaiser-Jeep Corporation 154
Kaiser Motors Corporation 22, 154
Kaiser-Willys Corporation 22
Kellogg, Tom 141
Klausmeyer, Otto 85

labor relations *see* Studebaker labor relations
Lark *see* Studebaker Lark
Litchfield, Edward H. 60, 88, 89
Loewy, Raymond 6, 85–87, 141, *142*
low-priced three 17

Macauley, Alvan 4–5, 132

MacMillan, C.M. 139
Management Advisory Agreement 35
Mason, George 22, 153
Maxwell, Duncan 125
McCulloch Corporation 91, 138
McKinnon Industries Engines 96, 98
McRae, Duncan 38–39, 61, 85, 107
Mercedes-Benz 51, 53, 68
Milligan, Melvin 139
Minkel, Lewis 83, 85, 89, 91
Molded Fiberglass Co. 141–142
Motor Life 100, 101, 102, 103, 105, 106, 108, 109, 113, 114, 120, 125, 128
Motor Trend 101, 102, 105, 107, 108, 115, 116, 120, 126, 127, 128

Nance, James J. 6–8, 13, 22, 31, 34, 37, 131, *132*, 133–138, 152–154
Nash automobile 6, 154
Nerpel, Chuck 123, 125

Onan engines and generators 93
overhead valve 6 engine *see* Studebaker overhead valve 6 engine

Packard, James Ward 3–4
Packard, William Doud 3
Packard Clipper *32*, 38, *41*, 42, 100–101, *159*
Packard Dealer Council 40
Packard Executive 38
Packard Hardtop *32*, *45*
Packard Hawk *44*, 105, *106*, 107, 108, 162, *165*
Packard integration into South Bend 39–45
Packard Motor Car Company 3–7
Packard 1957 model year 100–101
Packard 1958 model year 104–108
Packard Predictor *37*
Packard Sedan *44*, 107, *160*
Packard Station Wagon *45*, 107
Pasajlich, Novak *49*
Paxton superchargers 141
Pennington, Loren E. 75
Pierce-Arrow 4–5
Plymouth automobile 17–80
Plymouth Valiant 17, 120–122
Popular Mechanics 109–110
Porta, A.J. 41, 73, 85, 89, 91

Quinn, Richard 148

Rambler 113, 115–117, 120–122, 127, 154
Reuther, Walter 62
Rockne (automobile) 4, 12, 14, *16*
Rockne, Knute 14
Romine, Otis 75–76
Romney, George 22, 153–154
Roos, Delmar G. (Barney) 11–12, 14

Schaeffer Refrigeration 96
Schmidt, William 38
Skelton, Owen R. 11
Skillman, Sydney 64
Slick, Thomas W. 12
Snaith, W.T. 85
Sonnabend, Abraham 91–93
Sparrow, Stanwood W. 12
specifications *see* Studebaker-Packard specifications
Speed Age 102, 103, 105, 106, 107, 114
Stevens, Brook 139, 142
STP *see* Chemical Compounds Division
Strauss, Morris 93
Studebaker, Clement *see* H & C Studebaker
Studebaker, Henry *see* H & C Studebaker
Studebaker, John Mohler 3–4
Studebaker Avanti 88, *95*, 96, 141, *142*, 143, 153
Studebaker body rust 129–130
Studebaker Brothers Manufacturing Company *95*
Studebaker Canada 146–150
Studebaker Champion 5, 8, 15, *16*, *20*, *47*, *51*, *103*, 104, 155, 158
Studebaker Commander *21*, *47*, *65*, *97*, *103*, 104, 108–110, 158
Studebaker Corporation 144, 152; finances 142–144, 145–150, 155, 157
Studebaker Cruiser 82, *84*, *94*, *95*, 128, 129, *161*
Studebaker Daytona *96*, *149*
Studebaker Drivers Club 146, 148
Studebaker Econ-O-miler taxi 63, *71*, 82, 110–111, *112*
Studebaker factory *26*
Studebaker-Garford 4
Studebaker, H & C 3
Studebaker Hawk 76, 77, *78*, 79, 82, *84*, *94*, 96, 124–125, *126*, 162, 164; Golden Hawk 23, *30*, *51*, 102–103, 162, *163*, *164*; Gran Turismo Hawk 23, 139, *140*, 162, *165*
Studebaker labor relations 61–63, 135, 139–141
Studebaker Land Cruiser 30, *158*
Studebaker Lark 9, *61*, 63, *66*, *67*, *69*, *70*, *71*, 73, *74*, *81*, *82*, *83*, *94*, 96, 114–115, *116*, 117–119, 120–124, 126–128, 153, 155, *160*, *161*; advertising 64–69; development of 56–58, 61, 72; four cylinder engine 85–90; long-range planning for 83, 85, *86*, *87*, 88–90, 151–152; success of 65–67
Studebaker 1957 model year 102–104

Studebaker 1958 model year 108–112
Studebaker 1959 model year 112–119
Studebaker 1960 model year 119–124
Studebaker 1961 model year 124–128
Studebaker overhead valve 6 engine 126–127, 129
Studebaker-Packard advertising 64, *65*; Lark advertising 64–69
Studebaker-Packard Corporation 5–8, 22, 27, 29, 65–67, 89; finances 27, 59–60, 129, 136–137
Studebaker-Packard dealers 42, 43, *63*, 64, 83, 85
Studebaker-Packard specifications 166–168; automobiles 169–171; trucks 171–173
Studebaker President *65*, *159*
Studebaker President Classic *30*, 41, *47*, *51*, 129
Studebaker Provincial Station Wagon *111*
Studebaker Scotsman 46, *48*, 50, 72, 108, 109–110, 112
Studebaker Speedster *25*
Studebaker Starlight *23*, *53*, *163*, 164
Studebaker Starliner *23*, *163*
Studebaker trucks 18, 76; Champ 73, *75*, 76, *77*, 124; M-Series *21*; Military *19*; R-Series *50*, 75, 76; Scotsman *49*; Transtar *49*
Studebaker Weasel 18, *19*, 20

Teague, Richard 38–39
Thompson, Josephine *see* Churchill, Josephine Thompson
trucks *see* Studebaker trucks

United Auto Workers 61–63; *see also* Studebaker labor relations

Vail, Ralph 12, 16
Vance, Harold 5–6, 12, 16, 61
Victor, Royal 64, 91, 144, 145
Vieth, Bob 102

Warren, Donald 105–106
Weasel *see* Studebaker Weasel
Wherry, Joe H. 101, 107–108, 124
Whipple, Jim 115, 120–122
White, Lawrence 42
White Motor Company 11–12, 146
Whitmer, A. D. 85
Willys 22
World War II 18–21

Zeder, Fred M. 111

www.ingramcontent.com/pod-product-compliance
Lightning Source LLC
Chambersburg PA
CBHW081559300426
44116CB00015B/2937